Thomas Jefferson's Paris

Entrance to the Cour du Louvre

Thomas Jefferson's Paris

by
Howard C. Rice, Jr.

Princeton University Press
Princeton, New Jersey

PUBLISHED BY PRINCETON UNIVERSITY PRESS, 41 WILLIAM STREET,
PRINCETON, NEW JERSEY 08540
IN THE UNITED KINGDOM, BY PRINCETON UNIVERSITY PRESS,
CHICHESTER, WEST SUSSEX
COPYRIGHT © 1976 BY PRINCETON UNIVERSITY PRESS
ALL RIGHTS RESERVED

Library of Congress Cataloging in Publication Data
Rice, Howard Crosby, 1904-
Thomas Jefferson's Paris.
Includes bibliographical references and index.
1. Paris–Description.   2. Paris–History.
3. Jefferson, Thomas, Pres. U.S., 1743-1826.   I. Title.
DC707.R52   944′.361′0350924   75-30203
ISBN 0-691-05232-8
ISBN 0-691-00776-4 pbk.

FIRST PRINCETON PAPERBACK PRINTING, 1976;
REISSUED WITH A THIRD PRINTING, 1991

PRINCETON UNIVERSITY PRESS BOOKS ARE PRINTED ON ACID-FREE PAPER
AND MEET THE GUIDELINES FOR PERMANENCE AND DURABILITY OF THE
COMMITTEE ON PRODUCTION GUIDELINES FOR BOOK LONGEVITY OF THE
COUNCIL ON LIBRARY RESOURCES

10 9 8 7 6 5 4

COMPOSED IN LINOTYPE MONTICELLO
TEXT DESIGNED BY BRUCE D. CAMPBELL;
COVER DESIGNED BY DONALD HATCH
PRINTED IN THE UNITED STATES OF AMERICA BY
PRINCETON ACADEMIC PRESS

Cover: The Pont Neuf and Hotel de la Monnaie seen from the Quai du Louvre,
by A. J. Noel, ca. 1780. Cliché: Musées de la Ville de Paris
© by SPADEM 19.

Je me suis élancée dans les siècles à venir, et j'ai distingué la jeunesse américaine lisant avec ardeur et admiration tout ce qu'on aura recueilli de vos voyages. Lorsque la richesse de son sol et l'excellence de son gouvernement auront porté l'Amérique Septentrionale au plus haut degré de splendeur, que le midi suivra son exemple, que vous aurez donné des soins à la moitié du globe, on cherchera peut-être les vestiges de Paris comme on fait aujourd'hui ceux de l'antique Babylone, et les mémoires de Mr. Jefferson conduiront les voyageurs avides des antiquités romaines et françaises qui se confondront alors.

I have been projected into future ages, and have seen the youth of America reading with enthusiasm and admiration all that has been collected about your travels. When the wealth of her soil and the excellence of her government have elevated North America to the summit of greatness, when the southern continent has followed her example, when you have succored half the globe, then perhaps, people will search for the vestiges of Paris as they do today those of ancient Babylon, and the memoirs of Mr. Jefferson will guide travellers eagerly seeking the antiquities of Rome and of France, which will then be as one.

—MADAME DE TESSÉ
*in a letter to Thomas Jefferson,
30 March 1787*

The ornament on the recto of this page is a sketch of Madame de Tessé's parting gift to Jefferson, now lost. In the donor's mind, the "pedestal" was an altar—*un autel*—for the groves of Monticello dedicated to the Supreme Ruler of the Universe, "under whose watchful care the liberties of North America were finally achieved, and under whose tutelage the name of Thomas Jefferson will descend forever blessed to posterity." See page 98, note 24, and List of Illustrations.

Preface

Thomas Jefferson resided in Paris from August 1784 to September 1789. Although he visited other cities as a tourist, these five years represent his longest period of urban living in Europe, or even in America. Upon his return to the United States and assumption of his duties as Secretary of State, he resided for a few months in New York and then, for the better part of three years (1791–1793), maintained his own household in Philadelphia. At the time of his occupancy of the White House as President (1801–1809), Washington, D.C., was a city in name only. Jefferson was happiest when living at Monticello, where "all his wishes ended" and where, as he had hoped, his days ended on July 4, 1826.

This book, evoking in words and pictures the city of Paris as Jefferson knew it under the reign of Louis XVI, had its beginnings some thirty years ago when I was searching for Jefferson letters and related documents for the new edition of *The Papers of Thomas Jefferson*, then being initiated at Princeton University under the direction of Julian P. Boyd. It owes its inception to the latter's challenge: "I would suggest that we ought to try to locate and identify not only some of the principal buildings in which Jefferson himself had an interest, but also some of the principal public buildings and residences where he was accustomed to do business or to be entertained. For example, do we know *where . . .?*"

Taking my clues from Jefferson's letters, travel memoranda, and account books, I have attempted to find out, not merely what the places were, but how they looked in Jefferson's day and what has happened to them since. Jefferson was himself a talented amateur architect, interested, too, in city planning, gardening, engineering problems, and new inventions. Following in his footsteps and noting the sights that caught his eye provide a valuable clue to his tastes and criteria, which in turn helped shape the taste of the young American republic. Jefferson's French friends and acquaintances as well as concerts, theatres, art exhibitions, bookshops, and printing establishments likewise come within the purview of this book. I think of it, not as a formal biographical account of the American Minister's mission, but rather as a series of explorations —of "perlustrations," to borrow one of his words—in Paris with Jefferson. Following the principle of selection adopted for the illustrations, the maps are authentic documents of the Louis XVI period. Modern explorers should have no difficulty in matching them up with the corresponding maps and guidebooks of the present day.

Some of the material that I gathered long ago has found its way into the Princeton University Press edition of *The Papers of Thomas Jefferson*, especially the volumes (vii-xv) covering the Paris years, and into articles by myself and others. Meanwhile, I have added to my store and now, thanks to the prerequisite nod of encouragement from Herbert S. Bailey, Jr., Director of the Princeton University Press, have been able to condense and distill my accumulation.

Over the years I have had the pleasure and satisfaction of exchanging information and ideas with many Jefferson scholars and connoisseurs: among them, Gilbert Chinard, Marie Kimball, Fiske Kimball, Edward Dumbauld, Dumas Malone, Frederick D. Nichols, and James A. Bear, Jr. Julian P. Boyd and others who have been associated with the publication of *The Papers*—Lyman H. Butterfield, Mina R. Bryan, William H. Gaines, Jr., Alfred L. Bush, and above all, France Chalufour Rice—have nourished and sustained my interest in the subject, as have friends and colleagues in the Library of Congress and the libraries of the University of Virginia, the Massachusetts Historical Society, and Princeton University. More recently, Charles E. Greene of the Princeton Library, Gail Filion (editor) and Bruce Campbell (designer) of the Princeton University Press, and John F. Peckham of The Meriden Gravure Company have played an essential role in bringing the book to fruition.

As this is as much a book about Paris as about Jefferson, I am equally indebted to the many French friends and historians who have shared my interests. The footnotes and list of sources for the illustrations, hereinafter, inadequately record my obligations. I would however underscore such institutions as the Archives Nationales (including the Minutier Central des Notaires de la Seine), the Bibliothèque Nationale (especially its department of prints, the incomparable Cabinet des Estampes), the Musée Carnavalet, the Bibliothèque Historique de la Ville de Paris, the Musée de Blérancourt, and the Muséum National d'Histoire Naturelle. Thinking of the scholarly librarians, archivists, and curators—past and present—whom I have known there, I can echo Jefferson's words: "the communicative dispositions of their scientific men . . . the ease and vivacity of their conversation, give a charm to their society, to be found nowhere else." I hope they will accept this book as an expression of my esteem and an appropriate acknowledgment of their courtesies.

Though the idea for this book did indeed take shape thirty years ago, I might add that it really began even earlier. Writing these lines in retirement, I take some satisfaction in recalling that I first saw Paris in September 1925. This preface thus becomes also an *envoi*, addressed to friends of half a century: Parisians by birth, adoption, or inclination.

Brattleboro, Vermont   H. C. R., Jr.
September 1975

Contents

Thomas Jefferson's Paris

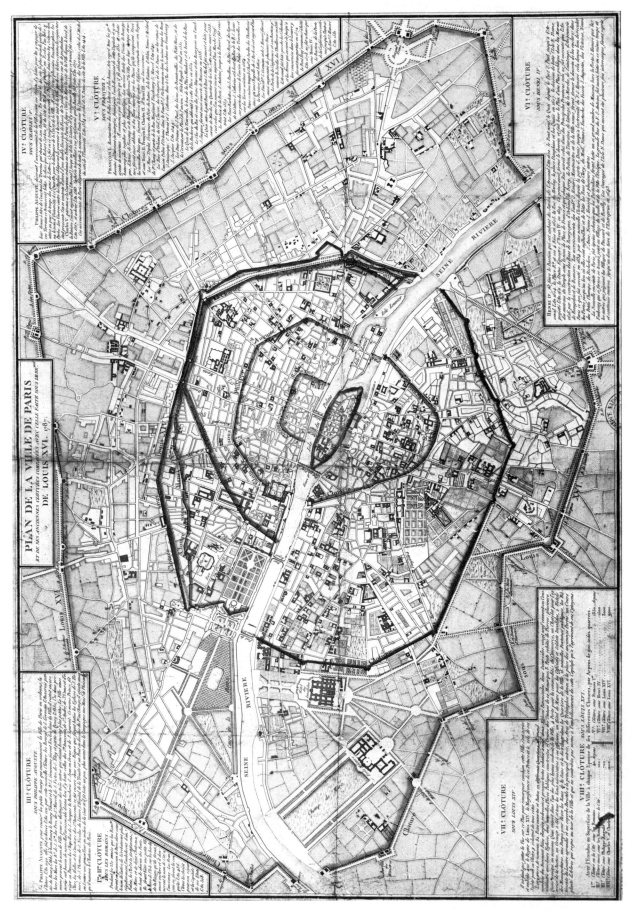

1. Paris in 1787, showing new Wall of the Farmers-General

Chapter 1

A Summary View of Jefferson's Paris

FROM its beginnings as a cluster of huts on an island in the Seine, Paris has grown in ever-expanding circles. The map of its growth suggests the cross-section of the trunk of some great tree. The concentric rings, now broad, now thin, record the fair weather and the droughts in the city's history. If we trace the ring that represents the limits of the Paris that Thomas Jefferson knew—the Paris of the 1780's—we find that it covers but half the area of the Paris we know today. If we take as our modern point of reference, not the city's legal limits, but the whole metropolitan area of Greater Paris, then Jefferson's Paris appears to us not much bigger than Roman Lutetia appeared to Jefferson's contemporaries. Paris, being highly conscious of its own history, has always enjoyed making such comparisons. There was published in 1787, for example, a finely engraved map showing the successive rings of the city's growth (Fig. 1). It was an appropriate time to print such a record, for in the 1780's a new city wall, the Wall of the Farmers-General, was being built.

This new "wall of circumvallation," as Jefferson called it, was not a fortification like several of the earlier city ramparts or the later wall built by Thiers in the 1840's, but a tax barrier designed to make the collection of municipal customs duties more effective. As such it was not popular and served to increase public criticism of the Farmers-General, the forty financiers to whom the King farmed out the internal revenue of his kingdom. The new wall ("*clôture*," as it is termed on the map shown here) provoked a storm of pamphlets, satirical verse, puns and other witticisms—the most famous of which is the now proverbial "*le mur*

murant Paris rend Paris murmurant." The wall was inextricably related to the problems of public finance then agitating the country—problems that had been aggravated by France's participation in the War of American Independence. The architect charged with the construction and design of the wall and the tollhouses punctuating it, Claude-Nicolas Ledoux, was inevitably drawn into the great debate.[1] The Wall of the Farmers-General was authorized in 1782; in January 1785 the plans drawn up by Ledoux were approved and work was begun. Supported by the Minister of Finance, Calonne, Ledoux's fortunes suffered an eclipse when his patron was replaced in 1787 by Loménie de Brienne. Reinstated in his functions after much intrigue, Ledoux was again dismissed in 1789 by still another Minister of Finance, Monsieur Necker.

The general hostility to the new wall made it difficult for people to view objectively Ledoux's designs for the tollhouses (*bureaux*) which were to flank each of the forty-seven gates (*barrières*). Even Jefferson, echoing the current mood, referred sarcastically to "the palaces by which we are to be let in and out."[2] Ledoux himself apparently did not associate the tollhouses with oppression or vexations. He saw in them a magnificent opportunity to create for Paris a garland of gateways, of propylaea, worthy of the great city. Harking back to Palladio and to Piranesi as sources of suggestion, Ledoux devised a series of variations on classic themes, in which mass, material, light and shade, rather than superficial decoration, created the design (Figs. 2, 3, 4, 5, 6, 7). In spite of mutilation during the Revolution, when some of them were sacked as symbols of oppression (see Fig. 171), most of the gatehouses survived down to the

2. Pavillon de Saint-Denis, one of Ledoux's tollhouses for the Farmers-General Wall

middle of the nineteenth century. Four of them are still standing today: the Rotonde de Monceau (Parc Monceau), the Rotonde de la Villette (Place de Stalingrad), the Barrière du Trône (Place de la Nation, Cours de Vincennes), and the Barrière d'Enfer (Place Denfert-Rochereau). Situated along the line of the old Farmers-General Wall, on avenues still anachronistically referred to as the outer bulwarks (*les boulevards extérieurs*), they provide convenient landmarks for staking out Jefferson's Paris. More than that, they greet us at the entrance to the eighteenth-century city as symbols of the new architecture of the day and as evidence that Paris under the reign of Louis XVI was, as Jefferson phrased it, "every day enlarging and beautifying."

Turning from Ledoux's new palaces along the city limits and penetrating into the heart of the city, the Ile de la Cité, we find there symbols of the older Paris that was fast disappearing. The bridges that linked the island with the right and left banks—forming part of the great north-south axis of the city—were still lined with houses as they had been for centuries. But, in 1787, Jefferson was able to report among the "wonderful improvements" in Paris: "one of the old bridges has all its houses demolished and

a second nearly so"[3] (Figs. 8, 9). "Come hither, stranger," exulted one of Jefferson's French contemporaries, "come and behold the view we have prepared for you: the city has indeed changed in appearance in the past quarter century! We've waged such war against the Visigoths, we've protested so long in our books, that the barbarians have not been able to shut their ears to our cries of derision: they have mended their ways in spite of themselves. Triumphantly do I pace these unshackled bridges, pointing the finger of scorn at the Rue de la Pelleterie which still dares obstruct my view!"[4] Another contemporary, seeking to epitomize in lapidary inscriptions the architectural achievements of the reign of Louis XVI, included in his litany the words: "Ponts Découverts"[5] (Fig. 10).

Bridges, too, provide convenient landmarks for measuring the city's growth. In Jefferson's day only a handful of bridges spanned the Seine: the Pont au Double, the Pont Saint-Charles, the Petit Pont, and the Pont Saint-Michel, leading from the Left Bank to the Ile de la Cité; and the Pont Notre-Dame and the Pont au Change, leading from the Island to the Right Bank. The Pont de la Cité linked the big island with the smaller Ile Saint-Louis,

3. Barrière d'Enfer

4. Barrière du Trône

while the Pont de la Tournelle and the Pont Marie, joining the Ile Saint-Louis to either bank, were the easternmost bridges in Paris. In the other direction the Pont Neuf, the "new bridge" completed in the reign of Henri IV, crossed the western tip of the Ile de la Cité. Beyond this there was only the Pont Royal, built in the reign of Louis XIV, crossing the river near the Château des Tuileries. Downstream to the west of the Pont Royal there were no more bridges within Paris, and, beyond the city limits, none at all until one reached the Pont de Sèvres on the road to Versailles.

New bridges were, however, being planned and one of these was finally begun during the period of Jefferson's residence in Paris. This was the Pont Louis XVI, designed by Perronet, which was to cross the Seine from the Place Louis XV (Place de la Concorde) to the Palais Bourbon, thus providing a more direct route from the Faubourg Saint-Honoré to the Faubourg Saint-Germain. Work on the Pont Louis XVI was started in 1787, although the symbolic first stone was not laid until 11 August 1788. In the presence of many royal officials (including Jefferson's friend Ethis de Corny) there was placed beneath the cornerstone a box containing

among other things six exemplars of the medal struck to commemorate the occasion (Fig. 11). The bridge, which was not completed until several years later, has undergone many transformations and changes of name (now the Pont de la Concorde), but Duvivier's medal preserves the appearance of the Pont Louis XVI as it was originally conceived.

Walls and bridges were by no means the only wonderful improvements that Paris displayed for the visitor's admiration. The city had

5. Rotonde de la Villette

[5]

indeed greatly changed in appearance during the quarter-century preceding Jefferson's arrival there. The Place Louis XV designed by the architect Jacques-Ange Gabriel had been completed in the 1770's; the enlarged Palais Royal (Victor Louis) was opened in 1784, with work still in progress; the dome of the Halle aux Bleds (Legrand and Molinos) had been finished in 1782. A new Théâtre Italien (Jean-François Heurtier) had been built between 1781 and 1783, a new Théâtre Français (De Wailly and M.-J. Peyre) opened its doors in 1782, while the new Mint (Jacques-Denis Antoine) was erected on the Quai de Conti in the 1770's. To all of these we shall return for closer inspection. Churches, too, were being built or improved. Soufflot's grandiose temple, the Church of Sainte-Geneviève (our Panthéon), crowning the Montagne Sainte-Geneviève in the Latin Quarter, was finally completed only in 1789 (Fig. 12). A new north tower was being added under Chalgrin's supervision to the Church of Saint-Sulpice. On the Right Bank a new Church of the Madeleine was under construction (although it was not to receive its final form until early in the nineteenth century). Brongniart had just finished a Doric chapel and cloister for the Capuchin Noviciate (Saint-Louis d'Antin, Lycée

7. Rotonde de Monceau, twentieth-century view

Condorcet) (see Fig. 49). In the Faubourg du Roule, Chalgrin was completing the basilica known as the Church of Saint-Philippe du Roule.

Public buildings like those just mentioned account for only a part of the changes in Paris. *"On bâtit de tous côtés,"* wrote Sébastien Mercier, "—there's money only for building. Huge mansions are springing up as if by magic, and whole new quarters are being formed of mag-

6. Ledoux's Rotonde de Monceau, drawing by Maréchal, 1787

8. Demolition of houses on the Pont au Change. Painting by Hubert Robert, 1788

nificent dwellings."[6] We shall often have occasion to borrow a phrase from Sébastien Mercier, whose *Tableau de Paris* remains the incomparable and inexhaustible chronicle of Louis XVI Paris. Jefferson himself was familiar with the book. The *Tableau de Paris*, he wrote to his friend James Madison when sending him a copy, "is truly a picture of private manners in Paris, but presented on the dark side and a little darkened moreover. But there is so much truth in

9. Demolition of houses on the Pont Notre-Dame. Painting by Hubert Robert, 1786

its ground work that it will be well worth your reading. You will then know Paris (and probably the other large cities of Europe) as well as if you had been here years."[7] Jefferson did not need to read Mercier to know that building was going on everywhere in Paris. "The stone of Paris," he observed, "is very white and beautiful, but it always remains soft, and suffers from the weather."[8] The scaffolding, the piles of stone, the sound of the stonecutter's chisel and carpenter's hammer, met him at every turn. Moreover, he himself was to rent, successively, as his Paris residence, two of the new mansions in two of the new quarters.

The "new quarters" of Jefferson's day were chiefly those included in the wide ring of territory between the old boulevards of Louis XIV Paris and the Wall of the Farmers-General. As one example we may take the neighborhood of the Chaussée d'Antin. This thoroughfare stretched northward from the old boulevard toward the slopes of Montmartre, crossing at

right angles the Chemin de Saint-Lazare, which skirted the base of the hill. The old semi-rural estates here began to be cut up into building lots by the middle of the eighteenth century, but not until the reign of Louis XVI did the builders hold full sway. Here, along the Chaussée d'Antin and the streets that soon branched out from it, Ledoux and other fashionable architects designed houses for bankers, speculators, and opera singers. And here, in the Cul-de-sac Taitbout, Jefferson lived during his first year in Paris. In the autumn of 1785 he moved to another new quarter, the Faubourg du Roule, where he resided in the Hôtel de Langeac for the last four years of his stay in France. Until the middle of the eighteenth century a royal nursery (*pépinière*) had extended from the Champs-Elysées northward to the Chemin du Roule (now the Rue du Faubourg Saint-Honoré), covering an expanse bounded approximately by the present Rue de Berri and Rue La Boétie. In 1772 this property came into the possession of

10. The city enlarged and beautified under the reign of Louis XVI

11. Pont Louis XVI. Medal by Duvivier, 1788

VUE GEOMETRALE DU PORTAIL DE LA NOUVELLE EGLISE DE ST. GENEVIEVE PATRONE DE PARIS

12. Soufflot's original plan for the Church of Sainte-Geneviève. Engraving acquired in Paris by Jefferson

the Comte d'Artois who, following the example of other princely speculators, soon had it cut up into building lots and thus started another new real estate development. The Hôtel de Langeac, where Jefferson made his home, was situated on a portion of the former Pépinière bordering the Champs-Elysées.

Not all the new residences were confined to such new quarters as the Chaussée d'Antin and the Faubourg du Roule. The *hôtels* that Jefferson came to know in the Faubourg Saint-Honoré and in the Faubourg Saint-Germain dated in most cases from the early years of the century; they were to him, not the latest examples of modern building, but yesterday's or day-before-yesterday's houses. Nevertheless, even here, there

were occasional new structures going up. Along the Seine, for example, not far from the Prince de Condé's recently enlarged Palais Bourbon, the Hôtel de Salm stood forth in all its fresh whiteness—inviting the admiration of all visitors to the capital, not the least of whom was Thomas Jefferson (Figs. 13, 14).

If there is any truth in the French saying "*Quand le bâtiment va, tout va*," then the Paris of the 1780's was most certainly a prosperous growing city. Indeed, some appreciation of this building fever is necessary to understand the generally optimistic mood in which public opinion approached the beginning of the French Revolution. Later apologists of the Ancien Régime, the victims of the Revolution, have looked

13. Construction of the Hôtel de Salm. Jefferson was "violently smitten" with this mansion designed by Pierre Rousseau

back nostalgically to the Paris of the 1780's as the time of the only true *douceur de vivre*. In so doing they have transfixed the city in their own static memories and made it seem stationary and unchanging. Yet, when one attempts to live in the Paris of the 1780's with Jefferson and see it from day to day through his eyes, it is impossible not to feel it as a living, forward-looking, rapidly evolving city.

In some respects the Revolution marked a pause in the city's growth. The physical appearance of Paris did not change much in the decade of the 1790's. There was little new construction, nor was there any significant destruction of the existing buildings. To be sure, royal statues were toppled, crown properties were nationalized and "*défleurdelysés*," religious edifices were laicized, mansions of the émigrés found new owners, and the way was thus prepared for speculators and future changes. It was primarily, however, a period in which old buildings were put to new uses. Mercier, when he published his *Nouveau Paris* in 1798, as a sequel to his earlier *Tableau*, could note changes in names, in speech, in manners and dress, but the old landmarks had not changed, for, as he

aptly remarked, "*l'oiseau passe, le nid demeure*" —the birds have flown but the nest remains.[9]

It was not until the early years of the nineteenth century, under the reign of Napoleon, that the "beautifying and improving" of Paris was resumed, often along lines that had already been envisaged by the architects and planners of the Ancien Régime. And it was not until the middle of the century, during the Second Empire, that Baron Haussmann began the transformations that gave Paris the characteristic appearance we associate with the modern metropolis. But even Haussmann and his collaborators did not really obliterate the old. Taking the landmarks created by earlier generations as their fixed points, they set them off, linked them together with new thoroughfares, and in so doing superimposed on the older city a new network of avenues. Beneath this modern design the warp and woof formed by the older streets remain, and thus Jefferson's Paris is still there for us to explore. Haussmann's avenues have shifted the emphasis away from the older arteries. Dust and smoke and weather, the great levelers, have often reduced to a common hue the new buildings of successive generations. Our task here is not so much to reconstruct in our imagination houses that have disappeared as it is to view familiar streets in the light of their older significance and look with fresh eyes at buildings that are still standing.

Every man creates for himself his own image of a city. The houses he lives in, the places he works, the friends he visits, the shops he frequents—all of these, as much as any systematic sight-seeing, make his city different from the next man's. Jefferson's Paris as we are evoking it here is of course a distorted view of the Paris of the 1780's. If, for example, we take the great north-south axis formed by the Rue Saint-Jacques and the Rue Saint-Martin as a dividing line, we find that Jefferson's Paris lies principally in the western half of the city. His business, his friendships, his avocations took him seldom to the working-class districts of the Faubourg Saint-Marcel or the Faubourg Saint-Antoine, or to the Marais which had been the center of fashion a century earlier. The "center" of Jefferson's Paris was roughly the rectangle bounded by the Place Louis XV, the Tuileries, the Louvre, the Palais-Royal, and the Rue Saint-

Honoré. With this we shall begin our account. Then, still on the Right Bank, we shall proceed outward toward the new quarters where Jefferson lived, first the neighborhood of the Chaussée d'Antin and the Boulevards, then the Grille de Chaillot and the Faubourg du Roule. Crossing over to the Left Bank, we shall visit the Faubourg Saint-Germain where several of Jefferson's friends lived and where his daughters were in boarding school—not forgetting a special trip out to the Jardin du Roi on the southeastern edge of the city. Finally, there are the *"environs de Paris,"* the towns then beyond the city wall. One excursion will take us out through the villages of Passy and Auteuil, through Sèvres and Chaville, to Versailles. Another will lead through the Bois de Boulogne and across the ferry to Suresnes and Mont Calvaire. In this same westerly direction we shall also cross the Pont de Neuilly and proceed to Louveciennes, Marly, Saint-Germain-en-Laye, the Désert de Retz, and the Château de la Roche-Guyon. Finally, we shall survey the city as Jefferson saw it during the concluding months of his residence there in the spring and summer of 1789.

14. Festival of Pales. Model by J.-G. Moitte for bas-relief, Hôtel de Salm

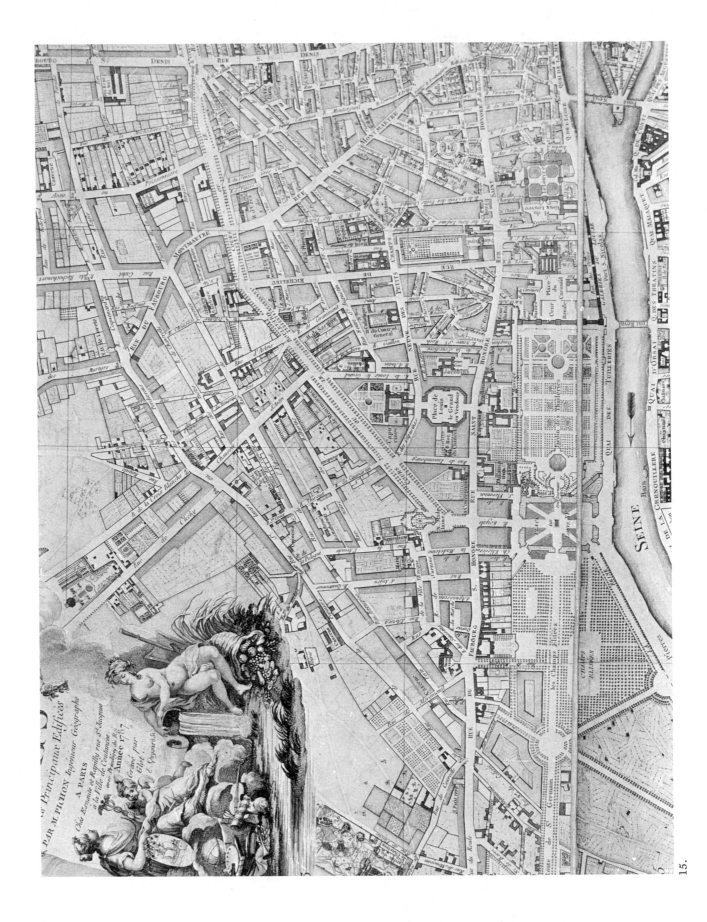

15.

Chapter 2

The Center of Jefferson's Paris
Palais Royal, Halle aux Bleds, Rue Saint-Honoré

THOMAS Jefferson, his eleven-year-old daughter Martha ("Patsy"), and his Negro servant James Hemings arrived in Paris on the 6th of August 1784. They had landed at Le Havre on July 31st, stopped two days in Rouen, then spent August 5th and 6th driving up the Seine valley to Paris. They spent the night of the 5th in the village of Triel and proceeded next day through Saint-Germain-en-Laye, Marly, and Nanterre, across the Bridge of Neuilly into the city. Their carriage took them from Neuilly into the Champs-Elysées, down this avenue to the Place Louis XV, thence along the Rue Saint-Honoré, until it brought them to the Rue de Richelieu, where they found lodgings at the Hôtel d'Orléans, adjoining the Palais Royal. Here they stayed for only a few days before moving to a Left Bank hotel also called the Hôtel d'Orléans.

These facts may be deduced from Jefferson's meticulously kept Account Book, which, in lieu of a diary, provides a daily record of his movements during his five years in Europe[1] (Fig. 16). The Account Book, besides informing us that Jefferson paid 72 *livres* for "house rent for 6 days in the Hotel d'Orleans rue Richlieu," also tells us that during these first days in Paris he hired a valet de chambre named Marc, bought "clothes for Patsy," and for himself lace ruffles, a sword, belt, and shaving apparatus. He "paid Molini for books 58 *livres*," the first of his many Paris book purchases, and for 3 *livres* bought "a map"—no doubt a street map similar to the one reproduced here (Fig. 15).

The Hôtel d'Orléans, one of the many hotels for travelers in this vicinity, faced the Rue de Richelieu (present No. 30) and extended back

16. Jefferson's Account Book

[13]

17.   *Vue du Nouveau Palais Royal*

to the Rue de Montpensier, which bounded the Gardens of the Palais Royal on the western side.[2] It was an obvious place for a foreign visitor to stop upon his first arrival in Paris, for the new Palais Royal was at the center of the city's life. Sébastien Mercier called it "the capital of Paris." "There," he wrote, "you can see everything, hear everything, learn everything. . . . There is no spot in the world comparable to it. Visit London, Amsterdam, Madrid, Vienna, you will see nothing like it: a prisoner could live here free from care for years with no thought of escape."[3] Mercier was speaking of the "new" Palais Royal as he knew it about 1788. He would not have used such superlatives a decade earlier, as it was only during the period of Jefferson's residence in Paris that the Palais Royal attained its pivotal position.

The Palace itself was of course not new and had served in turn various members of the royal family before passing in 1780 into the hands of Louis-Philippe-Joseph d'Orléans (1747–1793), then Duc de Chartres, who became Duc d'Orléans upon his father's death in 1785 and was later

known as "Philippe-Egalité." The Duke's attempts to play a political and military role had met with little success. His conduct as a naval commander in the Battle of Ouessant (1778), for example, had been widely criticized. He thus sought popularity and prestige as a man of fashion and arbiter of taste, and like so many of his aristocratic but impecunious contemporaries, caught the prevalent fever for real estate speculation. To realize his scheme for transforming his palace, the Duke turned to the architect Victor Louis, who had achieved fame with his designs for the Theatre of Bordeaux.[4] The gardens extending northward from the old palace were framed by new constructions, adjacent properties were acquired (to the dismay of dispossessed owners), and a spacious enclosure formed. This rectangle was bounded by the Rue Saint-Honoré (Place du Palais Royal) on the south, the Rue de Montpensier (parallel to the Rue de Richelieu) on the west, the Rue de Beaujolais on the north, and the Rue de Valois. The architect's most distinctive achievement was the arcaded galleries extending from street level above the *entresol* and forming a covered promenade around the perimeter of the gardens (Fig. 17). Shopkeepers whose establishments opened into the galleries, like occupants of the upper stories, were constrained by the terms of their deeds or leases to preserve intact the external appearance of the property.

By 1784 this new Palais Royal was open for business and pleasure, though masons and carpenters continued to work on various parts of it. In 1787, when reviewing recent urban improvements, Jefferson pointed out that "the Palais Royal is gutted, a considerable part in the center of the garden being dug out, and a subterranean circus begun wherein will be equestrian exhibitions, &c."[5] (Fig. 18). Observing such changes with the eye of an architect and builder, Jefferson could also appreciate the speculative aspects of the Palais Royal development. Soon after his arrival in Paris he described it to his Virginian friend, Dr. James Currie, as "a particular building lately erected here, which has greatly enriched the owner of the ground, has added one of the principal ornaments to the city and increased the convenience of its inhabitants." Seeking some potentially profitable investment for their own funds, Jefferson and his secretary William Short had discussed the possibility of a similar plan for Shockoe Hill in Richmond, the growing capital of Virginia. It would be, Jefferson told Currie (whose participation he invited), "a whole square in Richmond improved on some such plan, but accommodated to the circumstances of the place" and "would be very highly advantageous to the proprietors, convenient to the town and ornamental."[6] Although the scheme proposed to Dr. Currie was soon dropped, it provides a hint of how Jefferson's Paris observations stimulated his imagination and suggested applications in his native land.

During his sojourn in Paris Jefferson returned many times to the Palais Royal, enjoying it as an "ornament" while appreciating it as a "convenience." "Although everything increases, triples, and quadruples in price here," Mercier warned, "there seems to reign some charm that attracts money from all pockets, especially from foreigners, who go mad over this convenient assemblage of delights: it is a privileged spot where you can find in no time anything that

your situation may require."[7] Jefferson occasionally bought books here—from De Bray, for example—although his principal purchases were reserved for Left Bank dealers. One day he paid 36 *f* "for 12 ivory handled knives at the Prix fixe." This "Magasin d'effets précieux à prix fixe," under the management of "le Sieur Verrier et Cie" (located on the first floor of one of the new buildings and entered from arcade No. 9), carried a large stock of objects in marble, bronze, and porcelain, paintings, furniture, jewels, clocks, fine textiles, etc., consigned by owners on a commission basis and all labeled with a fixed price not subject to bargaining.[8] Another day Jefferson bought "a pendule at the Palais Royal," probably also at Verrier's Prix fixe.

Upon still another occasion Jefferson "paid for dinner at Palais Royal 24 *f*." Although his Account Book does not specify which of the many restaurants it was, it might have been Beauvillier's, Labarrière's, the Taverne Anglaise, the Grotte Flamande, Février's (No. 113), or perhaps the Café Mécanique (No. 121). This latter establishment boasted dumb-waiters connected with the kitchens below and concealed in the large column-shaped legs of the tables.[9] Customers were thus served with no waiters present.

In addition to the restaurants, the Palais Royal's "assemblage of delights" included such attractions as the Théâtre de Beaujolais (Nos. 68–

VUE INTERIEURE DU CIRQUE,
au Jardin du ci-devant Palais Royal.

18. Subterranean circus in the center of the Palais-Royal garden

75, the present Théâtre du Palais Royal) where marionettes and child-actors performed, "Les Fantoccini" (Italian marionettes, No. 54), Séraphin's *ombres chinoises et marionnettes* (Nos. 119–120), a *Spectacle des Pygmées français*, Curtius's wax-works (No. 17), as well as the theatre known as Les Variétés. With the encouragement of the Duc d'Orléans, the Théâtre des Variétés Amusantes had moved in 1785 from the Boulevards to the Palais Royal, where a large wooden structure was built for it next to the palace on a site known today as the Parterre d'Enée[10] (Fig. 19). Jefferson witnessed several performances here. Among his papers is a note from Madame de Marmontel inviting "Monsieur de Gefferson" to share with her the Baron de Breteuil's box at the Variétés for Dumaniant's new play, *Guerre ouverte, ou Ruse contre Ruse*, which had opened on 4 October 1786.[11] The play enjoyed considerable success

20. Chessmen belonging to Jefferson

not only in Paris and the French provinces but in other European capitals as well. In London it had a long run at Covent Garden as *The Midnight Hour, or War of Wits*. Antoine-Jean Bourlin, alias Dumaniant, was one of the star actors of the Variétés as well as the author of many of its plays. Jefferson attended a performance of his *Le Dragon de Thionville* (29 December 1786) and of his *La Nuit aux aventures, ou les Deux Morts vivans* (25 October 1787).[12] *Le Revenant, ou les Deux Grenadiers* by De Senne, another of the plays seen by Jefferson at the Variétés (12 January 1787), portrayed a young French grenadier, reported missing overseas, who unexpectedly returns from the recent war thanks to an American officer who had carried him from the battlefield and dressed his wounds. As the American minister to the French Court, Jefferson no doubt appreciated the topical allusions to the grenadier's benefactor and "*sa généreuse nation*" and to "*nos braves Alliés*."

More serious diversions were also available in the Palais Royal. Above the Café de Foy (arcades Nos. 57–60), was a Salon des Echecs where "gentlemen of the Court and the Town" could match wits at chess[13] (Fig. 20). Jefferson, who had played the game since his student days in Williamsburg, paid his admission fee of 96 *f* on 6 February 1786 and added to his collection of chessbooks a copy of the *Traité des échecs du Café de Foy*. In the Palais Royal proper there was a splendid art gallery of Old Masters (Jefferson viewed it upon one occasion in the Marquis de Chastellux's company), a Natural History Cabinet, a Cabinet of Medals, as well as an exhibit of scale models of tools and

19. Variétés Amusantes

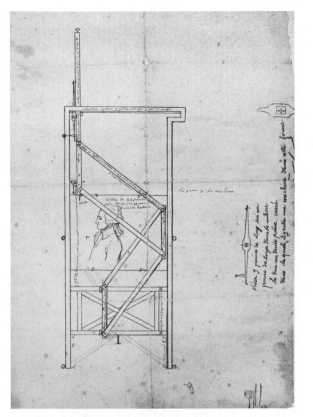

21. The Chrétien-Quenedey Physiognotrace

machines constructed from plates in the *Ency-clopédie* by Périer Frères for the education of the children of the Duc d'Orléans.[14]

It was in the Palais Royal, too, that Jefferson learned of a new invention called the *physiono-trace*, a mechanical device for tracing profiles invented by Gilles-Louis Chrétien and exploited commercially by him in partnership with Edme Quenedey (Fig. 21). In 1788 Chrétien and Quenedey set up business in the vicinity of the Palais Royal. According to one of their an-nouncements, tickets for sittings could be ob-tained "at the Palais Royal, under the first arcade on the right when entering from the Cour des Princes, at the shop of M. Bevalet, Jeweller, No. 180, where frames for these little portraits may also be obtained."[15] On 22 April 1789 Jefferson and his compatriot Gouverneur Morris (who had arrived in Paris earlier that year and was then staying at a hotel in the Rue de Richelieu) stopped in at Bevalet's to get an appointment for a physiognotrace sitting, but it was too late in the day and they had to return next morning.

"Can get only one Ticket," Morris noted in his diary, "Go with this to the Rue Croix des Petits Champs where he sits." Morris waited another month for his own sitting. Meanwhile, Jefferson had returned to Quenedey's studio on 29 April to pick up and pay for his finished profiles: 6 *f* for the initial sitting and 30 *f* for the engraved plate and a dozen prints therefrom[16] (Figs. 22, 23).

22. Jefferson, drawn from life by Quenedey, 1789

23. Gouverneur Morris, drawn from life by Quenedey, 1789

galleries with her two daughters; the virtuous wife, the honest citizeness, dare not be seen beside the bold courtesans, whose finery, manners, bearing, and often even their words, force one to flee, bemoaning the general corruption of both sexes."[18]

* * * * * * * * * * *

Not far to the east of the Palais Royal was a newly laid out circle, in the center of which stood the municipal grain market, the Halle aux Bleds. Arthur Young described it as "by far the finest thing" he had seen in Paris: "a vast rotunda, the roof entirely of wood, upon a new principle of carpentry . . . so well planned and so admirably executed that I know of no public building that exceeds it in either France or England."[19] The site near the Church of Saint-Eustache had been acquired by the City of Paris

24. "At eleven o'clock it is day chez Madame. . . ."

More than anything else, the Palais Royal was a place to observe the latest fashions and hear the latest gossip—the "empty bustle of Paris," Jefferson called it when writing to a young American woman eager for news of Paris. Describing the daily round of a lady of fashion, he continued: "At eleven o'clock it is day chez Madame. The curtains are drawn. Propped on bolsters and pillows, and her head scratched into a little order, the bulletins of the sick are read, and the billets of the well. She writes to some of her acquaintances and receives the visits of others. If the morning is not very thronged, she is able to get out and hobble round the cage of the Palais Royal: but she must hobble quickly, for the Coeffeur's turn is come; and a tremendous turn it is!"[17] (Fig. 24). According to Mercier, an honest and beautiful woman could hobble around the Palais Royal gardens "without having to complain of a glance"—that is, if the hour were noon or late afternoon. But, once evening had come, it was a different story. Then, Mercier cautioned: "a mother dare not cross the noisy

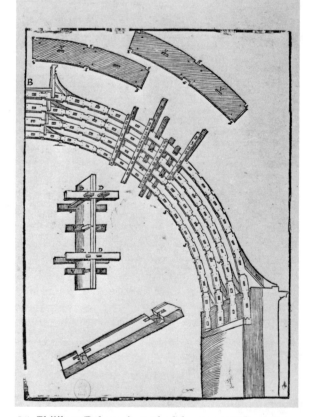

25. Philibert Delorme's method for constructing a dome

26. The new Halle aux Bleds and the Column surviving from the sixteenth century. Drawing by Maréchal, 1786

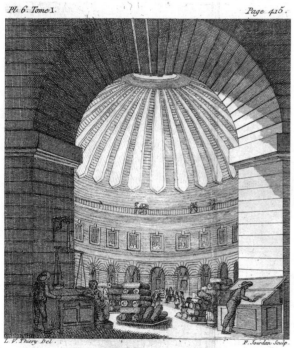

VUE INTÉRIEURE DE LA NOUVELLE HALLE

27. The Halle aux Bleds "flooded with daylight"

in the mid-eighteenth century. By 1767 a circular edifice built around an open court and designed by Le Camus de Mézières was completed. Some ten years later the task of covering this courtyard was entrusted to the architects J.-G. Legrand and Jacques Molinos, who revived a method of construction used by the Renaissance architect Philibert Delorme (Fig. 25). The light weight of the structure enabled the builders to insert in the space between the ribs twenty-five windows radiating from the central lantern and flooding the interior with daylight (Figs. 26, 27). The work was accepted on behalf of the city in 1782. Shortly thereafter the new-domed market was the scene of a public festival celebrating the Peace Treaty of 1783, and several years later in July 1790 a commemorative ceremony in honor of Benjamin Franklin was held within its black-draped walls.[20]

The Halle aux Bleds inevitably attracted Jefferson's attention and, indeed, came to occupy a special place in his memories of Paris. While representing the United States in France, Jefferson also handled various matters for the state of Virginia. He was, for example, in correspondence with his Virginia colleagues concerning designs for public buildings in Richmond, including the Capitol as well as a prison and a public market.[21] With the future welfare of his native state in mind, he set out one day in August 1786 to study the Paris grain market. He was accompanied by John Trumbull, the Connecticut-born painter then residing in London, who was also a bit of an architect. Less intent than Jefferson upon public welfare, Trumbull had invited his acquaintances, Richard and Maria Cosway, to join the party.[22] The English miniature painter (who had come to Paris to paint the children of the Duc d'Orléans) and especially his artist wife (Maria Hadfield, born in Italy of English parents) were soon competing with the "sticks and chips" of the market for Jefferson's attention (Fig. 28). His previous engagements, including a dinner with the elderly Duchesse de La Rochefoucauld, were speedily

MARIA COSWAY

Published as the Act directs ap Jan 1785 by G Bartolozzi & to be had at M.r Torres Hay Market 22.

28.

canceled by "lying messengers." The new acquaintances dined together (no doubt in the Palais Royal), then drove to Saint-Cloud, from Saint-Cloud to Ruggieri's, from Ruggieri's to Krumpholtz'—"and if the day had been as long as a Lapland summer day, you would still have contrived means among you to have filled it."

The meeting at the Halle aux Bleds marked the beginning of a series of sight-seeing expeditions, doubly charming to Jefferson because of the presence of a charming companion.[23] These "follies" continued until mid-September, when the usually decorous American minister, in a moment of exuberance, attempted to vault over a little fence in the Cours la Reine—only to fall and dislocate the wrist of his right hand. Having performed the last sad office of handing the Cosways into their carriage at the "Pavillon of St. Denis" (see Fig. 2), Jefferson's left hand then penned a twelve-page letter ("three mortal sheets of paper") to Maria in the form of a Shandean dialogue between "my Head" and "my Heart."[24] In it he lived over again in his imagination the well-filled days that had elapsed since the meeting at the Halle aux Bleds.

The ways by which the example of the Paris market contributed, via Jefferson's Head, to the one at Richmond are unknown, as only fragmentary documents concerning the latter structure are extant. We know, however, that Jefferson often recalled the Legrand and Molinos dome in later years. In 1802, for example, when unsuccessfully proposing to Congress a plan for a lock-dock, he suggested a "roof of the construction of that over the meal market at Paris, except that that is hemispherical, this semi-cylindrical. For this construction see Delorme's architecture, whose invention it was."[25] Jefferson had several editions of Delorme's *Inventions pour bien bâtir* in his own library and included it among the basic architectural works recommended for the University of Virginia.[26] Again, in 1805, when discussing with Benjamin H. Latrobe the dome covering the House of Representatives in the Capitol at Washington, he proposed the Halle aux Bleds as a model.[27] Latrobe feared that such a method of lighting the hall presented many disadvantages, such as troublesome sunlight and possible leakage. "A single leaky joint," he maintained, "dropping upon the head or desk of a member will disturb the whole house." Jefferson eventually deferred to Latrobe's judgment, but with this rejoinder: "I cannot express to you the regret I feel on the subject of renouncing of the Halle aux Bleds lights of the Capitol dome. That single circumstance was to constitute the distinguishing merit of the room, and would solely have made it the handsomest room in the world, without a single exception. Take that away, it becomes a common thing exceeded by many."

Jefferson probably did not realize, when he was writing to Latrobe, that the Legrand and Molinos dome as he had known it in Paris was already a thing of the past. In the course of repair work in 1802, a soldering-stove set fire to the wooden frame and the entire dome collapsed. When rebuilding it in 1809–1811, the architect Bélanger, assisted by the engineer Brunet replaced the woodwork with iron ribs—an early use of structural iron and forerunner of later architectural developments.[28] Eventually the entire building was demolished to make way for the Bourse du Commerce, completed in 1889 and still standing on the circular site of the old Halle aux Bleds. Next to it stands a curious column, the same that stood beside the meal market of the 1780's. It had been erected in 1572 on the grounds of the Hôtel de Soissons for Catherine de Médicis, who, tradition says, wound her way up its inside staircase to read the stars with her astrologer. The column (designed by the Renaissance architect Jean Bullant) escaped demolition at the time the eighteenth-century market was being built through the efforts of M. de Bachaumont, a connoisseur and antiquary who purchased the column and presented it to the City of Paris. Thus, thanks to M. de Bachaumont's interest in historic preservation, a classic column still marks the spot where Jefferson met Maria Cosway one summer day in 1786. (In 1975 it stood precariously on the brink of a great abyss created by the demolition of Baltard's nineteenth-century markets.)

✳ ✳ ✳ ✳ ✳ ✳ ✳ ✳ ✳ ✳ ✳ ✳

In the 1780's the Rue Saint-Honoré was the "main street" of the Right Bank.[29] No thoroughfare ran parallel between it and the Seine embankment. The present Rue de Rivoli (named

for one of Bonaparte's early victories) was cut through only during the First Empire. In its place, a labyrinth of small streets branched off from the Rue Saint-Honoré and filled the space now occupied by the Gardens of the Louvre, while private gardens in the rear of the houses along the western part of the street stretched back to the Tuileries Gardens. Even today the Rue Saint-Honoré is a narrow, busy street. It must have seemed even narrower and busier when all the traffic was channeled there. *"Gare! Gare! Gare les voitures!"* was Mercier's advice to poor pedestrians, who must expect to be spattered, crowded against the walls (there were no sidewalks), knocked down by a carriage, a hackney coach, or worse still, by a one-horse cabriolet driven at breakneck speed by some young man of fashion.[30] Despite such hazards, Jefferson soon became familiar with the whole length of the street from its eastern reaches near the Halle aux Bleds to the western end, where it intersects the Rue Royale and becomes the Rue du Faubourg Saint-Honoré.

Opposite the Palais Royal, on a triangular site bounded by the Rue de Chartres and the Rue Saint-Thomas-du-Louvre, was a fashionable new music hall, or "vauxhall," known as the Panthéon. According to Thiéry's guide for travelers, classic colonnades, Chinese pagodas, and ingenious lighting effects all contrived to create there an atmosphere of "gaiety and voluptuousness."[31] The hall of this Panthéon was occasionally used for less frivolous entertainment. Jefferson attended several concerts there, including a benefit, on 27 May 1789, for "Mr. George Bridgetower, a young negro from the British colonies, aged nine."[32] In the course of the program, which included a Haydn symphony, young Bridgewater (the son of an African father and Polish mother) executed a violin concerto by Giornowich, another by Viotti, and a rondeau by Grosse.

Continuing westward along the Rue Saint-Honoré, one soon came to the Church of Saint-Roch, on the right, and beyond that the Convent of the Jacobins. When Jefferson passed by, it was still an innocuous convent. Several years later, as the meeting place of the Revolutionary Jacobin Club, its name spread throughout the western world and gave birth to an epithet with which Jefferson was frequently damned by his political enemies. Beyond the Jacobins was the town house of the Comte and Comtesse d'Houdetot.[33] Madame d'Houdetot, the "Sophie" of Rousseau's *Confessions* and one of Franklin's fervent feminine admirers, specialized in Americans. Jefferson inherited her friendship from his predecessor, made dutiful calls at the Saint-Honoré *hôtel* and at her country place in Sannois (where he once lost 18 *sous* playing lotto), though never as frequently as the "old countess" (as he referred to her) would have liked. Their chief bond was a common interest in the two young sons of Saint-John de Crèvecoeur, who were at school in Paris while their father was serving as French consul in New York.

On the other side of the street was the mansion of the Noailles family, part of which has been incorporated in the present Hôtel de St. James & Albany. Adrienne de Noailles, at the age of fourteen and a half, was married to the Marquis de Lafayette (then only sixteen) in the chapel there in 1774, and continued to live with her family while her husband gained fame and glory in America. Farther along the street came the convent of the Feuillants and an adjoining building, the "Maison des Feuillants," a recently built apartment house designed by Jacques-Denis Antoine (still extant at present Nos. 229–235 Rue Saint-Honoré).[34] Like many of their Paris contemporaries, the Feuillant fathers evidently appreciated real estate as a revenue-producing investment. Among those living in their new style apartment house were Jefferson's acquaintances, Abbé Morellet, the abbé's niece Madame de Marmontel, and her husband, the secretary of the French Academy. Abbé Morellet prepared the French version of Jefferson's *Notes on the State of Virginia*, which appeared in 1786 as *Observations sur la Virginie, par M. J.****. Marmontel, whose *Contes Moraux* Jefferson had read (the English version, *Moral Tales*) as a youth in Virginia, was a dabbler in economic and political theory, a contributor of articles on literary criticism to the *Encyclopédie*, and the author of libretti for several of the Grétry light operas that Jefferson heard while in Paris.

Next, opening out from the Rue Saint-Honoré opposite the Maison des Feuillants, came the Place Vendôme or Place Louis le Grand, the

square laid out by J.-H. Mansart during the reign of Louis XIV. Many of the residents in the square or vicinity were men of wealth and patrons of the arts. Mercier claimed that one of the great attractions of this neighborhood for aspiring young writers and artists was the good tables set there. One such patron was Monsieur Chalut de Vérin, a Farmer-General, whose collections of art and natural history were said to fill and overflow thirteen rooms on the first floor of his mansion at what is now No. 17 Place Vendôme (next door to the Ritz). "When a person

29.

wants to assemble such a collection," snaps Thiéry's *Guide*, "it would be advisable for him to consult artists or enlightened connoisseurs in order to avoid confusion and select only choice pieces."[35] Although Jefferson's own comments have not survived, he must have inspected the collections when he dined at Chalut de Vérin's, as he did upon at least one occasion.[36] The Farmer-General was a brother of Abbé Chalut, whom Jefferson counted among his literary friends, as had Franklin and John Adams. Close by the Place Vendôme, in the Rue des Capucines, lived the banker Ferdinand Grand, the official banker of the United States, upon whom Jefferson depended for his monthly salary advances and expense account.[37] Though he at times found Grand "a very sure banker, but a timid one" (especially when "very small demands for current occasions" were refused) Jefferson could nevertheless testify to Grand's indispensable services to the United States in the days when American public finances were in a precarious state.

The Rue Saint-Honoré boasted more than churches, convents, and private residences. Then as now, fashionable shops occupied the lower floors of many of the buildings. Jefferson made many purchases all along the street. From Noseda, a dealer in scientific instruments, he bought thermometers, a pedometer, reading glasses, and such novelties as phosphoric matches[38] (Fig. 29). From the jeweller Daguerre (who enjoyed royal patronage), Jefferson bought lamps for his residence, and from Dupuis, whose shop "Au Puits" was situated at the eastern end of the street, a variety of household furnishings. Jean-Baptiste Odiot, a goldsmith "At the Sign of the Cross of Gold" near the Church of Saint-Roch at the corner of the now obliterated Rue des Frondeurs, executed after Jefferson's designs a silver *fontaine* (tea or coffee urn) and a pair of goblets[39] (Fig. 30). Nor was Jefferson insensible to the fact that the Rue Saint-Honoré was the capital of *la haute couture* (Fig. 31). He himself subscribed to the *Cabinet des Modes*, sent fashion plates to feminine friends in America, and relayed gossip about Mademoiselle Rose Bertin, the dressmaker to Queen Marie-Antoinette, who

31. Les Jolies Couturières

30. Silver Goblets executed by J.-B.-C. Odiot after Jefferson's design

launched those mountainous hats and billowing dresses that were everywhere to be seen in Jefferson's Paris. It was from Mademoiselle Bertin's shop (the location changed with her changing fortunes) that the celebrated *poupée de la Rue Saint-Honoré*, dressed in the *dernier cri*, left for her periodic travels to the capitals and courts of all Europe.[40] Although the style-setting doll seems not to have crossed the Atlantic at this time, she provided Jefferson with a moralizing simile when he remembered her years later. Speaking of fashions in medical treatment, he wrote to a friend: "I have lived myself to see the disciples of Hoffmann, Boerhave, Stahl, Cullen, Brown, succeed one another like the shifting figures of a magic lantern, and their fancies, like the dresses of the annual doll babies from Paris, becoming, from their novelty, the vogue of the day, and yielding to the next novelty their ephemeral favor."[41]

VUE PERSPECTIVE DE LA PLACE LOUIS XV,
prise du Côté des Champs Elisées.

A.P.D.R.   Ile de France   N° 9.

32.

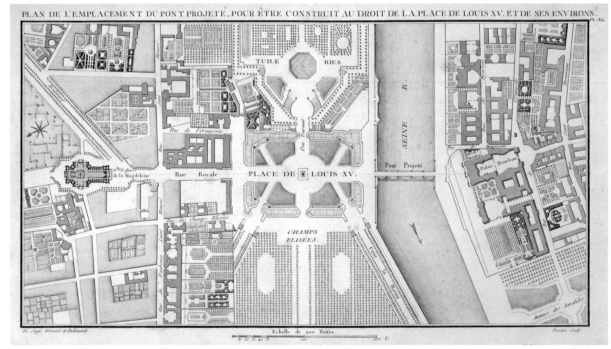

PLAN DE L'EMPLACEMENT DU PONT PROJETÉ, POUR ÊTRE CONSTRUIT AU DROIT DE LA PLACE DE LOUIS XV, ET DE SES ENVIRONS.   Pl. XI.

Echelle de 200 Toises

33.

Chapter 3

The Center of Jefferson's Paris
Place Louis XV, Tuileries, Louvre

THE Place Louis XV, said Arthur Young, "is not properly a square, but a very noble entrance to a great city."[1] It was in 1748 that the City of Paris, wishing to commemorate popular rejoicing over the reputedly miraculous recovery of Louis XV, *le bien aimé*, had voted to erect an equestrian statue of the monarch. As a site for the memorial, the King himself placed at the city's disposal certain vacant lands adjoining the Tuileries and the Champs-Elysées. Work on the square, planned as a grandiose setting for the statue, was begun in 1757 under the supervision of Ange-Jacques Gabriel (the architect who had won laurels with his Ecole Militaire) and was completed some twenty years later when Louis XVI was on the throne.[2] When Jefferson passed through the square, upon his first entrance into the great city, it was one of the latest sights for travelers to see (Figs. 32, 33). The American Minister soon acquired more than a tourist's impression and came to know the Place Louis XV better perhaps than almost any spot in Paris. To supplement his own observations he added to his library Pierre Patte's lavishly illustrated folios, *Monumens érigés en France à la gloire de Louis XV*, a work that provided models for architects and city planners throughout Europe and, Jefferson hoped, possibly in America as well.[3]

In the center of the square, on the axis extending from the Château des Tuileries to the summit of the Champs-Elysées, stood Edme Bouchardon's statue of Louis XV (Fig. 34). When approached from either direction, Jefferson discovered, it became an interesting study in perspective and led him to reflect on equestrian statues in general. Writing to the Virginia delegates in Congress concerning a proposal for an eques-

STATUE EQUESTRE DE LOUIS XV A PARIS.
Composée et Exécutée en Bronze par M. Bouchardon.

34.

trian statue of Washington, he described Bouchardon's Louis XV as "probably the best in the world, and it is the smallest here." "Yet," he continued, "it is impossible to find a point of view from which it does not appear a monster, unless you go so far as to lose sight of the features and finer lineaments of the face and body. A statue is not made, like a mountain, to be seen at a great distance. To perceive those minuter circumstances which constitute its beauty you must be near to it, and, in that case, it should be so much above the size of the life, as to appear actually of that size from your point of view. I should not therefore fear to propose that the one intended by Congress could be considerably smaller than any of those to be seen here; as I think it will be more beautiful, and also cheaper. I have troubled you with these observations as they have been suggested to me from an actual sight of works of this kind."[4] Several months after transmitting these observations, Jefferson established his residence in the Hôtel de Langeac, a mansion about two-thirds the way up the Champs-Elysées, from which point he could discern the mass of the statue at the foot of the tree-lined thoroughfare (see Fig. 68). It thus became a familiar landmark and a convenient milestone as well: when calculating by means of a pedometer his rate of walking, he noted that the distance from his house at the Grille de Chaillot to the Louis XV statue was 820 double steps.[5]

Looking from the royal statue (where an Egyptian obelisk now stands) toward the Seine, Jefferson would have seen no bridge there, though there had been talk of one since early in the century. The proposed new bridge already had a name—Pont Louis XVI, the engineer Perronet had earlier drawn plans, which had been published in a royally sponsored volume, but it was not completed until 1791, after Jefferson left Paris[6] (see Fig. 11). Throughout his stay, whenever he went from his Champs-Elysées residence to visit friends in the Faubourg Saint-Germain, he had either to be ferried across the river or take the more circuitous route via the Pont Royal.

Framing the square on its northern side, flanking the Rue Royale, were the Hôtel du Garde-Meuble (now the Ministry of the Navy) and its sister mansion (in which the Hôtel Crillon is now located), both designed by Gabriel.[7] Completing the perspective at the left, on the site occupied today by the United States Embassy, was the residence of Grimod de La Reynière, for which Clérisseau had designed a neo-Pompeian salon. At the right, still standing at the corner of present Rue de Rivoli and housing branch offices of the Embassy, was Chalgrin's Hôtel de La Vrillière, also known from the names of subsequent owners as Saint-Florentin, Infantado, Talleyrand, or Rothschild. Jefferson greatly admired Gabriel's façades, especially the Garde-Meuble, which he ranked, along with the Galerie du Louvre and the two fronts of the Hôtel de Salm, among the "celebrated fronts of modern buildings." A few years later, when dis-

cussing plans for the city of Washington with Major L'Enfant, he sent a roll of city plans and engraved plates collected in Europe and suggested the front of the Garde-Meuble as a possible model for the President's house.[8]

The Hôtel du Garde-Meuble housed offices and workshops of the administrative services responsible for furnishing the royal palaces (equivalent to the present Mobilier National) and served as a storehouse for furniture, tapestries, and objets d'art. The Crown jewels as well as a collection of ancient and exotic arms, such as Henri IV's sword (see Fig. 173), made it also a museum to which the public was admitted on certain days. It was doubtless to view these treasures that Jefferson, with Mrs. Cosway by his side, "paid seeing Gardes meubles, 12 f" on 9 September 1786.

Beyond the Garde-Meuble, at the head of the Rue Royale, a new Church of the Madeleine, intended to complete Gabriel's scheme for the Place Louis XV, was under construction.[9] Contant d'Ivry's original plans had been discarded following his death in 1777. The new designs of G.-M. Couture, like those of his predecessor, were currently debated in the Academy of Architecture and among carping connoisseurs. Work ceased entirely in 1791, was resumed in 1806 (by the architect Pierre Vignon, who began transforming the church into a "Temple of Glory"), but was finally completed and the church consecrated only in 1842. What Jefferson saw, therefore, was not today's familiar Madeleine, but a mere construction site where columns were barely rising above ground. An entry in his Account Book—"pd. at Madelaine 1 f 4"—suggests that he inspected M. Méraud's scale models of the church (one from Contant d'Ivry's plans, another from Couture's) that could be seen in the model-maker's workshop within the construction enclosure.[10]

Models such as these were of particular interest to Jefferson at that time because he was searching for an architect to help him perfect designs for the Richmond Capitol. Finding the style of architecture in Paris "far from chaste," he sought "an architect whose taste had been formed on a study of the antient models of this art."[11] His choice, a happy one, eventually fell upon Charles-Louis Clérisseau, who had studied twenty years in Rome and given proof of his taste in his engraved plates of the *Monuments de Nismes*. The French architect and Jefferson —*"un amateur zélé de ma chère antiquité,"* as Clérisseau characterized his friend[12]—together drew up plans for the Capitol in Richmond. Though its appearance, both exterior and interior, has been modified during the past two centuries, drawings and a scale model in plaster (executed by Fouquet, who had worked for Choiseul-Gouffier, author of the *Voyage pittoresque de la Grèce*) survive as evidence of the original Jefferson-Clérisseau conception.[13]

* * * * * * * * * * * *

The *pont tournant*, the swivel bridge that connected the Place Louis XV with the Jardin des Tuileries in Jefferson's time, has disappeared, but the entrance to the gardens is still framed by horseshoe-shaped walks leading up to the terraces and is still flanked by Coysevox's winged horses bearing Fame and Mercury (see Figs. 156, 172), brought here from Marly early in the eighteenth century. The formal gardens with the octagonal *bassin* and the circular pool along the central *allée* were laid out by André Le Nôtre during the reign of Louis XIV.[14] The Tuileries Palace formed a backdrop and did so until 1871, when it was burned during the Commune and its ruins razed. Along the Seine stretched the still familiar Terrasse du Bord de l'Eau, balanced on the opposite side of the garden by the Terrasse des Feuillants, which was sacrificed when the Rue de Rivoli was cut through.

Very soon after his arrival in Paris Jefferson came to the Tuileries Gardens, along with the rest of Paris, to witness a balloon ascension by the Robert brothers on Sunday, 19 September 1784. This was the twenty-fourth recorded as-

35. Place Louis XV with the Robert Brothers' balloon rising above the Tuileries Gardens, 19 September 1784. Drawing by De Machy. (The dome of the Madeleine at the head of the Rue Royale is the artist's anticipation)

MÉMOIRE

SUR LES EXPÉRIENCES

AÉROSTATIQUES

FAITES PAR MM. ROBERT FRERES,

Ingénieurs-Pensionnaires du Roi.

A PARIS,

DE L'IMPRIMERIE DE PHILIPPE-DENYS PIERRES,

Imprimeur Ordinaire du Roi, &c. N. P.

M. DCC. LXXXIV.

36.

At least one of the other foreigners present was impressed by the order and decorum. "I have seen ten times the bustle," wrote Dr. Johnson's friend Mrs. Piozzi, "and ten times the difficulty at a crowded playhouse in London, than the Parisians made when all the City was gathered together. Nobody was hurt, nobody was frightened—nobody was even *incommoded*: some comforts must then be confessed to result from a despotic Government."[17] There were, however, a few mishaps. The balloon had been filled with "inflammable air" (hydrogen) the previous afternoon, thanks to a new device invented by Vallet. At 11:30 on Sunday morning it was brought along the central allée of the Garden to the platform erected over the oval pool in front of the Château. The curious crowd closed in to see what was inside the gondola and broke the "rudder" affixed to the "stern" of the ship. Fortunately this accident caused no delay in the scheduled count-down. The two Robert

37. La Jolie Loueuse-de-chaises

cension since Pilâtre de Rozier and the Marquis d'Arlandes had flown over Paris in their hot-air-filled *montgolfière* from the Château de la Muette to the Butte des Cailles on 1 November 1783, and the third flight of the Robert brothers in their hydrogen-filled balloon.[15] Even before he had come to Europe Jefferson was interested in "aerostatics" and had tabulated all the information he could gather about the earliest flights.[16] In Philadelphia, in May 1784, he had even watched an air-filled balloon rise to a height of 300 feet, but this was not a passenger-carrying vehicle. It was in the Tuileries Gardens that he first saw human beings borne aloft. On Sunday morning Jefferson followed the crowd to the Château des Tuileries, where three of the six entrances to the Garden were open for ticket-holders. He had purchased his ticket the previous day for 6 *livres*, admitting two, at the "cabinet" of MM. Robert in the Place des Victoires. Elaborate preparations, including explicit traffic regulations, duly announced in the *Journal de Paris*, had been made by the city authorities.

38. View from the Terrasse des Tuileries. (The Hôtel de Salm, not visible here, would have been farther to the left)

brothers and their brother-in-law Colin Hullin climbed into their rudderless ship and at exactly two minutes before noon rose into the air amidst the acclamations of the crowd (Fig. 35).

By ten minutes before two the balloon had disappeared over the Paris horizon. The three travelers floated over Clermont-en-Beauvaisis, over Montdidier, and finally, at forty minutes past six, came successfully to earth at Beuvray, near the city of Béthune in the province of Artois—thus establishing a record for the longest flight to date. Paris was abuzz with rumors. On Tuesday and Wednesday the *Journal de Paris* published letters from provincial correspondents who had seen "them" passing over, but not until Thursday the 23rd was it able to print the Robert brothers' own letter confirming their successful descent (Fig. 36).

Throughout his stay in Paris, Jefferson kept abreast of the latest aerostatical experiments. He reported to his scientifically minded correspondents in America the first cross-Channel flight made on 7 January 1785 by Jean-Pierre Blanchard and the Boston-born Londoner Dr. John Jeffries, and then in June of that year the fatal accident of Pilâtre de Rozier and his companion Romain, "the two first martyrs to the aeronautical art."[18] The following year he watched M. Tétu take off in his balloon from the Luxembourg Gardens.[19] It was thus as an experienced observer that Jefferson, when back home in America, watched Jean-Pierre Blanchard ascend over the Philadelphia rooftops for the first successful air voyage in the United States on 9 January 1793.

While the Tuileries Gardens occasionally offered great public spectacles such as balloon ascensions, Jefferson came to know the place more intimately as a retreat for strolling and reverie. Even then it was one of the city's public parks, though notions of "public" have changed somewhat over the years. Thiéry's guidebook specified that "La populace ne peut entrer dans cette promenade que le jour de la Saint Louis."[20] Jefferson noted in his Account Book that he had "paid subscription for seats at the Tuileries 3 f 12,"[21] his seasonal tribute for chair rental (Fig. 37). No spot in the garden was more attractive than the terrace overlooking the Seine (Fig. 38). "While I was in Paris," he wrote to Mme de Tessé, "I was violently smitten with the Hôtel de Salm, and used to go to the Tuileries almost daily to look at it. The *loueuse de chaises*—inattentive to my passion—never had the complaisance to place a chair there, so that sitting on the parapet, and twisting my neck around to see the object of my admiration, I generally left it with a *torti-colli*."[22]

* * * * * * * * * * * *

The Château des Tuileries, when Jefferson knew it, was a royal palace in name only.[23] During the sixteenth and seventeenth centuries it had grown, pavilion by pavilion, only to find itself abandoned by its royal residents who henceforth lavished their wealth and attention upon Versailles or Marly (Fig. 39). By the 1780's it served mainly as an apartment house for aristocratic beneficiaries of royal pensions, while certain of its *salles* were used for receptions and concerts. To John Trumbull, fresh from Benjamin West's London studio, the Tuileries was "the vilest possible jumble of antique and Gothic, perfectly, utterly bad."[24] Jefferson associated it with the so-called *concerts spirituels*, the symphony concerts of eighteenth-century Paris. Founded in 1725 by Philidor, the concerts, held on Sundays and religious holidays, were originally intended to provide "spiritual" music on days when the Royal Academy of Music was closed.[25] The scope had been extended to include profane as well as sacred music, which prompted Mercier to say that the only difference between the Opera and the Concerts Spirituels was the costumes, since the same singers merely changed theatres on feast days.[26] After being held for many years in the Salle des Suisses in the central

pavilion of the Château, the concerts were transferred in the spring of 1784 to the Salle des Machines in the northern wing of the palace.[27] The hall, which took its name from the elaborate stage machinery constructed there earlier in the century, had at one time housed the Opera and more recently, the Comédie Française. As a result of successive transformations it was but a truncated version of the original hall when the Concerts Spirituels, under the direction of the singer M. Legros, took it over.

Jefferson first attended concerts in the Salle des Machines in September and October 1784, and subsequently returned there ten or a dozen times.[28] Admission to the concerts, which took place at 6 or 6:30 P.M. and generally lasted about two hours, was 6 *livres* for the best seats. The programs in the 1780's followed a standard pattern with at least one, sometimes two Haydn Symphonies played by an orchestra of 58 pieces, followed by shorter selections—motets, arias, oratorios, interpreted by French and Italian singers (Fig. 40). Italian names predominate among the composers as well as the interpreters: Anfossi, Sacchini, Alessandri, Prati, Cimarosa, Jomelli, Bonesi, and the popular Piccinni among them. The French were not absent: compositions by Rigel figure in the programs, while Gossec's trio "O salutaris" was a perennial favorite. German names such as Händel (but not Bach) occasionally appear. At the Tuileries Jefferson heard many of the famous performers of his day: the harpist Krumpholtz, for example, and the young violin virtuoso Rodolphe Kreutzer (to whom Beethoven later dedicated his "Kreutzer Sonata").

The Concerts Spirituels, with the Opera and the light operas of the Théâtre Italien, consti-

Vue du Château des Tuileries du Côté du Jardin.

39.

CONCERT.

Aujourd'hui 15, Concert Spirituel au Château des Tuileries.

Prem`ère partie. Symphonie de M. *Haydn*, après laque'le Mlle *Vaillant* chantera un Air Italien de M. *Sacchini.* — Mlle *Rcfe* exécutera un Concerto de harpe de M. *Krumpholtz.* — M. *Babni* chantera, pour la 1re fois, un Air Italien del Signor *Cimarofa.* — M. *Reichardt*, Maître de Mufique de la Chapelle du Roi de Pruffe, fera exécuter deux Chœurs de fa compofition, paroles latines.

Seconde partie. Nouvelle Symphonie de la compofition de M. *Reichardt*, après laquelle Mlle *Vaillant* chantera un Air Italien du même Auteur. — M. *Kreutz*, de la Mufique du Roi, exécutera un nouv. Concerto de violon de fa comp. — M. *Babini* chantera un Air Ital. del Sig. *Sarti.* — MM. *Lais, Cheron* & *Rouffeau* chanteront *O Salutaris*, Motet fans accompagnement de M. *Goffec*, demandé.

On commencera à 6 heures précifes.

SPECTACLES.

ACADÉMIE ROYALE DE MUSIQUE. Demain 16, DIDON, Tragédie en trois actes, paroles de M. *Marmontel*, mufique de M. *Piccini.*

THÉATRE FRANÇOIS. Aujourd'hui 15, *Reláche.*

Mercredi la 74e reptéf. de *la folle Journée.*

40. *Journal de Paris*, 15 August 1785

tuted the main part of Jefferson's musical fare during his years in Paris. No doubt he also heard chamber music in the *salons* of his friends and at home pulled the bow of his own violin—until the injury to his wrist interfered. He had a harpsichord made according to his specifications by Kirkman of London and saw to it that his daughters had lessons from the best masters, such as Claude Balbastre, the eminent Parisian organist and harpsichordist.[29] From time to time he purchased sheet music that would in later years strike echoes in his memory and be a source of pleasure to the whole Monticello family[30] (see Fig. 62).

* * * * * * * * * * * *

The Louvre, like the Tuileries, was serving many purposes in the 1780's. It had long since ceased to be a royal residence but had not yet been raised to the dignity of a national museum of art.[31] Though plans for a comprehensive museum, taking as a nucleus the various royal col-

lections already in the Louvre, were being discussed, the transformation formally began as a result of a decree of the National Convention in 1793. Meanwhile, private lodgings for royal pensionaries, artists' studios, and the offices of divers royally sponsored institutions were located here and there in the rambling palace. The Grande Galerie du Louvre, then as now, stretched along the Seine embankment until it joined the Cour Carrée, the quadrangle built on the site of the mediaeval fortress and constituting the Louvre proper (Fig. 41). On the ground floors of the Grande Galerie, just beyond the Pont Royal, were royal stables. Farther along was the Imprimerie Royale, the venerable printing office that boasted a magnificent collection of type-fonts dating from the time of Garamond. In this same part of the palace, up one flight, was the Monnaie des Médailles, with workshops for striking medals as well as a numismatics museum.

The several royal academies had their secretariats and meeting rooms in the buildings enclosing the Cour Carrée of the Louvre. Not until 1806 were their headquarters transferred across the Seine to the Collège des Quatre Nations with its familiar "Coupole." Among the "forty immortals" of the Académie Française, Jefferson knew, for example, the Marquis de Chastellux, Malesherbes, Condorcet, Saint-Lambert, Marmontel, Target, and Abbé Morellet. Condorcet and Malesherbes were also members of the Académie des Sciences, as were such acquaintances as the Duc de La Rochefoucauld, the Maréchal de Castries, Jean-Baptiste Le Roy, Daubenton, and Buffon. The royal academies were subsequently abolished by the National Convention, though they continued in fact as the different "classes" of the National Institute of France. Jefferson was later to resume acquaintance with a younger generation of academicians. In 1801, when he was President of the United States, he was elected a foreign associate of the Institute, "Classe des Sciences morales et politiques," through the influence of men such as Volney, Cabanis, Destutt de Tracy, and Dupont de Nemours. After 1803, as a consequence of further reorganizations decreed by Napoleon, Jefferson was ranged among the foreign associates of the Institute's "Classe Histoire et littérature ancienne," and after 1816

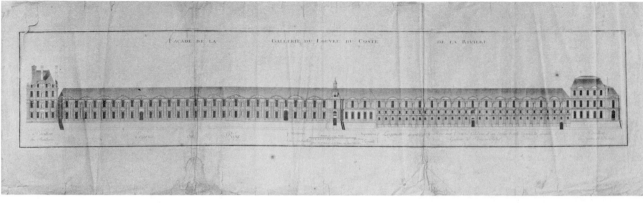

41. Engraving acquired in Paris by Jefferson

(with the restoration of the Bourbons), became a foreign associate of the Académie Royale des Inscriptions et Belles-Lettres.[32]

The Louvre, while not today's museum, nevertheless had many art connotations for Jefferson. Both the Académie Royale de Peinture et de Sculpture and the Académie d'Architecture had collections and headquarters there. Artists' studios and lodgings were found in various odd corners of the buildings. A German visitor seeking out the studio of M. and Mme Suvée, mentions the long badly lighted corridors, the endless stairways, and the artists' apartments like little birds' nests up beneath the roof. Nevertheless, it was considered a great good fortune in Paris for an artist to obtain a dwelling in the

LAUDA-CONATUM
EXPOSITION au SALON du LOUVRE En 1787.
à Paris, chez Bonier, Peintre, Rue Guénégaud N° 24, et à Londres N° 7, S.t Georges Row, Hyde Park.

42.

Louvre.[33] Several of the painters with whose work Jefferson became acquainted lived in the Cour du Louvre—Hubert Robert and David, for example, and De Machy, the author of several of the Paris views reproduced in this volume. His good friend Clérisseau, the architect, also had an atelier here.

Every other year, for a month beginning on Saint Louis' Day (August 25), the Royal Academy of Painting and Sculpture held an exhibition in the Salon Carré situated at the eastern end of the Grande Galerie du Louvre.[34] This particular *salon*, designed by Le Vau in the seventeenth century as one of the numerous saloons or drawing-rooms of the royal palace, eventually contributed the term "salon" to the vocabulary of the international art world. The exhibitions of 1785, 1787, and 1789 are a good index to the artistic fashions and prevailing taste at the time of Jefferson's residence in Paris. He himself commented, in a letter written in 1787 to John Trumbull, then in London: "The Salon has been open four or five days. I inclose you the list of it's treasures. The best thing is the Death of Socrates by David, and a superb one it is. A crucifixion by Roland in imitation of Relief is as perfect as it can be. Five peices of antiquities

by Robert are also among the foremost. Many portraits of Madme. Lebrun are exhibited and much approved. There are abundance of things in the stile of mediocrity. Upon the whole it is well worth your coming to see. You have only to get into the Diligence and in 4. days you are here"[35] (Figs. 42, 43).

Jefferson might also have told Trumbull that he would see at the Salon two busts by Houdon: General Washington "made by the author at this General's estate in Virginia" and the Marquis de Lafayette, commissioned by the "States of Virginia."[36] (Jefferson's own bust by Houdon would be exhibited two years later at the Salon of 1789.) The "peices of antiquities by Robert" singled out for mention in Jefferson's letter had been commissioned by the King for the palace at Fontainebleau. This series by Hubert Robert, "Robert des Ruines," included the Pont du Gard, the Maison Carrée at Nîmes, and other Roman monuments that Jefferson had studied during his journey in southern France the previous spring (Fig. 44). Among the "much approved" portraits by Madame Vigée-Lebrun were those of Queen Marie-Antoinette and her children (Fig. 45); Madame Molé Raymond (the lady with a muff); the actress Madame Dugazon

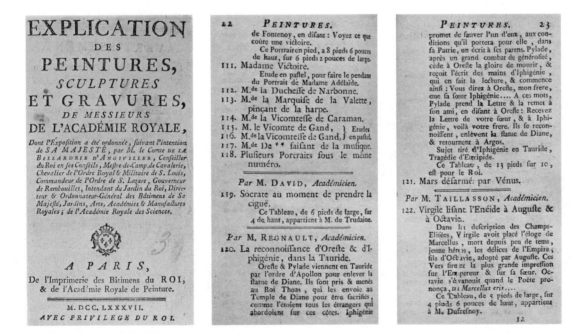

43. "I inclose you the list of it's treasures."

44. Maison Carrée, Arènes, and Tour Magne at Nîmes, by Hubert Robert

45. Marie-Antoinette and her children, by Madame Vigée-Lebrun

in the title-role of "Nina, the love-distracted maid"; as well as a self-portrait with her daughter. Jefferson's own approval of the portraits seems to have been qualified. "I do not like Madme. le Brun's fan colouring," he later asserted when searching for an artist to do a portrait of Lafayette for his Monticello gallery of American worthies, "and of all possible occasions it would be worst applied to a hero."[37] But he had no such reservations about David's heroics. "In fact," as he wrote upon another occasion, "I do not feel an interest in any pencil but that of David"[38] (Fig. 46).

The names of David, Vigée-Lebrun, Hubert Robert, and Houdon are still well-known. Equally significant as an index to the taste of Jefferson's Paris are the many lesser-known artists represented in the Salon of 1787. Listed in the catalogue, for example, is the academician Roland de la Porte, whose "crucifix imitant le relief en talc, sur un fond violet" Jefferson found so "perfect."[39] Roland de la Porte, accomplished in the art of *trompe-l'oeil*, represented the still-life tradition, as did Madame Vallayer-Coster and Van Spændonck. Jean-Baptiste Huet showed animals and pastoral scenes; De Machy and the Chevalier de Lespinasse, scenes and views of Paris. Alongside Madame Vigée-Lebrun's portraits hung others by Madame Labille-Guyard, Mosnier, Roslin, Vestier, and Weyler. But the genre dominating all others in the Salon of 1787 —as it did in 1785 and in 1789—was the historical canvas: "Saint Louis landing in Egypt" (Robin), "Henry the Fourth and Sully" (Vincent), "The Farewells of Hector and Andromache" (Vien), "Priam Asking Achilles for Hector's Body" (Doyen), "Ulysses Arriving in

46. "The best thing is the Death of Socrates by David, and a superb one it is."

Circe's Palace" (La Grenée the younger), "Virgil Reading the Aeneid to Augustus and Octavia" (Taillasson), and "Cicero Discovering the Tomb of Archimedes at Syracuse" (Valenciennes). To this same category belongs the "Marius at Minturnæ" by Jean-Germain Drouais, a pupil of David, which captured Jefferson's imagination when he saw it on display at the residence of the young artist's mother.[40]

Perhaps the most memorable feature of the Louvre for Jefferson was neither the treasures he saw at the Salon nor the academic meetings he attended there but the great colonnade along the eastern side, which he referred to as the "Galerie du Louvre." This façade, designed by Claude Perrault and others, built during the reign of Louis XIV, was intended to be a grandiose entrance, a front, to the palace. At the time of its completion, the King's attention was focused on his new residence in Versailles, so that the planned demolition of the maze of small streets filling the area between the Louvre and the church of Saint-Germain l'Auxerrois was held in abeyance. "Disengaging" the Colonnade was one of the urban improvements being completed when Jefferson reached Paris. Nineteenth-century additions to the Louvre and the destruction of the Château des Tuileries have opened up other perspectives which make it seem today that the Louvre "faces" in the opposite direction toward the Place de la Concorde and the Champs-Elysées. Yet, when Jefferson was in Paris he could contemplate the disengaged Perrault Colonnade from the vantage point of the Rue des Poulies (now the Rue du Louvre) and think of it as truly a "front" (Fig. 47 and Frontispiece, above). He classified it among "the celebrated fronts of modern buildings, which have already received the approbation of all good judges," obtained engraved plates of it, and recommended it to the attention of the planners of the new capital city of Washington, D.C.[41]

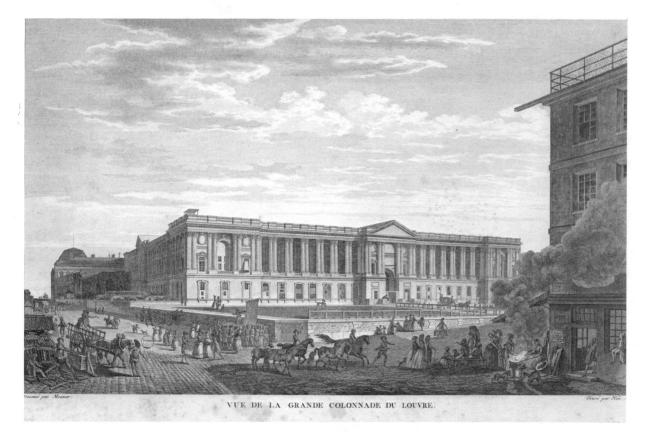

VUE DE LA GRANDE COLONNADE DU LOUVRE.

47.

MONTMARTRE

RUE DU FAUBOURG S. MARTIN

FAUBOURG S. DENIS

RUE S. DENIS

RUE S. MARTIN

MONTMARTRE

RICHELIEU

RUE DES PETITS CHAMPS

Place de Louis le Grand ou Vendome

48.

Chapter 4

New Quarters: The Chaussée d'Antin
and the Boulevards

MOVING away from the Louvre and the Palais Royal in the center of Jefferson's Paris and following the Rue de Richelieu northward, one soon reached the ring of tree-lined promenades known as the Boulevards. Along their course the Porte Saint-Denis and the Porte Saint-Martin, the triumphal arches erected in the seventeenth century to commemorate the victories of Louis XIV, stood as reminders (as they still do) that the Boulevards had once been the bulwarks or outer city walls. The city gates had already been moved out to the foot of the hill of Montmartre, and in the 1780's the new Wall of the Farmers-General would carry them half way up its slopes to the very base of the *Butte*. (Fig. 48.)

Beyond the Boulevards new streets had been laid out and built up only a few years before Jefferson's arrival in Paris. Lands adjoining the road called the Chaussée d'Antin, for example, had come into the hands of real estate speculators and developers in the late 1760's and 1770's. Architects such as Brongniart and Ledoux set the style for the buildings in this new residential quarter.[1] Most of the elegant private mansions have disappeared from the Chaussée d'Antin and other streets in this neighborhood (roughly the present Ninth Arrondissement), but the chapel and cloister designed by Brongniart for the Capuchin Novitiate are still standing in the Rue Caumartin (Church of Saint-Louis d'Antin and Lycée Condorcet) as a monument to the Neo-Classic style that once prevailed in this part of Jefferson's Paris (Fig. 49).

* * * * * * * * * * * *

On 16 October 1784, after two months in temporary lodgings, Jefferson signed a nine-year lease for "un hotel sis à Paris rue et Cul de sac Taitbout Chaussée d'antin," for which he agreed to pay annual rent of 4,000 *livre*s in quarterly installments.[2] Actually, as his Account Book records, he paid 1,500 *livres* each quarter, there evidently being a private agreement in addition to the formal lease signed by Jefferson, by the lessor, Guireaud de Talairac, by Maître Rendu, the notary who drew up the document (for a fee of 72 *livres*), and as the law required, by a second notary, Maître Foacier (Fig. 50). From this lease and other papers in Maître Rendu's archives we learn that M. François Guireaud de Talairac lived with his wife, Dame Louise-Elisabeth Wurmser, in the Rue du Mail near the Church of Saint-Eustache, held the minor judicial office of "conseiller du Roy, juge rapporteur du point d'honneur," and, significantly, that he was a building contractor and

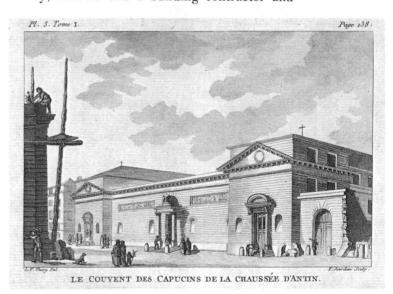

49. Designed by Brongniart. Bas-reliefs by Clodion

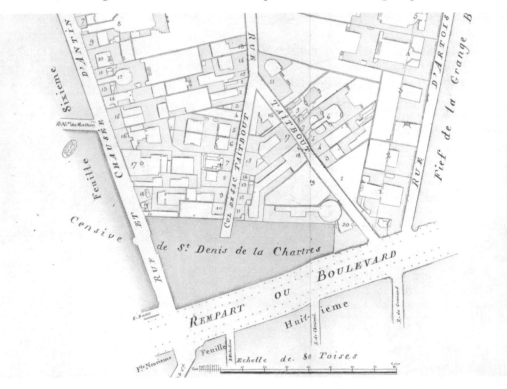

50. Lease for Jefferson's house in the Cul-de-sac Taitbout

owned other property in the Chaussée d'Antin development.

The lease describes the house as comprising "three main parts (*corps de logis*), a courtyard, and two gardens." Further details were deemed unnecessary as "the said Sieur Jefferson" stated in the presence of the notary that he was familiar with the house, "having seen and visited it."

Apparently no picture of this house has survived, but the outlines of its three corps de logis, forming a letter E joined to the adjacent house of similar form, can be distinguished on a contemporary street plan (Fig. 51). A doorway led from the street into the courtyard, then a more elaborate doorway, probably with a pillared porch and ascending steps, led into the central

51. The Cul-de-sac Taitbout house leased by Jefferson from Guireaud de Talairac is Number 5 on this plan

part of the house. Beyond this was a rectangular garden and the third corps de logis. At the rear of the property was a very small triangular plot, presumably the second of the two "gardens" mentioned in the lease. Compared with the more spacious mansions in the neighborhood, this was a relatively small town house, without grounds or a view. It was, however, of very recent construction, as the Cul-de-sac Taitbout, branching off from the Rue Taitbout, had been opened up only about 1775. Later on, in 1799, the Cul-de-sac was extended southward to the Boulevard des Italiens and was renamed Rue du Helder after the French victory in the Netherlands. Still later, the final extension of Boulevard Haussmann left a small triangle now called Place Adrien Oudin to mark the spot where the Cul-de-sac Taitbout once branched off from the street of that name. Jefferson's residence would have been on the other side of Boulevard Haussmann, at or near the corner of Rue du Helder.

The "Hôtel Têtebout," as Jefferson generally called it,[3] was rented unfurnished. The Minister resident soon found that his "first expences, or Outfit"—household furniture, carriage, apparel, "all plain"—exceeded his year's salary.[4] Leaving to his maître d'hôtel such purchases as "brooms and other small affairs for the house," he himself selected furniture, carpets, linen and blankets (with an *armoire* to keep them in), clocks, silver, and dishes (Fig. 52). While disavowing

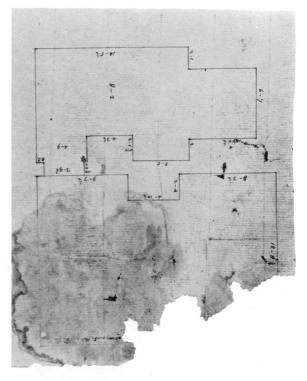

53. Jefferson's sketch for work on the Cul-de-sac Taitbout house

any "ambition for splendor," but never one to be satisfied with inferior quality, Jefferson made extensive purchases of damask from the firm of Barbier & Tetard, bought *toile de Jouy* at the Hôtel de Jabac in the Rue Neuve de Saint Merri (the Paris salesroom for the Oberkampf factories at Jouy-en-Josas), made substantial payments to a *tapissier* named Bohain, to a *serrurier*, and to many other craftsmen.[5] A fragmentary drawing preserved among Jefferson's papers suggests that he made minor modifications in the house itself (Fig. 53). He once asserted that "Nothing can be worse done than the house-joinery of Paris," and in a moment of apparent exasperation noted in his Account Book: "pd a menuisier for nothing 48 *f*."[6]

During this first year in Paris, Jefferson bought many books and had bookshelves built to hold them. He rented a pianoforte for 12 *f* a month, bought music as well as a music-stand, and acquired engravings and paintings to hang in his *hôtel*. While living in the Cul-de-sac Taitbout he attended at least two art auctions: the De Billy sale (16–19 November 1784) in the

52. Louis XVI armchair purchased by Jefferson in Paris

54. Art sale at Paillet's auction rooms in the Hôtel Bullion. Painting by De Machy

salle de vente of M. Paillet in the former Hôtel Bullion, Rue Platrière (Fig. 54), and the Dupille de Saint-Séverin sale (2–26 February 1785) held in the deceased collector's *hôtel* in the Marais, Rue Saint-Louis (Rue de Turenne).[7] The American envoy purchased five items at the Saint-Séverin sale (Fig. 55), including a "Herodiade with the head of John the Baptist," listed in the catalogue (No. 248) as the work of the seventeenth-century French painter Simon Vouet. This Herodiade (a copy rather than an original Vouet), like many of the books and household furnishings purchased in Paris, followed Jefferson back to America and can be seen at Monticello today (Fig. 56).

The establishment in the Cul-de-sac Taitbout required an appropriate household staff.[8] The head servant was Marc, the *maître d'hôtel* who remained in Jefferson's employ until July 1786, when he was dismissed and replaced by Adrien Petit. Marc handled the household accounts (not always wisely, as his employer eventually dis-

covered) and directed the other servants: Legrand, the *valet de chambre*, and Saget, the *frotteur*, whose business was to rub floors. Tile or parquet floors would not bear water, as Abigail Adams explained to her sister, so that "the method of cleaning them is to have them waxed, and then a man-servant with foot-brushes drives round your room dancing here and there like a Merry Andrew." A coachman named Vendôme completed the roster of Jefferson's regular employees. During most of this period he rented horses and carriage, as there were no stables with the Taitbout house. Nor was a full-time gardener necessary there. Jefferson had brought with him from Virginia his Negro servant James Hemings, who fell sick soon after their arrival in Paris. Upon his recovery (thanks to Dr. McMahon, a nurse, and a "chirurgeon") "Jem-me" was apprenticed to a *traiteur* (caterer) by the name of Combeaux—the first of several such apprenticeships—to learn what he could of the secrets of French cooking. During the first year

55. According to this marked copy of the sale catalogue, a St. Peter by Guido Reni, No. 36, went to the American Envoy for 72 *livres*, 10 *sols*

56. Herodiade with the head of John the Baptist, copied from Simon Vouet. Purchased by Jefferson at the Saint-Séverin sale, No. 248

in Paris Jefferson had no regular *cuisinier*, relying on a *traiteur* for the main dishes served at his table. His weekly accounts with Marc record the sums paid by the latter to the traiteur as well as a New Year's *étrenne* to the caterer's errand boy. Wine, brandy, China tea, and other appropriate accompaniments to the caterer's fare were purchased directly from the purveyors.

With a house of his own, Jefferson was able to offer hospitality to other American sojourners in Paris. David Humphreys of Connecticut, secretary to the American Commissioners, and William Short of Virginia, who arrived in November 1784 to serve as Jefferson's secretary, lived under Jefferson's roof for extended periods. John Quincy Adams, then seventeen and living with his family at Auteuil, was a frequent visitor. Years later, when referring with pride to John Quincy's election to the presidency, his father wrote to Jefferson: "I call him our John because, when you were at the Cul de sac at Paris, he appeared to be almost as much your boy as mine."[9]

In spite of such pleasant companionship, Jefferson's year in the Cul-de-sac was not an entirely happy one. The circle of his French acquaintances was still limited, he was not yet at ease with a foreign language, and he was in poor health. In January 1785 came the crushing news of the death of the youngest of his three daughters, Lucy Elizabeth, who, with her sister Mary (Polly), had been left in Virginia in the care of their relatives Francis and Elizabeth Eppes. The news revived Jefferson's grief over the death of his wife, who had succumbed a few months after Lucy Elizabeth's birth in 1782. "I have had a very bad winter," he told James Monroe, "having been confined the greatest part of it. A seasoning, as they call it, is the lot of most strangers, and none, I believe have experienced a more severe one than myself."[10]

Jefferson lived in the Cul-de-sac Taitbout for only one year. On 10 September 1785 he gave M. Guireaud de Talairac the customary six months' notice that he would terminate the lease on 10 March 1786.[11] The landlord, he later said, "was sufficiently litigious, and desired to continue the lease, but knew he could not."[12] Thus Jefferson paid the additional six months' rent for which he was liable and, in October 1785, moved out of the Cul-de-sac to a more sightly and stately mansion, the Hôtel de Langeac at the corner of the Rue de Berri and the Champs-Elysées.

* * * * * * * * * * *

The properties on Jefferson's side of the Cul-de-sac Taitbout extended back to others fronting toward the Chaussée d'Antin. The entrance to the Chaussée was from the Boulevard, with a police station, the Dépôt des Gardes Françaises, at the right and the impressive Hôtel de Montmorency, designed by Ledoux in 1772, on the opposite corner. Along its course were other attractive new houses such as Ledoux's pavilion built in 1770 for the opera-singer Mlle Guimard (Fig. 57) or Madame de Montesson's mansion designed by Brongniart (1770–1771).[13] Jefferson, with his connoisseur's eye, no doubt took note of these examples of the modern style of building, but the house that retained a special place in his memory was the one where his friends the Cornys lived.[14] Monsieur Ethis de

57. Mlle Guimard's house in the Chaussée d'Antin, designed by Ledoux

Corny, *Procureur du Roi et de la Ville*, had served for a year or more in America as commissary for the French army. His second wife, *née* Marguerite-Victoire de Palerne, became a special favorite among Jefferson's Parisian friends, one of that "little coterie" that included John Trumbull, Maria Cosway, and Angelica Schuyler Church. The Cornys' house was on the west-

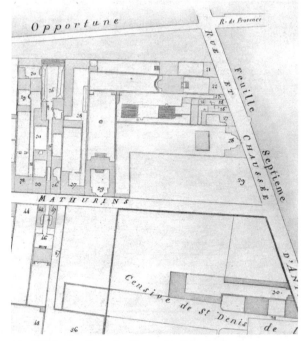

58. Ethis de Corny's Chaussée d'Antin house is number 22 on this plan

ern side of the Chaussée d'Antin near the corner of the Rue de Provence, about where the Galeries Lafayette is now located. A contemporary street plan shows it to have been a spacious residence with a large garden behind it (Fig. 58). Jefferson once referred to it as a house "where all is beautiful."[15] As for many of Jefferson's other friends, the French Revolution marked the end of the *douceur de vivre* for Madame de Corny. In 1801 she resumed correspondence with him, when she was a lonely widow withdrawn from society, living in a small apartment with only a pot of flowers on the window-sill to satisfy her passion for trees and gardens.[16]

* * * * * * * * * * * *

Not far beyond the Cornys' house, the Chaussée d'Antin met the Rue Saint-Lazare, the winding street skirting the base of the hill of Montmartre. Beyond this junction the Rue de Clichy led out of the city over the western flank of the hill. Several notable semi-rural estates graced its course, among them the "Folie Boutin" or "Tivoli," the residence of M. Boutin, Treasurer of the Royal Navy[17] (Fig. 59). His famous hillside gardens boasted a formal Italian garden and, farther up, an English garden where, "strolling through irregular groves," one met with "knolls, bridges, an antique tomb shaded with cypresses, a sheepfold, and many rare shrubs mingled with exotic plants and flowers."

Boutin's English garden, with its various *fabriques* and "natural" planting, was characteristic of the style that had become the rage throughout Europe. Breaking with the venerable French tradition of formal, well-clipped gardens, these modern designs owed not a little to English models and to such theoretical works as Whately's *Observations on Modern Gardening* (1770) and Chambers' *Dissertation on Oriental Gardening* (1772), an expanded version of his earlier essay "Of the Laying out of Gardens among the Chinese" (1757). Jefferson had long been familiar with the new doctrine. As a young man in his twenties, when planning Monticello, he outlined a scheme for the grounds, embracing a deer park, cascades, a Grecian or Chinese temple, as well as a graveyard in an "unfrequented vale" among "antient and venerable oaks inter-

spersed with gloomy evergreens."[18] Thus, when he visited M. Boutin's "Tivoli" and other such gardens in France or England, Jefferson was pre-conditioned to appreciate them. As an American exotic himself, he could contribute knowledge of the foreign trees and shrubs then being naturalized in Europe. His *Notes on the State of Virginia*, for example, include an authoritative list of plants native to Virginia—medicinal, esculent, ornamental, and useful for fabrication—with the Linnæan names added for the information of foreigners. When inviting Jefferson to dine with him in the company of the Comte de Moustier and other mutual acquaintances, Monsieur Boutin acknowledged the gift of the *Notes* and of some seeds of *Juniperus Virginiana* with a promise to reciprocate with seeds of the dry rice from Cochin China.[19]

The subsequent fate of Boutin's folly is typical of others in the neighborhood. Boutin himself fell victim to the guillotine in 1794. His confiscated property came into the hands of speculators who transformed it into a popular amusement park.[20] Even in Jefferson's time, however, the world of entertainment and pleasure that was to make Montmartre world-famous a century later had begun to creep up the slopes of the hill. A short distance east of Boutin's residence, in the vicinity of Notre-Dame de Lorette, was Ruggieri's, where Jefferson and Maria Cosway

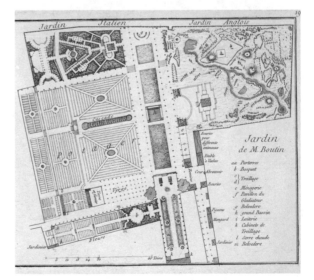

59. Estate of M. Boutin. The Rue de Clichy leading up the slope of Montmartre ran parallel to the lower border of this plan

tarried during the escapade following their first meeting at the Halle aux Bleds. Ruggieri's, "somewhat like the Vauxhall in London" where dancing under the trees could be enjoyed, took its name from a family of Italian pyrotechnicians who had emigrated to France earlier in the century.[21] Since 1783 their establishment had been featuring elaborate displays of fireworks combined with pantomime. The subjects ranged from "The Death and Funeral of Marlborough," "Theseus delivered from Inferno by Hercules," "The Siege of Delhi by Thomas Koulikan King of Persia," to topical extravaganzas such as "The Inauguration of the Louis XVI Bridge by Minerva and the Arts" (1788). The night Jefferson and Mrs. Cosway were there, the program included "The Forges of Vulcan beneath Mount Etna" and "The Combat of Mars."

The streets reaching out over the open spaces on this edge of Paris retained their semi-rural character. Along the Rue des Martyrs, up the hill from Ruggieri's, was the countrylike town residence of Jefferson's esteemed friend Lamoignon de Malesherbes.[22] This "good and enlight-

60. "M. de Malesherbes, who plants whole forests. . . ."

ened minister" was, in Jefferson's opinion, "unquestionably the first character in the kingdom for integrity, patriotism, knowledge, and experience in business."[23] He was, furthermore, "the most curious man in France as to his trees" and had collected a notable library. Jefferson favored him with the *Notes on the State of Virginia* and supplied him with such American species as the cranberry and pecan nut as well as a "prodigious quantity" of *Juniperus Virginiana* seeds, which were nursed in Malesherbes's Montmartre garden before being transplanted to his country estate southeast of Paris. Jefferson was familiar with both the nursery in the Rue des Martyrs and the arboretum at the Château de Malesherbes, which he visited when attending Court at Fontainebleau in October 1785. In 1792 Malesherbes, Jefferson's senior by some twenty years, undertook at his own request the defense of Louis XVI—only to follow the King to the guillotine (Fig. 60). Years later Jefferson received a copy of the *Vie et écrits de Malesherbes* (1820) with a covering letter from the author, Boissy d'Anglas, recalling their meetings long ago at Malesherbes's house in Paris.[24] To young Frenchmen of the 1780's like himself, Boissy d'Anglas testified, Malesherbes "was our Jefferson."

Another house in this vicinity known to Jefferson was the Comte de Moustier's residence at the upper end of the Rue Rochechouart.[25] Jefferson made the acquaintance of Moustier prior to the latter's departure for the United States in the autumn of 1787 as Minister Plenipotentiary from the French Court. The diplomat's sister-in-law, the Marquise de Bréhan, and her young son accompanied him to America. Jefferson did his best to prepare them for life overseas, and they continued to exchange letters, but neither the Comte nor the Marquise seems to have been wholly happy there. Madame de Bréhan was even less happy in the changed and changing Paris she found upon her return in the autumn of 1789.

* * * * * * * * * * * *

Back on the Boulevards again, we find several more landmarks of Jefferson's Paris. Just beyond the old Porte Saint-Martin (Bullet's Arch of

VUE DU THÉATRE DE L'OPERA.
On voit dans l'éloignement les Portes S.t Martin et S.t Denis.

Lallemand del.   Née Sculp.

61.

Triumph) stood the new Opera[26] (Fig. 61). It had previously been located in the Palais Royal, where it was consumed in a disastrous fire on 8 June 1781. The "temporary" hall erected near the Porte Saint-Martin in the record time of seventy-five days by the architect Lenoir le Romain was inaugurated on 25 October 1781 by a free performance celebrating the birth of the Dauphin. This gala opening reassured those who were skeptical about the solidity of the rapidly constructed building, while elaborate precautions against fire and conspicuously posted firemen allayed fears of a new catastrophe. The operatic repertory of the Royal Academy of Music was primarily "grand opera" in the tradition of Quinault, Lulli, Rameau, and Gluck, whose busts ornamented the front of the new theatre. Jefferson attended several performances here: Grétry's oriental fantasy La Caravane du Caire, as well as Piccinni's "lyrical tragedies," Didon and Pénélope.[27] "The new

opera of Penelope by Marmontel and Piccini succeeds," he reported to Abigail Adams (then living in London). "Mademoiselle Renaud, of 16. years of age, sings as nobody ever sung before. She is far beyond Madame Mara in her own line of difficult execution. Her sister of 12 years of age will sing as well as she does."[28] A song from Sacchini's Dardanus, another of the Opera's creations of this period, lingered long in Jefferson's memory, evoking happy days in Paris with Maria Cosway[29] (Fig. 62).

Close by Jefferson's first Paris residence was the Théâtre des Italiens, situated just across the Boulevard from the Rue Taitbout. It was indeed so close that letters were often addressed to Mr. Jefferson at the "Cul de sac rue Tetebout près la Comédie Italienne." The theatre, which gave its name to this stretch of the Boulevards, was a glistening new building when Jefferson lived nearby. It had been built between 1781 and 1783 by the architect Jean-François Heurtier,

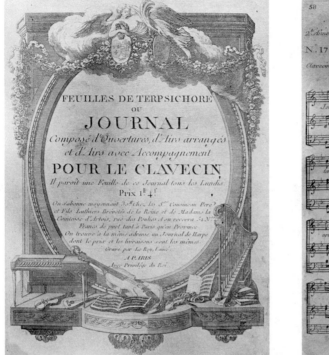

62. "*Jour heureux. . . .*" Music acquired in Paris by Jefferson

63.

the interior designed by De Wailly, on land separated from the grounds of the Hôtel de Choiseul[30] (Fig. 63). The real estate speculators had astutely drawn their lines in such a way that the theatre faced away from the Boulevard, leaving a narrow but desirable building lot along the main thoroughfare. The pattern has persisted to the present day, as have such street names as Favart, Marivaux, and Grétry, recalling writers and composers who contributed to the glory of the "Italiens." Heurtier's structure was eventually replaced by another on the same site, known to later generations as the Opéra Comique. The Théâtre des Italiens, with the Théâtre Français and the Opéra, was one of the three great theatres subsidized by the King. Its name stemmed from a company of Italian players, the "Comédiens ordinaires du Roi de la Troupe Italienne."[31]

65. Frontispiece of a volume of Florian's plays, including *Les Deux Billets*

64.

Although improvised plays with the stock characters of the *Commedia dell'arte* lingered on into the 1780's, the theatre's repertory by then consisted largely of light comedies or operettas known as *"comédies mêlées d'ariettes."*

Jefferson's Account Book records payments "for tickets at the Italiens" upon at least nine occasions, and there were no doubt others when he was an invited guest. The programs generally included a main spectacle and one or two shorter pieces. Jefferson witnessed performances of several of the successful hits of the pre-Revolutionary years, including Grétry and Marmontel's *Zémire et Azor*, Monsigny and Favart's *La Belle Arsène*, and Dalayrac and Marsollier des Vivetières' *Nina, ou la Folle par Amour*. Madame Louise Dugazon, who played the title-role of Nina the love-distracted maiden, inspired many artists of the period as well as a wry remark from Jefferson (Fig. 64). Describing a singer

Assaut donné à la forteresse par les troupes de Marguerite.

Richard Cœur de Lion Acte 3.ᵐᵉ Scène 10.ᵐᵉ

66. Scene from *Richard Coeur de Lion*

he heard in Marseille, he commented: "She is in the stile of Mde. Dugazon, has ear, voice, taste and action. She is moreover young and handsome: and has an advantage over Mde. Dugazon and some other of the celebrated ones of Paris, in being clear of that dreadful wheeze or rather whistle in respiration which resembles the agonizing struggles for breath in a dying person."[32]

The day he took Mrs. Cosway to the Théâtre Italien was a memorable one for Jefferson. The program that evening (9 September 1786) featured Grétry and Sedaine's light opera *Richard Coeur de Lion* and a one-act harlequinade in verse, Florian's *Les Deux Billets* (Fig. 65). An allusion in Jefferson's "Head and Heart" letter to Maria recalls their evening together: "If your letters are as long as the bible, they will appear short to me. Only let them be brimfull of affec-

tion. I shall read them with the dispositions with which Arlequin, in *les deux billets*, spelt the words 'je t'aime,' and wished that the whole alphabet had entered into their composition."[33]

We may suppose that Jefferson also remembered the haunting melodies of *Richard Coeur de Lion*, as did so many of his contemporaries (Fig. 66). He had heard it once before, in the spring of 1785, when living in the Cul-de-sac. His companion that evening was young John Quincy Adams who, years later, at the time he failed to be re-elected to the presidency, confided to his diary that he seemed deserted by all mankind, as in the song Blondel sang under the walls of Richard's prison: "O, Richard! O, mon Roi! / L'univers t'abandonne . . . !" "When I first heard this song, forty-five years ago, at one of the first representations of that delightful play,

[48]

it made an indelible impression upon my memory, without imagining that I should ever feel its force so much closer home. In the year 1829 scarce a day passed that did not bring it to my thoughts."[34] Still later, the diarist's grandson Henry Adams performed "an act of piety to the memory of my revered grandfather" by attending a revival of *Richard Coeur de Lion* at the Opéra Comique on 29 December 1891. For a moment he imagined himself as his grandfather might have been, a handsome young fellow, "with full dress and powdered hair, talking to Mme. Chose in the boxes, and stopping to applaud 'Un regard de ma belle.'" Unluckily, the world-weary globe-trotter discovered, "the Opéra Comique, which used to be the cheerfullest theatre in Paris, is now to me the dreariest, and poor Richard howled mournfully as though time had troubled him."[35]

Not far from the Théâtre des Italiens, at the corner of the Boulevard and the Rue Louis-le-Grand, opposite the Chaussée d'Antin, the multi-storied new building of Arthur & Grenard's Manufacture de Papiers Peints had become a conspicuous neighborhood landmark.[36] The older inhabitants, like the Maréchal de Richelieu, stigmatized it as a deplorable encroachment of industry into a peaceful residential district. Like the more famous Réveillon (located in the Faubourg Saint-Antoine), Arthur enjoyed a high reputation among wallpaper manufacturers. The firm employed some two hundred workers, producing the traditional "painted papers" printed from wooden blocks and a novelty known as *papier tontisse*, i.e. flock-paper, simulating velvet, brocade, or carved relief. Monsieur et Madame Arthur, as well as their son, were accomplished salesmen and took special pleasure, says Thiéry, in welcoming *amateurs* and acquainting them with all the operations carried on in the workrooms. They were generous, too, with their samples: one visiting English lady was given a piece representing a golden urn, "big enough to make a fire-screen." Jefferson bought "paper hangings" for his Hôtel de Langeac residence and, after his return to America, instructed William Short to make extensive purchases for him at "Arthur's on the Boulevards."[37] "The old man will interest himself for me, I wish he would send me specimens of his good Arabesques, noting the price of each." He also asked for "22 rouleaux of lattice or treillage paper," specifying that "This is in imitation of a treillage, with vines &c. on it." Long afterward, in the course of twentieth-century restoration work, traces of this paper were discovered in the North Octagonal Room at Monticello. The room, the so-called Madison Room, has now been repapered with a modern copy of the old design from Arthur's on the Boulevards (Fig. 67).

67. Arthur's "lattice or treillage" wallpaper

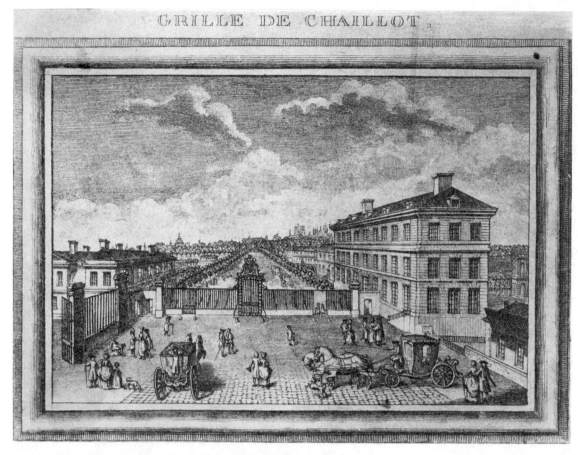

GRILLE DE CHAILLOT.

68. Looking eastward down the Champs-Elysées. Hôtel de Langeac at left

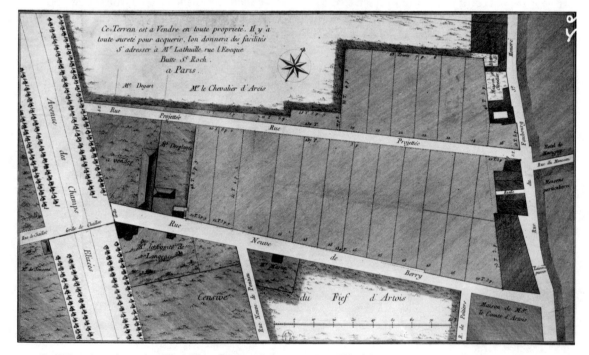

69. Building lots for sale. The "Rue Projetée" is now Rue Washington

Chapter 5

New Quarters: The Grille de Chaillot and the Faubourg du Roule

WHEN Jefferson arrived in Paris in August 1784, his mission was to join Franklin and Adams as one of the American commissioners for negotiating trade treaties with the European powers. Not until the following year was he appointed Franklin's successor as Minister to France. On 17 May 1785 Jefferson presented his letters of credence to the King at a private audience and "went through the other ceremonies usual on such occasions." Adams moved on to London as the first American Minister to Great Britain, while Franklin returned to America in July. "The succession to Dr. Franklin at the court of France," Jefferson later said, "was an excellent school of humility." "On being presented to any one as the Minister of America, the common-place question, used in such cases, was 'c'est vous, Monsieur, qui remplacez le Docteur Franklin?' . . . I generally answered, 'no one can replace him, Sir; I am only his successor.' "[1] Now facing a longer residence in Paris than originally expected, Jefferson again set about house hunting. "I have at length procured a house in a situation much more pleasing to me than my present," he wrote to Abigail Adams from his Cul-de-sac Taitbout *hôtel* on 4 September 1785. "It is at the grille des champs Elysees, but within the city. It suits me in every circumstance but the price, being dearer than the one I am now in. It has a clever garden to it."[2]

The new house, known as the Hôtel de Langeac from the name of its owner, was situated on a piece of the former Pépinière du Roule halfway up the Champs-Elysées, at the corner of the Rue de Berri, adjoining the Grille de Chaillot (Figs. 68, 69). Though the latter still marked the city limits when Jefferson moved

there, a new gate—one of Ledoux's "palaces"— would soon be erected farther up the avenue on the summit of the Montagne du Roule, the present Etoile. Across the Champs-Elysées from the Langeac property, also adjoining the Grille de Chaillot, was the Comtesse de Marbeuf's estate, originally laid out "in the manner of his country" by M. de Jansen, an Englishman. The "curious" Jansen gardens were adorned with an obelisk, a belvedere, and other fashionable *fabriques*.[3]

Jefferson took up residence in the Hôtel de Langeac on 17 October 1785. According to the notarized lease dated 5 September, the annual rent, payable in quarterly instalments, was 3,500 *livres* (Fig. 70). A private agreement of the same date placed the "real" rent at 7,500 *livres*, which was indeed dearer than the 6,000 *livres* paid Guéraud for the house in the Cul-de-sac.[4] In other respects, however, it was a far more attractive and spacious residence. The Hôtel de Langeac survived only until 1842, but earlier sketches, including a plan of the grounds drawn by Jefferson, preserve its appearance (Figs. 71, 72, 73). The pavilion, designed by the eminent architect Jean F.-T. Chalgrin, was a new, barely completed house when Jefferson moved into it. Originally begun in 1768 by the Comte de Saint-Florentin (later Duc de La Vrillière) for his mistress the Marquise de Langeac, work on it was interrupted in 1774, then resumed for the Marquise's son, the Comte de Langeac (1748–1832), Jefferson's landlord.[5] The latter, burdened with many titles, was also burdened with debts, as Jefferson learned when the Comte's creditors instituted garnishment proceedings in an attempt to collect the rent.[6] Langeac, among other things, was an amateur

70. Jefferson's lease for the Hôtel de Langeac

engraver, a man of taste, whose *pavillon* was deemed worthy of inclusion in Thiéry's *Guide des Amateurs*. The ingenious arrangement of the rooms and the ceiling in the oval salon representing the rising sun, painted by Jean-Simon Berthélemy, were singled out for special mention.[7]

The Hôtel de Langeac was rented to Jefferson unfurnished, as had been the smaller house in the Cul-de-sac. His increased expenses for furnishings and upkeep are reflected in his accounts. Furthermore, he was expected to maintain the "stile of living" established by Franklin —with "500 guineas a year less to do it on"— and this, as he said, "called for an almost womanly attention to the details of the household."[8] Among his regular expenses were annual payments of 50 *livres* for piped water from Périer Frères, managers of the Compagnie des Eaux de Paris. Their *pompes à feu* were situated by the Seine at the foot of the Colline de Chaillot, a few minutes walk from the Hôtel de Langeac (Fig. 74). These pumps, Jefferson explained

to a Virginian correspondent, were worked by a "fire engine . . . better called the Steam engine." One of the pumps could "raise 400,000 cubic feet (French) of water in 24 hours."[9] The site of the twin pumps (familiarly known to Parisians as "Augustine" and "Constantine" from the names of the Périer brothers) is commemorated by the Rue des Frères Périer, adjacent to the present Place de l'Alma.

Jefferson's new establishment required a larger staff of servants. Now that he had stables of his own, he acquired horses, carriages, and employed a regular coachman. The grounds and gardens in turn required a full-time gardener. The extensive grounds of the Hôtel de Langeac were evidently one of its great attractions for Jefferson. "I cultivate in my own garden here Indian corn for the use of my own table, to eat green in our manner. But the species I am able to get here for seed, is hard, with a thick skin, and dry," he told Col. Nicholas Lewis of Albemarle when asking him to send an ear of the "small ripe corn we call Homony corn" as well as seeds of the common sweet potato, watermelon, canteloupe, acorns of various sorts, and "a dozen or two bacon hams."[10]

Jefferson even experimented with grape growing. He found, for example, that vine cuttings from Hocheim and Rudesheim, which he visited in the company of Baron Geismar during his 1788 Rhine Valley excursion, were growing luxuriantly in his Paris garden. "If you ever revisit Monticello," he promised the Baron, "I shall be able to give you there a glass of Hock or Rudesheim of my own making."[11] During his years abroad Jefferson "examined into the details relative to the most celebrated wines of France," and made careful notes on viticulture as he observed it.[12] He established friendly relations with wine merchants such as Parent of Beaune, who stocked the Hôtel de Langeac cellar with the finest Burgundies, and with vineyard owners such as Dr. Lambert of Montpellier, who sent his choicest muscat from Frontignan in Languedoc, or the Comte de Lur-Saluces, whose Sauternes Jefferson judged "very fine." After his return to the United States, Jefferson continued for the rest of his life to import wines from abroad. The best French wines would be served by him in Philadelphia, at the White House, and at Monticello, following the tradition set in Paris.

The Hôtel de Langeac was Jefferson's home from his forty-second to his forty-sixth year, while serving also as the American Legation where the Minister transacted the official business of his country. The principal objects requiring his attention, he later said, were: "the receipt of our whale-oils, salted fish, and salted meats, on favorable terms; the admission of our rice on equal terms with that of Piedmont, Egypt and the Levant; a mitigation of the monopolies of our tobacco by the Farmers-general, and a free admission of our productions into their islands."[13] This characteristically modest summary takes no account of the countless other demands on the Minister's time. A succession of visitors found their way to the Grille de Chaillot: impecunious American seamen stranded abroad, French veterans of the American Revolution inquiring about arrearages due them from Congress, American travelers (such as John Ledyard or William Langborn, bound for Siberia) needing passports or expecting letters of introduction, hopeful young European adventurers setting out for the New World, authors and artists, inventors and land-jobbers, as well as an assortment of lame ducks and eccentrics, including the importunate John Paradise and his psychotic wife, Lucy Ludwell. The famous M. de Latude sometimes came "to take family soupe," and entertained Jefferson with anecdotes of his five and thirty years imprisonment in the Bastille and Dungeon of Vincennes.[14]

Although informal "family dinners" seem to have been the general rule at the Hôtel de Langeac, there were occasional "great dinners" like the one in December 1787 that included Mrs. Cosway, her friend Princess Lubomirska, and the Polish writer Julian Niemcewicz (with whom Jefferson later resumed acquaintance in America).[15] Children, too, tripped up and down the stately stairway of the mansion or romped in the gardens, as Jefferson's purchase of a "battledore & shuttlecock" suggests.[16] His daughters, Patsy and Polly, when released from their convent boarding school, came home to the Hôtel de Langeac, often with friends such as Kitty Church, the daughter of Angelica Schuyler Church, who was for a time their schoolmate

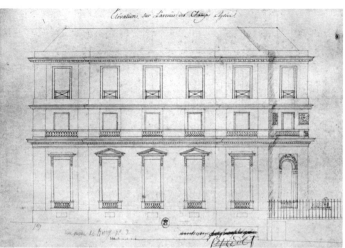

71. Hôtel de Langeac, southern side, along the Champs-Elysées

at the Abbaye de Panthemont. Among his parental responsibilities, Jefferson kept an eye on Ally and Louis, sons of St. John de Crèvecoeur, French consul in New York, who were pupils at MM. Loiseau and Lemoine's "Institution pour la jeune Noblesse" in the Rue de Berri just across the street from the Hôtel de Langeac, as was George Washington Greene, the son of General Nathanael Greene.[17]

Among the Americans who lived for a time at the Hôtel de Langeac was John Trumbull, whose acquaintance Jefferson made when he visited London in March and April 1786. Jefferson was deeply interested in Trumbull's "national work" of commemorating in a series of paintings

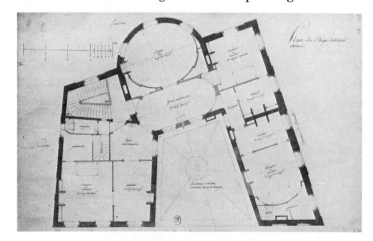

72. Hôtel de Langeac, plan of second floor. "Avenue de Neuilly" (i.e., Champs-Elysées) at right; Rue Neuve de Berri at bottom

the great events of the American Revolution. He invited the young artist (then studying with Benjamin West) to come to Paris to see the fine works of art there, and "to make his house my home."[18] During his first visit in the late summer of 1786, Trumbull, with the "information and advice" of his host, "began the composition" of his "Declaration of Independence." On a later visit, mid-December 1787 to mid-February 1788, he brought with him a canvas prepared for receiving portraits—John Adams was already painted in—and he could now paint Jefferson. This half-length portrait is slightly rejuvenated to suggest the subject's appearance a decade or so earlier.[19] The miniatures that

74. "A fire engine (better called the Steam engine) which supplies the greater part of the town with water."

Trumbull subsequently executed—one for Mrs. Church, one for Mrs. Cosway, and another for Martha Jefferson, especially the first two—show a more stylish Jefferson, with powdered hair and jabot, more as the American Minister appeared to his Paris contemporaries (Figs. 75, 76). During the period from December 1787 to February 1788 several French veterans of the American Revolution—Generals Rochambeau, Chastellux, the brothers Vioménil, Colonel Deux-Ponts, the Duc de Lauzun, Admirals de Grasse and Barras, among others—sat "in Mr. Jefferson's house" for the portraits that Trumbull inserted in his depiction of "The Surrender of Cornwallis at Yorktown." The artist regarded these "the best of my small portraits."

* * * * * * * * * * *

The Hôtel de Langeac made an excellent center for walking. Jefferson mentions his frequent excursions into the Bois de Boulogne and once remarked that in fair weather he walked four or five miles a day. One shorter circuit took him along the Rue de Berri to the Rue du Faubourg Saint-Honoré, then up this street (Rue du Faubourg du Roule, or Chemin du Roule, as this stretch was then generally called) to the top of the "Montagne du Roule" and thence back down the Champs-Elysées to the Grille de Chaillot. There were several examples of the new

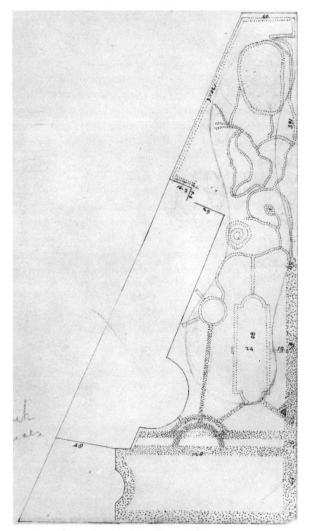

73. Grounds of the Hôtel de Langeac, drawn by Jefferson. Champs-Elysées at bottom

75. Jefferson, miniature by John Trumbull

76.

architecture in this neighborhood, such as the Ecuries du Comte d'Artois, designed by Bélanger, which stood at the corner of the Rue de Berri and the Rue du Faubourg Saint-Honoré (Fig. 77). Work on these stables for the King's brother had begun in 1778 but was not completed until ten years later.[20] On the other side of the thoroughfare the new parish church of Saint-Philippe du Roule caught Jefferson's eye

(Fig. 78). The church was built in 1772–1784 from designs by Chalgrin, the same who drew plans for the Hôtel de Langeac.[21] Architectural historians have hypothesized a resemblance to it in Jefferson's own design for Christ Church in Charlottesville, Virginia, completed in 1826, the year of his death, and subsequently demolished.[22]

Along the Chemin du Roule, on the left when proceeding out of the city, was the *folie* of the wealthy philanthropist Nicolas Beaujon (1718–1786). His "Hermitage" or "Chartreuse" boasted English gardens comparable to those of M. Boutin or M. Jansen.[23] Nothing is left of it today save some classic columns salvaged from Girardin's Chapelle de Saint-Nicolas and subsequently re-erected on the grounds of the Fondation Salomon de Rothschild farther up the street at the corner of present Rue Balzac. Another example of Girardin's work for his patron is intact: the model orphanage built in 1784–1785 on land acquired by Beaujon across the street from his Hermitage (present No. 206, Rue du Faubourg Saint-Honoré, now serving as offices for the National Police)[24] (Fig. 79). The "Hospice Beaujon," nationalized during the Revolution, was known as the Hôpital Beaujon until the 1930's, when the hospital was transferred to the suburbs while retaining the name of the eighteenth-century philanthropist. In Jefferson's day the name Beaujon was synonymous with great wealth, like Croesus, or like Rothschild or Rockefeller to later generations. When explaining to a French visitor that there were few great fortunes in America, Jefferson qualified his statement with the remark: "I do not mean to speak here of the Beaujons of America. For we have some of these tho' happily they are but ephemeral."[25]

Continuing up the Rue du Faubourg du Roule beyond Beaujon's Hermitage, the eighteenth-century stroller came to the Foundry of the City of Paris, where Bouchardon's equestrian Louis XV and other notable statues had been cast.[26] The sculptor Houdon had an atelier and lodgings here at the time Jefferson first knew him, but was subsequently evicted. "Driven in 1787 from these workshops," Houdon later recalled, "in three weeks I bought a house opposite, I built new furnaces, and there I cast my Apollo."[27] The new atelier, according to a contem-

77. Stables of the Comte d'Artois, designed by his architect, F.-J. Bélanger

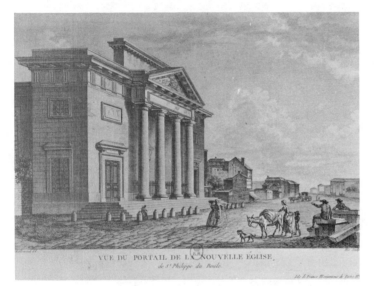

VUE DU PORTAIL DE LA NOUVELLE EGLISE,
de St Philippe du Roule.

78. Designed by Chalgrin, the architect of the Hôtel de Langeac

79. Hospice Beaujon. 206 Rue du Faubourg Saint-Honoré. Designed by N.-C. Girardin, as was Beaujon's chapel (Saint-Nicolas du Roule) on the other side of the street

porary newspaper, was "opposite M. de Beaujon's chapel" in the Rue du Faubourg du Roule. Houdon still kept possession of another studio in the Bibliothèque du Roi, Rue de Richelieu.[28]

Jefferson became acquainted with Houdon soon after his arrival in Paris and came to appreciate him as an artist "without rivalship" and as a disinterested, generous, and candid man, "panting after glory."[29] Having been commissioned by his native state of Virgina to obtain a fitting statue of General Washington, Jefferson inevitably turned to Houdon, "the first statuary of the world," who had already executed busts of two other American heroes, Benjamin

Franklin (Salon of 1779) and John Paul Jones (Salon of 1781), and who, furthermore, had already received from Virginia a commission for a bust of Lafayette. Jefferson's conversations with Houdon resulted in a formal agreement (8 July 1785) whereby the sculptor and his workmen journeyed to America for the express purpose of modeling Washington from the life. Houdon crossed the Atlantic in Franklin's company and spent a fortnight in October at Mount Vernon making the "necessary mould and measures" for the General's statue. On 4 January 1786 Jefferson could write Washington from Paris that Houdon was safely returned: "He has brought with him the mould of the face only, having left the other parts of his work, with his workmen to come by some other conveiance." When reporting the subsequent arrival of Washington's bust—which met "the approval of those who know the original"—Jefferson added the information that the sculptor would soon be taking a wife.[30] Houdon's marriage to Marie-Ange-Cécile Langlois (the subject of one of his most charming feminine busts) took place in the church of Saint-Philippe du Roule on 1 July 1786.

Jefferson became familiar with Houdon's studios in the course of his official business with the sculptor or when viewing the works on display there. On one occasion he gave a porter 3 ƒ "for seeing Houdon's Diana in bronze," and upon another noted down various prices: "Houdon's Diana in plaister is 25 guinees; his Frileuse, 15 guinees; his écorché in plaister, 12 louis"[31] (Fig. 80). John Trumbull, who saw Houdon's "little Diana in marble," accompanied by the sculptor and his new wife, thought it "a very beautiful figure—an honor not only to the artist, but to the country and age in which he lives."[32] Jefferson took a small plaster Diana back to America, remarking when he gave it to Joseph Hopkinson that it required careful handling and that "its nudity may be an objection to some to receive it as a deposit."[33]

Jefferson followed with special interest the progress of Houdon's Washington and was in fact concerned with it for years to come. Although a bust was shown at the Salon of 1787, the full-length marble statue was not completed until 1796 and reached its destined spot in the rotunda of the Capitol at Richmond only the following year (Fig. 81). Houdon's accounts were finally settled in 1803, but the inscription on the pedestal was not carved until 1814.

The bust of Lafayette also demanded Jefferson's continuing attention. The Virginia Assembly had originally commissioned a marble for Richmond, but later decided that a replica should be presented on Virginia's behalf to the City of Paris. Shortly before his own departure for America in 1785 and when the Marquis was about to set off on a tour in Germany, Houdon managed to model Lafayette's face (Fig. 82). The marble bust for Richmond eventually arrived there late in 1787. Jefferson made the arrangements for its shipment and later brought the pedestal with his own baggage in 1789 (Fig. 83). Meanwhile the marble for Paris

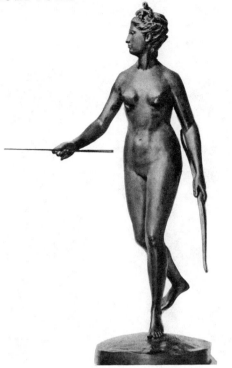

80. Houdon's Diana in bronze. Jefferson took back to America a reduced plaster version

(which was finished first) led Jefferson into a series of negotiations in which art and politics were delicately intertwined. The King, through the Baron de Breteuil, his Minister for Parisian affairs, eventually agreed to permit the City of Paris to accept Virginia's somewhat unprecedented gift honoring one of His Majesty's unorthodox subjects. The formal presentation, with Houdon present to unveil his work, was scheduled to take place in the great hall of the Hôtel de Ville on 28 September 1786. Before the day arrived, Jefferson had dislocated his wrist when walking in the Cours la Reine with Mrs. Cosway, and was thus unable to be present at the ceremony. William Short (also of Virginia) represented the Minister and read the prepared address, to which M. Ethis de Corny and other dignitaries responded in resounding phrases and appropriate classical references to the Colleagues of Fabius and the defeat of Hannibal, to Bayard and Henri IV, liberty and patriotism.[34] Lafayette himself was not present (he was mending political fences in Auvergne in view of the coming meeting of the Assembly of Notables), but was well represented by his wife, Adrienne. "I

81. Houdon's Washington. Capitol, Richmond, Virginia

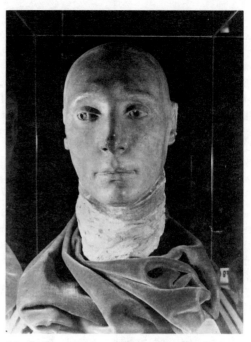

82. Lafayette's face. Plaster by Houdon

am persuaded," William Short confided to his Virginian friend and correspondent William Nelson, Jr., "that she did not receive more pleasure on the night of her marriage."[35]

The Paris marble bust of Lafayette fared less well than its Virginia counterpart, which, despite a mended broken nose, can still be seen in Richmond. On the 10th of August 1792 (the day the monarchy was overthrown), delegates to the Commune of Paris, meeting in the Hôtel de Ville, voted to "overthrow the busts of Bailly, Lafayette, Necker, Louis XVI, those charlatans of patriotism whose presence wounds the eyes of all good citizens." Thereupon, without waiting for workmen to arrive, forty arms were raised to cast down these "false idols," which "fell and were reduced to dust" amidst applause from the galleries.[36]

The closest bond between Jefferson and Houdon was forged by the sculptor's bust of Jefferson himself.[37] Little information about the circumstances of its execution has survived, probably because this was a personal rather than

83. Houdon's bust of Lafayette in marble. Capitol, Richmond, Virginia

an official commission, undertaken at Jefferson's or Houdon's own initiative or at the suggestion of friends. A bust of "M. Sefferson [*sic*], Envoyé des Etats de Virginie" was shown with other works of Houdon at the August 1789 Salon (Catalogue No. 241) (Fig. 84). Presumably, therefore, Houdon had modeled Jefferson's head sometime during the previous year. The sittings, concerning which Jefferson's papers are silent, may have taken place at the Hôtel de Langeac, or more probably in one of Houdon's studios. In later years the sculptor had a studio in the Palais des Quatre Nations. A painting by Boilly[38] shows him at work there about 1804, surrounded by his works: the Ecorché, Diana, the Frileuse, the busts of Buffon, Franklin and Washington . . . . Jefferson's bust is there, too, at home among his Parisian contemporaries (Fig. 85).

84. Houdon's Jefferson, in plaster

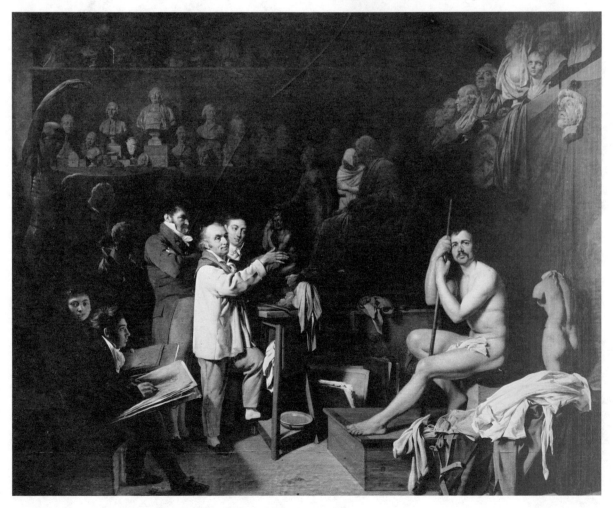

85. Houdon in His Studio. Painting by Boilly, 1804

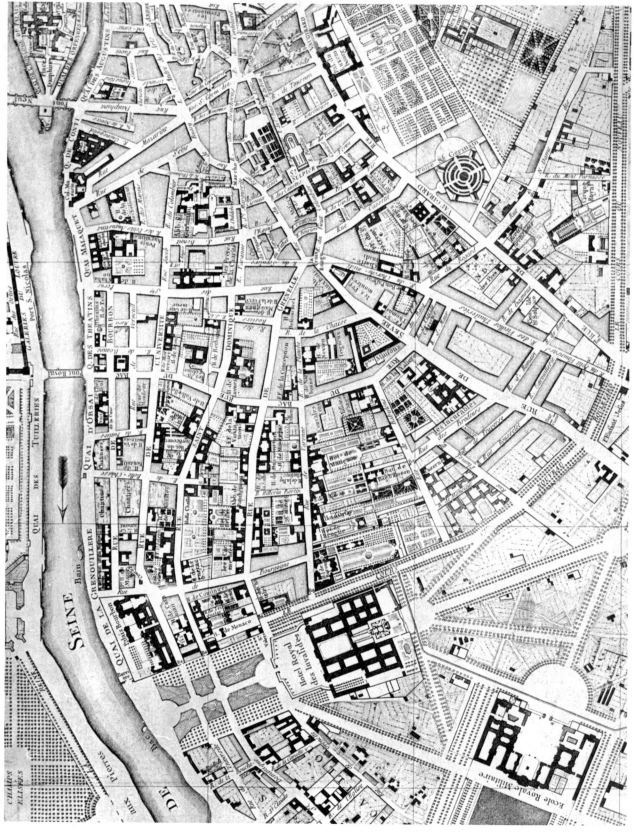

86.

Chapter 6

Left Bank: The Faubourg Saint-Germain

JEFFERSON's residences in the Cul-de-sac Taitbout and at the Grille de Chaillot were both on the Right Bank. He nevertheless became acquainted with the Faubourg Saint-Germain and other Left Bank neighborhoods soon after his arrival in Paris. From his first lodgings at the Hôtel d'Orléans (Rue de Richelieu), he moved to another hostelry of the same name in the Rue des Petits Augustins (present Rue Bonaparte), where he stayed from 10 August to 17 October 1784, while searching for a house of his own.[1] Jefferson often returned to this section of the city and, we may suppose, generally crossed the Seine via the Pont Royal (1685), then the westernmost Paris bridge. It spanned the river (as it still does) from the Pavillon de Flore to the Rue du Bac, whose name evokes a still earlier period when there was only a ferry here. (Fig. 86.)

One of the first to welcome Jefferson and his daughter to Paris was the Marquis de Chastellux, then living at the corner of the Rue du Bac and the Quais[2] (Fig. 87). The Marquis helped Jefferson find a suitable school for Martha (whose mother was still alive at the time of Chastellux's visit to Monticello in the spring of 1782),[3] and the two friends soon resumed in Paris the conversations begun in Virginia—on "the measure of English verse," on music and the fine arts, classical antiquity, and natural history. Chastellux's description of his visit to Monticello and tribute to his host was first published in Paris in 1786. "It might perhaps have passed in Europe at the time you wrote it and the exaggeration not have been detected," Jefferson told Chastellux, "but consider that the animal is now brought there, and that every one

will take his dimensions for himself."[4] Nevertheless, this portrait painted by a respected French man of letters must have excited interest in the Paris salons and corridors of government and considerably enhanced the American Minister's "image." Chastellux, who was married in 1787 to Miss Plunkett (Fig. 88), a protégée of the

87. Marquis de Chastellux

Duchesse d'Orléans, died suddenly a year later. "His loss," Jefferson later wrote to his widow, "was one of the events which most sensibly afflicted me while in France: and his memory continues very dear to me."[5]

It was Chastellux who said that "Mr. Jefferson is the first American who has consulted the Fine Arts to know how he should shelter himself from the weather." Close by Chastellux's Paris residence, along the Seine embankment, stood

88. Marquise de Chastellux. "She was Irish, of good family, and about twenty-eight years of age"

the Hôtel de Salm, an example of the Fine Arts that Jefferson could now consult without reference to his books.[6] This mansion, designed by Pierre Rousseau for the Prince de Salm-Kyrburg, was only just reaching completion when Jefferson knew it. Indeed, our street map designates the site *"chantiers,"* that is, construction in progress. "The two fronts of the Hôtel de Salm" were among those "celebrated fronts of modern buildings" that Jefferson cited as worthy models for his countrymen.[7] Like other Paris mansions, the Hôtel de Salm was set *entre cour et jardin*—the garden in this instance extending back to the Seine. The "garden front"—the one that Jefferson viewed with admiration from the Terrasse des Tuileries—thus faced the river (see Fig. 13), while the "courtyard front" faced the Rue de Bourbon (present Rue de Lille) (Fig. 89). Although the interior was gutted by fire at the time of the Commune in 1871, the shell of the building, with the contour of its original dome slightly changed, survives today as the Palais de la Légion d'Honneur.

Jefferson often passed by the Hôtel de Salm, and could watch it take shape, when bound for Lafayette's residence farther along in the Rue

de Bourbon. The Lafayette house, no longer in existence, once stood near the Palais Bourbon (see Fig. 33) on the site of present No. 119 Rue de Lille, the westernmost tip of the street dissevered by the Boulevard Saint-Germain.[8] In 1782, after Lafayette's return from the wars in America, he and his wife (who had until then resided with her family in the Hôtel de Noailles, Rue Saint-Honoré) at last acquired a home of their own. The Rue de Bourbon house, purchased from the Marquis de Bérenger, was remodeled and redecorated for them under the supervision of the architect Adrien Mouton. No picture of it seems to have survived, but its twin, extant in the courtyard of 121 Rue de Lille (Institut Néerlandais), where Turgot died in 1781, gives an idea of what it was like. It was in no way comparable to the sumptuous Hôtel de Salm, but, as Lafayette confided to a friend, it was nevertheless *infiniment gentille.*

The Marquis was again in America when Jefferson arrived in Paris, but took pains to send a letter of welcome. "My House, Dear Sir," he wrote from Hartford, Connecticut, "my family, and any thing that is mine are entirely at your disposal and I beg you will come and see Mde. de Lafayette as you would act by your brother's wife. Her knowledge of the country may be of some use to Miss Jefferson whom she will be happy to attend in every thing that may be agreeable to her. Indeed, my dear Sir, I would be very angry with you, if either you or she, did not consider my house as a second home."[9] Lafayette's Rue de Bourbon *hôtel*, presided over

VUE DE L'HÔTEL DE SALMS.

89. Hôtel de Salm. Entrance on Rue de Bourbon

90. *Dans tous les coeurs son mérite le place*
Anastasie, George-Washington, and Virginie de Lafayette, with bust of their father

masked by the other ministry buildings along the street. The Tessé residence, designed by the architect Debias-Aubry, was built in the 1720's by a Swiss banker (Antoine de Hogguer) for the actress Mademoiselle Desmares. The "Maison Desmares" was subsequently acquired by the Duc de Villeroy, who enlarged and embellished it in the 1740's with the assistance of J.-B. Leroux and Nicolas Pineau. The Hôtel de Villeroy became in 1767 a Crown property, the usufruct of which was granted to the Comte de Tessé, First Equerry of the Queen, as a perquisite of his office. This Rue de Varenne mansion, next door to the Hôtel de Castries (present No. 72), was the town house of the Comte and Comtesse de Tessé from 1769 until 1790, when, like other residents of the "noble faubourg," they set forth on their wanderings as émigrés. The Tessés also enjoyed the usufruct of another royal property, the Château de Chaville, their country house on the road to Versailles (see Chapter 8). The Comtesse de Tessé, who enthusiastically espoused the good causes and liberal ideas of her

by his wife Adrienne, became a familiar haunt to Jefferson, as it did to other Americans in Paris (Fig. 90). Among the latter were Otchikeita (Peter Otsiquette), a young Oneida Indian, and Kayenlaha, an Onondaga, whom the Lafayettes took into their household. This particular house was Lafayette's home for barely a decade. Following his departure from the country in 1792, it was confiscated as émigré property and, ironically, came for a time into the possession of an American citizen, William Rogers of New York, holder of a winning ticket (No. 573,726) in the first of France's National Lotteries. The tradition of open house for Americans was later resumed—in the Rue d'Anjou and at the Château de La Grange—and maintained generously and faithfully until the end of Lafayette's life.

When urging his wife to take good care of Jefferson and Martha, Lafayette suggested, among other appropriate courtesies, that she take them to call on Madame de Tessé.[10] The Comtesse de Tessé (née Noailles), Adrienne's aunt, also lived in the Faubourg Saint-Germain, at what is today No. 78 Rue de Varenne, the Ministry of Agriculture[11] (Fig. 91). The *hôtel* proper and its garden at the back are now

91. Former Hôtel de Tessé, Rue de Varenne

92. Madame de Tott painting portrait of
Madame de Tessé

niece's husband, adopted the American Minister with equal enthusiasm (Fig. 92). She was about Jefferson's age and the two had many interests in common: politics, the fine arts, Roman antiquities, and above all, horticulture and "pleasure gardening."[12]

✶ ✶ ✶ ✶ ✶ ✶ ✶ ✶ ✶ ✶ ✶ ✶

Convents as well as private *hôtels* contributed to the characteristic appearance of the Faubourg Saint-Germain—the Carmélites, the Dames de Bellechasse, the Abbaye aux Bois, among them. One of Jefferson's early excursions into this part of the city was to the Abbaye Royale de Panthemont in the Rue de Grenelle. On the advice of such friends as the Marquis de Chastellux, he selected Panthemont as an appropriate school for twelve-year-old Martha, who was joined there in 1787 by her younger sister, Mary. "I was

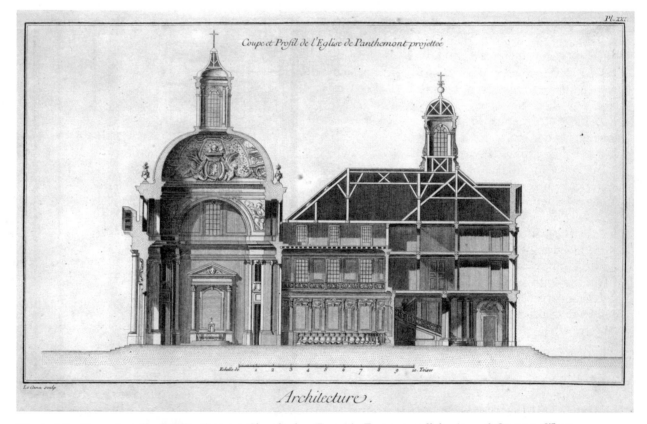

Coupe et Profil de l'Eglise de Panthemont projettée.

Architecture.

93. Architect's project for the Panthemont Church, by François Franque, collaborator of Contant d'Ivry

placed in a convent at my arrival," Martha wrote to an American friend a year or so later, "and I leave you to judge of my situation. I did not speak a word of French . . . . There are fifty or sixty pensioners in the house, so that speaking as much as I could with them I learnt the language very soon. At present I am charmed with my situation."[13]

Panthemont (or Pentemont) was presided over by a forceful and worldly abbess, Madame Béthisy de Mézières (related through her mother to the Jacobite family of Sutton d'Oglethorpe), who, upon the assumption of her duties in 1743, had inaugurated an ambitious building program.[14] Plans were drawn by Pierre Contant d'Ivry of the Royal Academy of Architecture, the cornerstone was laid by Cardinal Rohan in 1747, the new church was dedicated by the Dauphin in 1753 and completed in 1756 (Fig. 93). Improvements and additions to the buildings were continuing in the 1780's. When relaying convent news to her father, Martha Jefferson reported upon one occasion that "Every body here is very well, particularly Madame L'Abbesse, who has visited almost a quarter of the new building, a thing she has not done for two or three years before now."[15] A month or so later, when describing her own aches and pains, Martha added that "Mde. l'Abesse has just had a fluxion de poitrine and has been at the last extremity but now is better."[16] The Abbess indeed recovered and resumed her tours of inspection. In 1790 she was to suffer the ordeal of seeing her half-century's work undone when the community was dissolved and the buildings confiscated as national property. More fortunate than others of her class and calling, the old Abbess was allowed to remain in her convent as a *locataire de la nation* until her death there in 1794.

The Panthemont buildings, still standing, were used as a barracks during the Revolution and Empire. Eventually Contant d'Ivry's chapel was ceded by the City of Paris to the Eglise Réformée de France. Thus, since 1846, Protestant services have been held here in the former convent church, now known as the Temple de Pentemont at 106 Rue de Grenelle (Fig. 94). The other convent buildings, facing a courtyard entered from 39 Rue de Bellechasse (the street

94. Temple de Pentemont, 106 Rue de Grenelle

was extended southward to meet the Rue de Grenelle only in 1805), are now occupied by the Ministère des Anciens Combattants.[17]

Martha Jefferson's "classe" at Panthemont, she explained to an American correspondent, comprised four exceedingly large sleeping rooms, a parlor, and a classroom for lessons. The girls' uniform, as she described it, was "crimson made like a frock laced behind with the tail like a robe de cour, hoocked on muslin cuffs and tuckers."[18] The lessons, given in part by visiting "masters," included reading, arithmetic, history, geography, as well as needlework, music, drawing, and dancing. At one time Martha learned to draw flowers and "landskips" from M. Pineau and took lessons on the harpsichord from Claude Balbastre, the talented organist of Saint-Roch and Notre-Dame. Livy, or "Tite Live" as she said in her gallicized English, put her "out of her wits." "I have begun

95. Panthemont Account Book

it three or four times," she told her father in reply to his exhortations, "and go on so slowly with it that I believe I shall never finish it . . . . I read a little of it with my master who tells me almost all the words, and, in fine, it makes me lose my time."[19]

The pupils at Panthemont were under the immediate supervision of the *première maîtresse des pensionnaires*, Sister Tonbenheim (a Saxon by birth), whose name (generally misspelt) occurs frequently in the Jefferson correspondence. Through Sister Tonbenheim Jefferson made regular payments for his daughters, as recorded in both his own and the convent account books (Fig. 95). The rate for room and board, exclusive of the masters' fees and various extras, was at first 175 *livres* a quarter, later increased when the girls sat at the Abbess's table. In the Panthemont accounts, kept by Sisters de Vis, Amariton, and d'Elbée (*dépositaires de l'Abbaye*), the spelling of the girls' name varies— Gefferssone, Gefersone, Geferson, Gefferson, occasionally Jefferson—but it is always Mademoiselle (or les Demoiselles) *de* Jefferson. Martha's classmates called her "Jeff." (Figs. 96, 97, 98).

Martha's news that she was "placed in a convent" evidently caused some concern among friends and relatives in Virginia. Life at Panthemont was, however, far from cloistered. There were numerous *sorties*: an invitation from her father to dine with American guests at the Hôtel de Langeac—"Make it a rule hereafter," he admonished, "to come dressed otherwise than in your uniform"; an excursion to the opera with Madame de Corny; or a visit to Madame de Tessé's at Chaville with Madame de Lafayette and thence to Versailles to see the fountains play.[20] Furthermore, Panthemont itself was more than a boarding school for the *demoiselles pensionnaires*. It also served as a select residence for aristocratic spinsters, widows, ladies separated from their husbands or seeking refuge for other reasons. One such resident was an attractive young Creole from Martinique, Joséphine de Beauharnais, then estranged from her husband. Her sojourn at Panthemont, it is said, later stood her in good stead when she became Bonaparte's bride and eventually, *l'Impératrice Joséphine*. The presence of these *dames en chambre* contributed to the education of the younger boarding pupils. Echoes of their worldly gossip even crept into Martha Jefferson's letters. "There was a gentleman a few days ago," she told her father, "that killed himself because he thought his wife did not love him. They had been married ten years. I believe that if every husband in Paris was to do as much, there would be nothing but widows left."[21]

Panthemont had the reputation of being a safe place for young Protestants. "There are in it," Jefferson assured his sister Mrs. Bolling, "as many protestants as Catholics, and not a word is ever spoken to them on the subject of religion."[22] Jean-Armand Tronchin, the representative of Calvinist Geneva at the French Court, mentioned the English girls enrolled at Panthemont as evidence of its tolerant policy and cited as a further testimonial the fact that Mr. Jefferson's daughter was a pupil there. "Surely," he said of a Genevan orphan entrusted to the convent, "she will leave it as good a Protestant as when she entered."[23] Nevertheless, these young Protestants inevitably became familiar with Catholic beliefs and practices. Martha, very early in her stay at the convent, witnessed the ceremony of the taking of the veil in the company of her father, Mrs. Adams, and the latter's daughter, Abby, who penned a lengthy description in her diary.[24] "The ceremony lasted half an hour, while these poor girls were lying on their faces," Abby wrote, "and when they rise, it is called rising to the resurrection, after having been dead to the world. Then they went to the old abbess; she put upon them the nun's habit." One of the girls was French from "one of the first families of the kingdom," the other was Irish. "Thus these two girls are destined to pass their lives within the walls of this convent. They are not so strict as formerly. Miss Jefferson told me they were very cheerful and agreeable. They seemed to take pleasure in contributing to the happiness of the pensioners."

Among the souvenirs of Martha's schooldays in Paris is a small book entitled *Méthodes d'Instruction pour ramener les Prétendus Réformés à l'Eglise Romane*, inscribed on the flyleaf "Miss Jefferson panthmont march 21 1787" (Fig. 99). Her father apparently thought it worth preserving, for it was among the books he sold

96. "Mlle Martha *Jefferson*, fille de Monsieur Thomas Jefferson, Ministre Américain à Paris. MDCCLXXXIX." Miniature by Joseph Boze

97. *J'espère & J'aime*. Martha Jefferson 1788

98. Mlle Botidoux, one of Martha's schoolmates

to the Library of Congress in 1815.[25] According to a family tradition, Martha once informed her father that she desired to remain in the convent and dedicate herself to the duties of a religious life. Whereupon, the story ran, Jefferson "with a benignant and gentle smile" met his two daughters at Panthemont and straightway withdrew them from the convent. Martha did, at least in a passing phase, show "favourable dispositions for the Catholic religion" (as the papal nuncio in Paris, Dugnani, later told Bishop John Carroll of Baltimore), but the abrupt withdrawal is certainly an overdramatized version.[26] In the spring of 1789, when preparing to return to America and momentarily expecting his leave, Jefferson "gave Patsy for vales at Panthemont 81 ƒ" (that is, money for farewell gifts or gratuities), settled his accounts there "in full (625 ƒ -15-3)," and brought the two girls to live with him at the Hôtel de Langeac, where lessons with Balbastre and other masters continued throughout the summer. Martha's schooldays were soon to be over. She was married at the age of seventeen to Thomas Mann Randolph, Jr., at Monticello on 23 February 1790. An Episcopal clergyman, the Reverend James Maury, performed the ceremony.

* * * * * * * * * * * *

Jefferson's Left Bank saunterings were not limited to the Faubourg Saint-Germain. To the east of the Faubourg the Palais du Luxembourg, built by Salomon de Brosse for Marie de Médicis and occupied in the 1780's by "Monsieur" (the King's eldest brother, the Comte de Provence), provided, then as now, a convenient guidemark for strollers. Near the Luxembourg, along the Rue de Vaugirard, the Théâtre Français had in 1782 opened its doors in a new home built by the architects Charles de Wailly and M.-J. Peyre on the site of the former Hôtel de Condé[27] (Fig. 100). The building formed the central point of a characteristic piece of city planning, now largely forgotten though its main lines are still discernible. From the half-circle in front of the theatre, radiating streets named for dramatists were staked out: Racine, Voltaire (now Casimir Delavigne), Crébillon, and Regnard, with Corneille and Molière (now Rotrou) hugging the

MÉTHODE D'INSTRUCTION POUR RAMENER LES PRÉTENDUS RÉFORMÉS A L'ÉGLISE ROMAINE, Et confirmer les catholiques dans leur croyance.

Par M. DE LA FOREST, Cuftode-curé de Sainte-Croix de Lyon, docteur de la faculté de théologie de Paris, &c.

A PARIS, Rue & hôtel Serpente.

A LYON, Chez AIMÉ DE LA ROCHE, Imprimeur de la Ville, aux Halles de la Grenette.

M. DCC. LXXXIV. AVEC APPROBATION ET PRIVILEGE DU ROI.

99.

flanks of the building. To Parisians of the 1780's the new theatre seemed far from the center. They complained that cab-drivers took advantage of its remote situation.

Jefferson attended five or more performances at the Théâtre Français and thus had a taste of

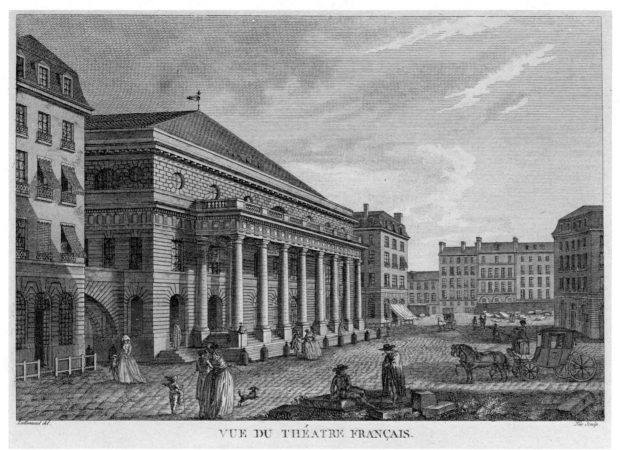

VUE DU THÉATRE FRANÇAIS.

100.

Racine (in *Les Plaideurs*), of Molière (*Amphitryon*), and of dramatists in the Molièresque tradition such as Lesage (*Crispin*) and Dancourt (*Les Trois Cousines*).[28] The Comédie's most notable new creation was Beaumarchais's *Le Mariage de Figaro, ou La Folle Journée*, which Jefferson saw on 4 August 1786—its ninetieth performance (Fig. 101). Written when its author was managing clandestine shipments of war supplies to the American rebels, *Figaro* had received the Royal Censor's approval only in 1784. In his capacity as American Minister and as a former wartime governor of Virginia, Jefferson was involved in the settlement of Beaumarchais's accounts—an "immense amount," he once said—with both Congress and the State of Virginia; upon at least one occasion America's creditor called in person at the Hôtel de Langeac.[29] As the author of the Declaration of Independence Jefferson was well prepared to

101. Mlle Contat in the *Mariage de Figaro*

102. The Pont Neuf and Hôtel des Monnaies from the Quai du Louvre. Painting by A.-J. Noël, ca. 1780

appreciate the "very daring spirit" of Figaro's witticisms. He acquired a copy of Beaumarchais's play and could thus meditate at leisure on its allusions to equality of birth, freedom of the press, and arbitrary imprisonment. "How fertile is the mind of man," as he said of Monsieur de Latude, "which can make the Bastille and Dungeon of Vincennes yield interesting anecdotes!"

In the lobby of the Théâtre Français (known to later generations as the Odéon) Jefferson could see Houdon's bust of Voltaire, still another reminder of the daring spirit he found in Paris. Such a bust was later to stand in the entrance hall at Monticello. The *Oeuvres complètes* of Beaumarchais were in Jefferson's library there, as were Voltaire's works printed on the press established by Beaumarchais at Kehl, conveniently located beyond the reach of censorship across the Rhine from Strasbourg.[30] This Kehl edition included notes by another of Jefferson's Paris acquaintances, the Marquis de Condorcet.

De Wailly's and Peyre's Théâtre Français burned in 1807 but was rebuilt by Chalgrin on the same plans, so that its present appearance is substantially what it was in the 1780's. Another Left Bank building dating from the Louis XVI period is the Hôtel des Monnaies, designed by Jacques-Denis Antoine, whose plans had won acceptance over those of several competitors (including Boullée).[31] The building facing the Quai de Conti, which has changed little in appearance or function over the past two centuries, was begun in 1768 and ready to house the Royal Mint by 1775 (Figs. 102, 103). Jefferson came to know it not only as the mint but also as the home of the Marquis de Condorcet, political reformer and mathematician, Secretary of the Academy of Sciences, and *Inspecteur général des monnaies*. This latter office (sinecure, said some) gave him the privilege of a residence in the Hôtel des Monnaies.

Jefferson's interest in coinage was both theoretical and practical. His *Notes on the Establishment of a Money Unit, and of a Coinage for the*

United States, prepared for Congress prior to his departure abroad, was reprinted for him in Paris in 1785 as a 14-page pamphlet that he had bound with some copies of his *Notes on Virginia*.[32] After his return from France, when he was Secretary of State, he published his *Report . . . on weights, measures, and coins* (New York, 1790) and was deeply concerned with the establishment of the United States Mint in Philadelphia, of which his scientifically-minded friend David Rittenhouse was the first director.[33] On a visit to the Hôtel des Monnaies in January 1787 in the company of Ferdinand Grand, banker of the United States in Paris, and of

104. Ecu de Calonne, 1786. Specimen coin designed and struck by J.-P. Droz

Matthew Boulton of London, Jefferson watched a demonstration of a machine capable of striking the two faces and edge of a coin at one stroke invented by the Swiss craftsman Jean-Pierre Droz.[34] Specimen 6-*livre* pieces (never circulated), known as the *écu de Calonne*, samples of which Jefferson obtained to send to America, were struck from Droz's labor-saving invention (Fig. 104). Droz did not at this time obtain employment in Paris but moved on to England where he worked under Watt and Boulton as coiner for the British Crown. For several years Jefferson hoped to bring Droz to the United States as coiner of the United States Mint, but the plan never materialized despite protracted negotiations.[35] Droz eventually returned to the Hôtel des Monnaies and is remembered there as the designer of the gold-pieces known as *napoléons*.

Jefferson's interest in coinage was closely related to the business of the medals voted by Congress to commemorate persons and events of the American Revolution.[36] While overseeing their execution in Paris, Jefferson gave his attention to the smallest details, consulting the Académie des Inscriptions et Belles-Lettres for the Latin inscriptions, and commissioning the foremost French medallic artists—Augustin Dupré, Benjamin Duvivier, Nicolas-Marie Gatteaux—to execute the designs. Jefferson thus had a share in the medals for Horatio Gates (Saratoga), Anthony Wayne and John Stewart (Stony Point), William Augustine Washington, John Eager Howard and Daniel Morgan (Cowpens), Nathanael Greene (Eutaw Springs), and John Paul Jones (Bonhomme Richard vs. Serapis) (Fig. 105). But of all the Paris-made American medals the one most truly his is the very rare

103.

"Diplomatic Medal," conceived by him as a parting gift to retiring envoys. Jefferson's very explicit ideas for the design, which he sent to William Short in 1790 after his own return to America, were faithfully translated in Augustin Dupré's medal[37] (Fig. 106). These American medals were presumably struck at the Monnaie des Médailles, the venerable royal institution housed in the Grande Galerie du Louvre[38] (see Fig. 41). The Medal Mint was moved across the Seine and incorporated in the Hôtel des Monnaies only in 1806, but even in Jefferson's day officials and craftsmen worked interchangeably on both sides of the river.

The Quai de Conti buildings of the Mint included quarters assigned to the Ecole Royale des Mines, with an extensive mineralogical "cabinet" assembled by B.-G. Sage, the school's director, as well as apartments for the *Inspecteur général des monnaies*. The incumbent of this post, the Marquis de Condorcet, was married in 1786 to Sophie de Grouchy, a budding lady-philosopher half his age, who welcomed scientists, literary figures, and foreign visitors to her Seine-side salon.[39] Jefferson placed Condorcet, with Rittenhouse and Madison, among "those worthy sons of science" that his Head so justly prized.[40] His library included Condorcet's scientific writings as well as such pseudonymous tracts for the times as *Lettre d'un Citoyen des Etats-Unis* (1788) and *Sentiments d'un Républicain* (1788).[41] He prepared notes for a trans-

105. Washington's set of American medals struck in Paris

[72]

106. *To Peace and Commerce*. Diplomatic medal designed by Augustin Dupré following Jefferson's specifications

107.

lation of Condorcet's *Réflexions sur l'esclavage des nègres* and discussed with him proposals for a French Constitution.[42] The esteem was mutual. "Whatever may happen here," Condorcet wrote on the eve of his friend's departure from Paris, "Monsieur Jefferson will always be the friend of the philosophers and of the free men of all countries."[43]

* * * * * * * * * * * *

Another "son of science" whose worth Jefferson appreciated was the Duc de La Rochefoucauld, who had translated under Franklin's aegis the *Constitutions des Treize Etats-Unis de l'Amérique* (printed by Philippe-Denys Pierres, Paris, 1783). The Duc lived in his family's mansion in the Rue de Seine, behind the Collège

des Quatre Nations only a short distance from the Hôtel des Monnaies (Fig. 107). The La Rochefoucaulds' house, Filippo Mazzei told Jefferson when briefing him on people worth knowing in Paris, "is devoted to Philosophy, and their garden to experiments for the improvement of knowledge."[44] The Duc's mother, the Duchesse d'Enville, a widow of seventy, who divided her time between the Paris town house and the ancestral château at La Roche-Guyon (see Chapter 9), was the ruling spirit of the family.[45] A friend of Voltaire, Choiseul, Turgot, and of her son's contemporary Condorcet, she had fallen under Franklin's spell and eagerly befriended all Americans. Mrs. Adams, when paying court, found "the old lady" seated in an easy chair with a circle of Academicians surrounding her.[46]

[73]

108.

109. Houdon's Condorcet in marble (1785), "which stood on a marble table in the salon of the Hôtel de la Rochefoucauld"

Though Mrs. Adams misjudged the Duchesse's age by ten years, she nevertheless avowed that "the old lady has all the vivacity of a young one —She is the most learned woman in France; her house is the resort of all men of literature, with whom she converses upon the most abstruse subjects."

"Be assured," Jefferson told the Duchesse d'Enville in a farewell letter, "that I shall ever retain a lively sense of all your goodness to me, which was a circumstance of principal happiness to me during my stay in Paris."[47] He retained similar lively memories of the younger members of the family, especially the "old Dutchess's" son, Louis-Alexandre, duc de La Rochefoucauld, and the latter's young second wife (who was also his niece and thus both granddaughter and daughter-in-law to the old lady). The Duc and

Jefferson were the same age, kindred spirits, whose acquaintance deepened under the stimulus of the events of 1789 (Fig. 108). On 17 September of that year, a week before Jefferson left Paris, La Rochefoucauld (fresh from the National Assembly at Versailles), Condorcet, and Lafayette were all three dinner guests at the Hôtel de Langeac, as was Gouverneur Morris, who noted in his diary that the conversation ranged from the current bread scarcity to the impending threat of a march on Versailles by the troops of the National Guard.[48] Jefferson (more optimistic than Morris) left Paris with the hope that his French friends, these three in particular, would, as he phrased it, "live long years of health and happiness to see in full ripeness the fruit of your own Revolution."[49]

Neither the Duc de La Rochefoucauld nor

[74]

Condorcet lived out the approaching storm. La Rochefoucauld was stoned to death at Gisors on 4 September 1792 before the eyes of his wife and his mother. That same week the Duchesse d'Enville's grandson, the Comte de Chabot, perished in the September massacres at the Prison de l'Abbaye. Condorcet's earlier refusal to intervene in the young prisoner's behalf added bitterness to the family's grief. With another turn of the revolutionary wheel, Condorcet, tracked down by Robespierre's police, took his own life in his hiding-place at Bourg-Egalité (*ci-devant* Bourg-la-Reine) in 1794. Shortly before his death, he wrote on the fly-leaf of a book his testamentary instructions concerning his daughter Elisa. He urged that she be taught English, as she might be forced to take refuge in England or in America. In the latter eventuality, Condorcet specified, she would find a protector in Franklin's grandson Bache—or in Jefferson.[50]

Of the trio who dined with Jefferson at the Hôtel de Langeac, only Lafayette, despite imprisonment in the dungeons of Olmütz, survived the Revolution and lived to embrace his old friend at Monticello in 1824. Meanwhile their correspondence had continued. In 1814, when informing Jefferson of the deaths of the Comte and Comtesse de Tessé, Lafayette cast a backward glance to the Paris of the 1780's: "You remember our happy hours, and animated conversations at Chaville. How far from us those times, and those of the venerable Hôtel de la Rochefoucauld!"[51]

Another reminder of those happy hours came to Jefferson from William Short, who had remained in Paris after Jefferson's departure and continued to frequent the Hôtel de La Rochefoucauld. His romance with the young Duchesse reads like a Henry James novel on the international theme.[52] (Fig. 109-A.) Short returned to America in 1802, but revisited Paris in 1808–1810 (at which time the widowed Duchesse de La Rochefoucauld married the Comte de Castellane). "Apropos of Philosophers," Short wrote Jefferson on 21 October 1819, "you recollect without doubt the marble bust of Condorcet [by Houdon] which stood on a marble table in the salon of the Hotel de la Rochefoucauld. When it was determined no longer to receive him in that house, it was thought *inconvenant* to keep the bust there. The grandchildren, who never liked him, availed themselves of this to have the bust transported to the *garde meuble* without consulting the old Lady . . . . she passed over this in silence . . . . It had cost her a great effort to signify to the original that his presence had become disagreeable; she had really a parental affection for him, and had given a remarkable proof of this at the time of his marriage. On her death [in 1797] I asked this bust of the granddaughter who gave it to me with great pleasure. It has been on its way ever since I left France . . . . It has finally arrived and is at present placed in the Philosophical hall [in Philadelphia] in the most suitable company, the busts of Franklin, yourself, Turgot"[53] (Fig. 109).

"I am glad that the bust of Condorcet has been saved and so well placed," Jefferson wrote in reply to Short's letter. "His genius should be before us; while the lamentable but singular act of ingratitude which tarnished his latter days, may be thrown behind us."[54]

Fig. 109-A. The Duchesse de la Rochefoucauld. Miniature preserved in a pocket-case owned by William Short

110.

Chapter 7

Left Bank: The Quartier Latin
and the Jardin du Roi

"WHILE residing in Paris I devoted every afternoon I was disengaged, for a summer or two, in examining all the principal bookstores, turning over every book with my own hands, and putting by everything related to America, and indeed whatever was rare and valuable in every science." Furthermore, as Jefferson told his friend Samuel Harrison Smith when offering his personal collection to the library committee of Congress, he had standing orders on the principal book marts of Europe—Amsterdam, Frankfurt, Madrid, and London—"for such works as could not be found in Paris."[1]

Although Jefferson made occasional purchases from Right Bank dealers (De Bray in the Palais Royal or Bailly in the Rue Saint-Honoré near the Barrière des Sergents), his book-collecting excursions generally took him to the Left Bank, the traditional center of the book trade, as did his errands to printers, publishers, bookbinders, engravers, and stationers. Several of the booksellers were located along the Quai des Grands Augustins, which stretched eastward from the Pont Neuf to the Pont Saint-Michel. When Jefferson knew it, buildings of the Convent of the Grands Augustins, extending back from the Quai to the Rue Christine, were still a prominent feature of the urban landscape, while the Quai itself, as it approached the Pont Saint-Michel, merged into a narrow street, now obliterated, called the Rue du Hurepoix (Fig. 110). Jefferson's accounts and correspondence show that he was acquainted with the bookshops of Royez, L.-N. Prévost, Pissot, J.-F. Froullé, and Barrois—all situated here on the Quai des Grands Augustins. (Fig. 111.)

"Address yourself to me as your bookseller,"

Jefferson told James Madison when preparing to leave for Europe.[2] Consequent to such offers, he served as an agent for Madison and other American friends throughout his stay in Paris. Soon after his arrival, for example, he placed with Royez (Librairie Nouvelle, Quai des Augustins) two subscriptions—one of them for Madison—to Panckoucke's new *Encyclopédie Méthodique*, publication of which had begun in 1782. The successive *livraisons* were to be supplied at the original subscribers' rate. Inquiries made on the eve of Jefferson's departure in 1789 revealed that Royez had mislaid the subscription papers. Whereupon, said Jefferson, "it was understood between him and me that there was an end of it."[3] Maintaining the *Encyclopédie Méthodique* up to date plagued Jefferson for years to come. He never did have the satisfaction of possessing a complete set, for the final *livraisons* were eventually issued by the original publisher's widowed daughter only in 1832.

L.-N. Prévost, another of the Quai des Augustins *libraires*, escaped Jefferson's strictures. Prévost was the Paris correspondent of Amand Koenig of Strasbourg, whose shop Jefferson visited during his 1788 journey to Holland and the Rhine Valley and who had "the greatest collection of Classics, and the finest editions, I met with in Europe."[4] Koenig filled orders with exemplary care and promptness, dispatching them by the diligence to Prévost in Paris. His arrangements with the diligence, Jefferson noted, "took all the expence and trouble off the hands of his customers."[5]

Editions of the Modern classics, as well as the Ancients, were scrutinized by Jefferson both as to format and price. He had occasion to discuss

111. *"Un Libraire sérieux, ne faisant que l'ancienne Librairie. . . ."*

with Pissot (who had been Franklin's bookseller) the latter's plan for reprinting the English classics (in collaboration with J.-J. Tourneysen, a Bâle printer) "cheaper than in England or even in Ireland," and sent specimen pages to Philadelphia in the hope that Franklin's grandson, B. F. Bache, might serve as Pissot's American distributor.[6] In line with the American Minister's general mission, this was still another way of encouraging trade with France and lessening commercial dependence on England. Jefferson also interested himself in another of Pissot's enterprises, the English-language publication of a weekly "English and American gazette" called *The General Advertiser*.[7] He welcomed the opportunity of transmitting American news to Pissot's paper as a corrective to the London

newspapers—"those infamous fountains of falsehood," as he characterized them.[8]

"While speaking of Froullé, libraire, au quai des Augustins," Jefferson wrote James Monroe when the latter was setting forth for Paris in 1795, "I can assure you, that, having run a severe gauntlet under the Paris book-sellers, I rested at last on this old gentleman, whom I found, in a long & intimate course of after dealings, to be one of the most conscientiously honest men I ever had dealings with. I recommend him to you strongly, should you purchase books."[9] Froullé, for his part, reciprocated these sentiments and esteemed the extensive bibliographical knowledge and exacting standards of "Monsieur Chefersone." "When I name a particular edition of a book," Jefferson told another bookseller, "send me that edition and no other . . . . I disclaim all pompous editions and all typographical luxury; but I like a fine white paper, neat type, and neat binding, gilt and lettered in the modern. stile."[10] Confessing that he "laboured grievously under the malady of Bibliomanie," he explained to a friend that he "submitted to the rule of buying only at reasonable prices, as a regimen necessary to that disease."[11]

Froullé, who was well-acquainted with Jefferson's book-buying habits, was both bookseller and publisher, with a shop at the corner of the Rue Pavée, now Rue Séguier, a street leading from the Quai to the Rue Saint-André-des-Arts. With the counsel of the Marquis de Chastellux, Jefferson negotiated with Froullé for the translation and printing of Dr. David Ramsay's history, which appeared in 1787 under Froullé's imprint as *Histoire de la Révolution dans la Caroline du Sud*.[12] He also paid Froullé for reprints of Franklin's "advice to emigrants" (*Avis à ceux qui voudraient émigrer en Amérique*), having found it a good regimen for those laboring under the malady of Americomanie.[13] At one time Jefferson discussed with Froullé a proposed translation of John Adams's *A Defence of the Constitutions of Government of the United States of America* (London, 1787-1788), but this work was not published in France until 1792, and then under the imprint of Buisson.[14]

Barrois, another of the Paris bookseller-publishers with whom Jefferson had dealings, resided in the Rue du Hurepoix at the far end of the Quai des Augustins. In contrast to "my Bookseller Frouillé, an extremely honest man," it was the "shifting conduct of Barrois" that Jefferson remembered. He consented somewhat reluctantly to Barrois's publication of Abbé Morellet's translation of his *Notes on the state of Virginia* in order to forestall a less desirable pirated edition. Morellet suggested the inclusion of a map, whereupon Jefferson himself painstakingly drafted one (based to a large extent on his father's earlier one, the 1750 Jefferson-Fry map of Virginia), had it engraved by Samuel Neale of London, and then corrected by the Paris engraver Guillaume-Nicolas Delahaye.[15] Jefferson promised the plate to the London publisher John Stockdale, who was bringing out the first trade edition of his book. Meanwhile he lent the plate to Barrois, assuming that it would be retained for a week or two at most. After waiting three months and after sending a stern note to Barrois (couched in his best French), followed by repeated urgent messages, Jefferson finally threatened to "apply to the police."[16] Barrois's "ill behaviour" was embarrassing to Morellet as well as to Jefferson, but strikes from the plate eventually appeared, in the form of a folding map, in both Stockdale's *Notes on the State of Virginia, Written by Thomas Jefferson* (London, 1787) and Barrois's *Observations sur la Virginie, Par M. J**** (Paris, 1786) (Fig. 112).

* * * * * * * * * * * *

Threading his way from the Quai des Grands Augustins over to the Rue Saint-Jacques, where the principal printers were located, Jefferson was perhaps distracted for a moment in the Rue Saint-André-des-Arts by the vinegars and mustards on display in the establishment of Maille, *vinaigrier-distillateur ordinaire du Roi*,[17] before pausing in the Rue Mignon at the bookshop of Molini, a specialist in Italian books who supplied several of Jefferson's desiderata in this field. Though such nineteenth-century arteries as the Boulevard Saint-Germain, the Boulevard Saint-Michel, and the Rue des Ecoles, have re-channeled the traffic in this quarter, fragments of the narrow older streets survive, as does the Rue Saint-Jacques, the main thoroughfare in Jefferson's day. There was then no Boul' Mich.

Jefferson first visited the printing establishment of Philippe-Denys Pierres in the Rue Saint-Jacques soon after he arrived in Paris, no doubt at Franklin's suggestion. He had brought with him from America the manuscript of his *Notes on Virginia*, composed in 1781–1782 in reply to a questionnaire circulated by M. de Marbois, then attached to the French Legation in Philadelphia. Jefferson soon discovered that printing costs in Paris were considerably less than those quoted to him in Philadelphia. He thus arranged with Pierres to have printed, at his own expense and for private distribution, some 200 copies of his book. The job was finished in May 1785, at which time Jefferson began presenting copies to selected friends in Europe and America, each inscribed with an admonitory message to guard it against "exposure to the public eye"[18] (Fig. 113). He subsequently had Pierres print cancel leaves, which he substituted for pages containing errors or misstatements, and also had several

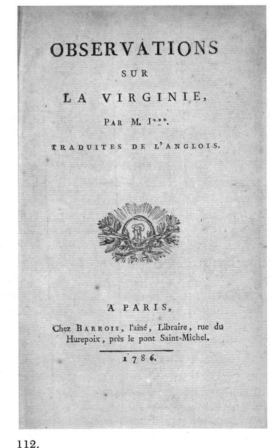

112.

NOTES on the ſtate of VIRGINIA;

written in the year 1781, ſomewhat corrected and enlarged in the winter of 1782,
for the uſe of a Foreigner of diſtinction, in
anſwer to certain queries propoſed by him
reſpecting

MDCCLXXXII.

Th. Jefferson having had a few copies of these
Notes printed to be offered to some of his friends,
and to some other estimable characters beyond that
line, presents one to Mons.ʳ de Marbois, under
the most just of all titles, his right to the original.
unwilling to expose them to the public eye, he
asks the favour of Mons.ʳ de Marbois to put
them into the hands of no person on whose care
& fidelity he cannot rely to guard them against
publication.

113. Printed by P.-D. Pierres, Paris, 1785

separate items printed (by Pierres or others),
which he had bound-in as appendices to some
copies of the *Notes*.[19] Most notable was the "Virginia Act for Establishing Religious Freedom,"
of which there were several different Paris printings, in the original English as well as in French
and Italian translations.

Jefferson also employed Pierres to print blank
passport forms and at one time even asked him
to have a small printing press made.[20] In 1786
Pierres published a *Description* of the improved
press that had been in operation in his Rue
Saint-Jacques shop since October 1784 and
received the approbation of the Academy of Sciences in 1786 (Fig. 114). According to the author's account he had earlier discussed his invention with Monsieur Franklin, who "possessed to
an eminent degree the science of typography."
A small model made by Baron de Tott was exhibited in 1784 to the King, who straightway
requested a similar small press, which Pierres
had made for His Majesty by Baradelle *l'aîné*, a

skillful Parisian instrument-maker. Jefferson no
doubt had something like this in mind. When he
inquired about type to go with the press, sug-
gesting Didot's "charming characters" and

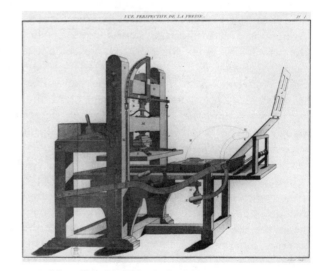

114. New Printing Press, designed by P.-D. Pierres

[80]

Greek characters from Foulis in Glasgow, Pierres replied with a show of ruffled professional pride that he himself could supply types "engraved by Garamond," no less beautiful than those mentioned by Jefferson. No evidence has been found to prove that Jefferson actually acquired the *"petite presse"* referred to in the exchange of letters dated January 1787. We can nevertheless conclude that he at least toyed with the idea of having his own private press at the Grille de Chaillot, following Franklin's example at Passy.

Another printer with whom Jefferson did business was Jacques-Gabriel Clousier—like P.-D. Pierres an *imprimeur du Roi*—whose shop was in the Rue des Mathurins (present Rue du

115. Printed for Jefferson by J.-G. Clousier, 1788

Sommerard) in the vicinity of the old Sorbonne. Jefferson's accounts attest that Clousier did a substantial amount of printing "for the United States" in 1788 and 1789. His work included a ten-page pamphlet containing in parallel columns the texts of the proposed Franco-American Consular Convention of 1784 and the new Convention as negotiated by Jefferson in 1788.[21] This example of what might be termed an early United States government document was printed by Clousier in Paris for "the use of the members" of the Continental Congress. Ratification of the Convention finally took place only after the establishment of the new government in 1789, thus making it the first treaty ratified by the United States Senate.

Clousier also printed both an English and a French edition of Jefferson's *Observations on the Whale-Fishery* (Fig. 115). This well-documented survey (not intended for public circulation and not to be confused with the later "Report on the Cod and Whale Fisheries" submitted by the Secretary of State to Congress in

116.

1791) brought together the material Jefferson had assembled while negotiating preferential treatment for French imports of American whale oil.[22]

Jefferson's Left Bank excursions often brought him in touch with bookbinders, engravers, and stationers. His accounts for 1785, for instance, record substantial payments to "Derosme" (Nicolas-Denis Derôme, le jeune), an outstanding binder of the time (Fig. 116), as well as to Jacques-Guillaume Hamerville, whose shop was in the Rue de la Charretière (behind what is now the Lycée Louis-le-Grand). Throughout Jefferson's stay in Paris there were payments for stationery and for bookbinding to Cabaret, at the sign of the Griffin, Rue de Seine

117.

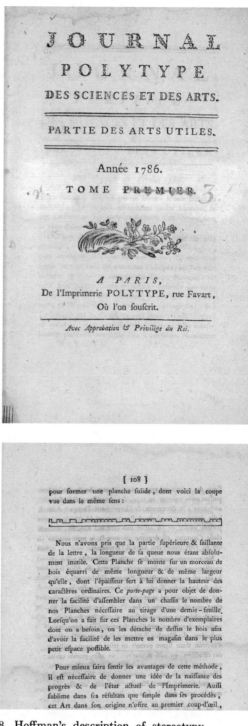

118. Hoffman's description of stereotypy

(Fig. 117). He had engraving done by Corneillon from whom he also bought "engraving utensils," drawing paper, and "pictures." The ruled drawing paper he used for his architectural drawings was obtained "Chez Crepy, rue S. Jacques à S. Pierre près la rue de la Parcheminerie."[23]

* * * * * * * * * * * *

The roll call of Jefferson's Paris printers would not be complete without the Alsatian, François-Ignace-Joseph Hoffman, whose Imprimerie Polytype was situated, significantly, not in the traditional Latin Quarter printers' homeland, but in the Rue Favart near the Théâtre Italien, not far from Jefferson's first Paris residence in the Cul-de-sac Taitbout.[24] The Hoffman shop was licensed in 1785 but subsequently ran afoul of the authorities for clandestine activities. Jefferson took a keen interest in Hoffman's innovations, describing them at length in letters to American correspondents. Hoffman's term "polytype" covered, somewhat confusingly, two distinct processes, though both made use of a special alloy of his invention. The first of these, described by Hoffman in his *Journal Polytype*, closely resembled what was subsequently known as stereotypy (Fig. 118). His "types for printing a whole page are all in one solid piece," Jefferson told Madison, "an author therefore only re-

119. Stereotype printing by Hoffman, 1786

120. Reproduced from Jefferson's handwritten copy by Hoffman's "art of multiplying originals"

prints a few copies of his work from time to time as they are called for. This saves the loss of printing more copies than may possibly be sold, and prevents an edition from being ever exhausted."[25] Attracted by such advantages, Jefferson at one time obtained Hoffman's estimate for reprinting his *Notes on Virginia* in this manner.[26] This project was never undertaken, but it is clear from an entry in Hoffman's record book, dated 25 October 1786, that he did print for "M. de Jefferson" Calonne's letter of 22 October, and delivered with the "planches polytypées" 150 copies of this 8-page leaflet[27] (Fig. 119). The letter thus stereotyped summarized the work of a special Comité du Commerce appointed by Calonne, Minister of Finance, to study problems of Franco-American trade. For Jefferson, who had labored long with this committee, the concessions outlined in Calonne's landmark letter

represented a considerable achievement and thus deserved wide circulation.[28] Calonne's six-man "American Committee" included Lafayette as well as Pierre-Samuel Dupont, an *inspecteur général du commerce* and *conseiller d'état* (then residing in the Cul-de-sac de la Corderie near Le Temple), whose acquaintance Jefferson would later resume in America.[29]

Hoffman's other "polytype" invention was a method for making facsimile copies of handwriting or drawing—"the art of multiplying originals," as he called it. According to Jefferson: "I called on the inventor, and he presented me a plate of copper, a pen and ink. I wrote a note on the plate, and in about three quarters of an hour he brought me one hundred copies, as perfect as the imagination can conceive."[30] On one such visit to the Rue Favart Jefferson wrote on the plate, using Hoffman's special ink mixed with an "earthy substance," the dinner invitation form of which a specimen has survived[31] (Fig. 120). What Hoffman did during his three quarters of an hour's absence can be deduced from descriptions of his procedure. Presumably he pressed the written-on copperplate face-down on a warm metal sheet (of his special quick-cooling alloy), thus producing an intaglio plate, from which impressions could then be printed in the ordinary manner.

* * * * * * * * * * * *

The Jardin du Roi, to the east of the Latin Quarter in what was once known as the Faubourg Saint-Victor, was a continuing source of interest to Jefferson during his years in Paris, and long thereafter. The Garden with its related buildings was situated at the eastern edge of the city on low ground where the Bièvre, or Rivière des Gobelins, flows into the Seine. Indeed, when speaking of it years later, Jefferson remembered it as being "in the country." (Figures 110, 121.)

This royal garden, established in 1635, was originally conceived as a practical school of botany with emphasis on medicinal plants.[32] Over the years its scope was gradually extended, especially after 1739, when Georges-Louis Leclerc, comte de Buffon, assumed the post of *Intendant*. With the help of his collaborators and an international network of correspondents, Buffon spectacularly enlarged the "King's cabinet," that is, the natural history collections, which came to encompass the whole range of the "kingdoms of nature," vegetable, animal, and mineral. These collections were the foundation of his vast publication issued by the Imprimerie Royale from 1749 on: *Histoire Naturelle, générale et partic-*

ulière, avec la Description du Cabinet du Roi. During the half-century of his directorship Buffon acquired adjacent properties and added many new buildings to the institution. By a decree of the National Convention (10 June 1793) the *ci-devant* Jardin du Roi became the Muséum National d'Histoire Naturelle, henceforth administered by the incumbents of the twelve professorial chairs established by the decree. Nevertheless, there was no essential break in continuity. Though further additions to the grounds and buildings have been made in subsequent years, the general pattern of the Jardin du Roi as Buffon left it, is still readily recognizable today—a green oasis in the heart of the twentieth-century metropolis.

Even before he reached Paris, Jefferson knew about the King's Garden and Cabinet, with which the name and fame of Buffon were so closely associated. When compiling his *Notes on the state of Virginia* he had pored over the

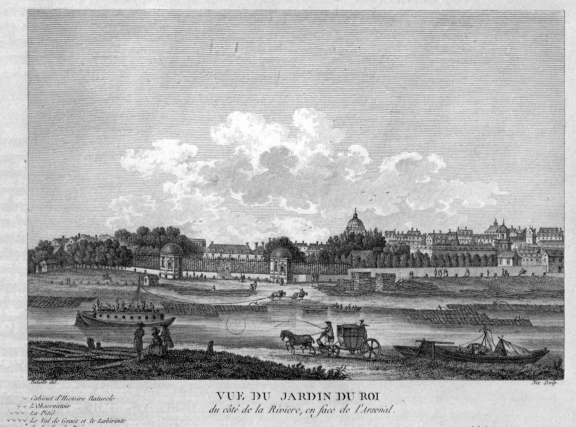

Cabinet d'Histoire Naturelle
L'Observatoir
La Pitié
Le Val de Grace et le Labirinte
du Jardin du Roi

VUE DU JARDIN DU ROI
du côté de la Rivière, en face de l'Arsenal.

Isle de France Monumens de Paris. N° 81

121.

Histoire Naturelle, whose author, "the best informed of any Naturalist who has ever written," had thrown "a blaze of light on the field of natural history."[33] "The wonder is," Jefferson wrote, "not that there is yet something in this great work to correct, but that there is so little." He was particularly interested, as were so many of his contemporaries, in Buffon's theories concerning the formation of the earth during the successive "epochs of nature" that eventually created an environment for Man. However, when applying his ideas to the New World, Buffon deduced conclusions that did not square with Jefferson's own observations. Buffon thought, for example, that the climatic conditions of the Americas produced animals inferior in size to those of the Old World and that the aborigines, too, were less developed. Certain of Buffon's disciples even extended the idea to the European settlers in America. Buffon's own statement—"I love as much a person who corrects me in an error as another who teaches me a truth, because in effect an error corrected is a truth"—prompted Jefferson to demonstrate that Buffon's conclusions respecting New World animals were based on insufficient evidence. Taking Buffon as his ground work, he included in his *Notes* (Query VI: Productions Mineral, Vegetable and Animal) a comparative table of quadrupeds "from mouse to mammoth" and also defended the Indians against Buffon's disparaging surmises.

As soon as Pierres had completed printing the *Notes*, Jefferson sent copies (via the Marquis de Chastellux) to Buffon and his chief collaborator Daubenton, who had compiled for the *Histoire Naturelle* the anatomical descriptions of quadrupeds.[34] As a tangible bit of evidence corroborating his own statistics, Jefferson soon thereafter sent a panther-skin foresightedly purchased in Philadelphia. In a letter acknowledging the skin of the "cougar," Buffon regretted that his health prevented him from offering his thanks in person, but hoped that Monsieur Jefferson would come with the Marquis de Chastellux to dine at the Garden at their convenience.[35] When he was not at Montbard—his Monticello in Burgundy—Buffon resided in the Intendant's house, which is still standing in the southwest corner of the Garden (Figs. 122, 123). Jefferson evidently dined there several times in the course of

122. Houdon's Buffon, in plaster, 1781

123. Buffon's House

[85]

the years 1786 and 1787.[36] In his memory these visits merged into a pleasant composite picture. "It was Buffon's practice," he liked to recall, "to remain in his study till dinner time, and receive no visitors under any pretence; but his house was open and his grounds, and a servant showed them very civilly, and invited all strangers and friends to remain to dine. We saw Buffon in the garden, but carefully avoided him, but we dined with him, and he proved himself then, as he always did, a man of extraordinary powers in conversation. He did not declaim; he was singularly agreeable."[37]

The conversations with Buffon ranged over many subjects. On one occasion Buffon recalled Cadwallader Colden's pamphlet on the *Causes of Gravity* sent to him by the author at the time of its publication (New York, 1745).[38] He had lent it to a friend who had never returned it. Could Jefferson find him another copy? Or again, the conversation turned on chemistry. Jefferson, extolling the treatise written by Buffon's colleague Fourcroy, thought this embryonic science "big with future discoveries for the utility and safety of the human race," while Buffon, "placing the toils of the laboratory on a footing with those of the kitchen," dismissed it as mere "cookery."[39]

Despite such digressions, Jefferson never lost sight of his American quadrupeds. In the autumn of 1787 he was at last able to present to the Cabinet du Roi "the spoils of the Moose, Caribou, Elk and deer" obtained for him by Governor John Sullivan of New Hampshire.[40] The skeleton of the moose, which Sullivan's hunters had shot high up in the Green Mountains of Vermont, was in good condition, though the skin had shed a good deal of hair during its Atlantic transit. Nevertheless, enough remained

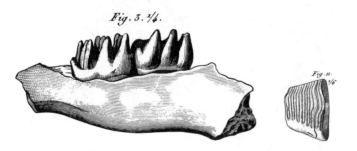

Fig. 3. ¼.

124. Fossils from Big Bone Lick presented to the Muséum in 1808 by Jefferson

to give an adequate idea of the animal, which, Jefferson hoped, could be stuffed and placed on its legs in the King's Cabinet. This *beau présent* was duly acknowledged on Buffon's behalf by Daubenton, *Garde et Démonstrateur du Cabinet*, as well as by the Comte de Lacépède, *Sous-démonstrateur*, who wrote that the donor had indeed many claims to public esteem, uniting as he did "the knowledge of the naturalist with the science of the statesman."[41] These specimens of American *Cervidae* apparently convinced Buffon of his errors for, according to Jefferson's recollection, he promised to correct them in subsequent editions of his book.

When Jefferson knew him, Buffon was an elderly and ailing man, suffering from stones, as did his friend and contemporary, Benjamin Franklin. Buffon died in his house at the Garden in the spring of 1788 at the age of eighty. Nevertheless, Jefferson's conversations on natural history were resumed with the younger savants he met at the Jardin du Roi and were to be an abiding source of satisfaction throughout his life. Faujas de Saint-Fond, for example, sent him a copy of his *Essai de Géologie, ou Mémoires pour servir à l'Histoire Naturelle du Globe* (Paris, 1803, 1809).[42] Lacépède sent in 1803 and 1804 his *Histoire Naturelle des Poissons et des Cétacées*, the concluding volumes of the *Histoire Naturelle* begun by Buffon in 1749.[43] Jefferson, for his part, reported on the transcontinental explorations of Lewis and Clark. In 1808, recalling that "the collection of the remains of the Animal incognitum (sometimes called Mammoth) possessed by the Cabinet of Natural history is not very copious," he assembled in the White House and sent to Lacépède a plentiful collection of bones obtained for him by William Clark at Big Bone Lick in Kentucky.[44] The gift was warmly received, studied by Lacépède and his colleague Cuvier, and placed on display at the Muséum. More resistant than the moose-skin from Vermont, these Kentucky fossil bones are still preserved in the Muséum's Laboratoire de Paléontologie, a modern offshoot of the old Cabinet du Roi.

In his *Recherches sur les Ossemens Fossiles, où l'on rétablit les caractères de plusieurs animaux dont les Révolutions du globe ont détruit les espèces* (second edition, 1821) Cuvier in-

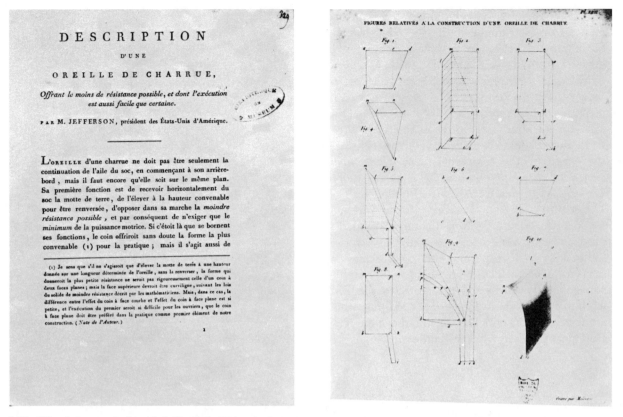

125. Thouin's translation of Jefferson's "Description of a Mould-board of the Least Resistance"

cluded a laudatory description of Jefferson's gift, assigning each bone to its appropriate place in his reconstituted skeletons of prehistoric animals. Several of these bones are shown in the engraved plates of Cuvier's landmark work, among them the lower molar tooth of *Elephas primigenius* and the lower-jaw of *Mastodon americanus*, which he conclusively established as two distinct species (Fig. 124). Long ago, in his *Notes on Virginia*, Jefferson had questioned Buffon's identification of the American "mammoth" as a mere elephant.[45] Thus, in this particular conversation, Jefferson, thanks to Cuvier, had the last word.

None of the acquaintances made at the Jardin du Roi gave Jefferson more lasting pleasure than that of André Thouin, a man of his own age, who was *Jardinier-en-chef* there in the 1780's. Following the reorganization of 1793, Thouin was named *Professeur de Culture* (i.e., plant culture in the broadest sense), a post he held until his death on 27 October 1824. Correspondence with Thouin was resumed about 1801

when Jefferson sent to Paris a copy of his "Description of a Mould-board of the Least Resistance" with a wooden block showing how to make one—"the combination of a theory which may satisfy the learned with a practice intelligible to the most unlettered laborer." He had been developing the theory and refining the practice ever since 1788, when the awkward form of the moldboard on the plows in use by Lorraine peasants led him to consider what its proper form should be.[46] His essay on the subject was sent in 1798 to Sir John Sinclair, president of the Board of Agriculture in London, and was published in the American Philosophical Society's *Transactions* for 1799. André Thouin's translation of Jefferson's paper was published in the *Annales du Muséum* (vol. I, 1802) and also issued as a separate pamphlet (Fig. 125). The Paris Agricultural Society, which named Jefferson a foreign associate at its meeting of 10 October 1804 and awarded him one of its gold medals the following year, testified that it was fitting to see the name and glory of the first Magistrate of a great Republic associated with the improvement of an instrument of tillage.[47] The wooden block sent by Jefferson as well as scale models derived from it were placed in the Muséum's *galerie des ustensiles d'agriculture* and are still preserved in the archives of its present-day counterpart, the Laboratoire de Culture[48] (Fig. 126). Year after year, in his course of lectures, Professor Thouin displayed these models to his students with the comment: *"Excellente invention d'un excellent homme, M. Thomas Jefferson, président des Etats-Unis d'Amérique!"*[49]

Recalling Jefferson's earlier gifts of American seeds to the Jardin du Roi, Thouin continued to send him each year a wide selection of "exotics" indigenous to Europe and other non-American parts of the world. (Figs. 127, 128.) Jefferson generally consigned the seeds to the Philadelphia nurseryman Bernard McMahon, others were given to David Hosack for the New York Botanical Garden, while still others were planted

126. Professor A. Guillaumin (titulary of the chair first held by Thouin) examining scale model of Jefferson's moldboard, at the Muséum, 1946

127. Jardin des Plantes. Drawing by J.-B. Hilair, 1794

128. André Thouin, ca. 1800

will contain all the fine flowers of France, and fill all the space we have for them."[51] Anne assured her grandfather that she would be with him in early March "to assist about the border which the old French Gentleman's present, if you mean to plant them there, with the wild and bulbous rooted ones we have already, will completely fill."[52] On other such occasions, as Jefferson's Garden Book records, he sowed Thouin's seeds of the *Cytisus laburnum* (Golden Chain Tree), "planted residue of the seeds of the *Genista juncea* [Spanish Broom] on both sides of the Upper Roundabout," and eventually had success with Sprout Kale, which he considered "among the most valuable garden plants."[53] (Fig. 129.)

In the spring of 1826, only a few weeks before his death on July 4th of that year, Jefferson was discussing plans for the Botanical School he hoped to see established at the University of Virginia. "For three-and-twenty years of the last twenty-five," he reminded Dr. Emmet, "my good old friend Thouin, superintendent of the garden of plants at Paris, has regularly sent me a box of seeds. . . . But during the last two years this envoi has been intermitted, I know not why."[54] Soon thereafter he learned from his neighbor, James Madison of Montpelier, that Thouin had died, but that the latter's successor [Louis A.-G. Bosc] was addressing the annual shipments to the care of the Agricultural Society of Albemarle. A box had already arrived in New York and was awaiting reshipment to Virginia. Other hands would now plant the seeds from Paris.

at Monticello. One such shipment contained seven hundred species: "On every paper is written the time for sowing it (according to the French calendar) and whether under frames, in open air & what sort of soil."[50] "I suppose," Jefferson told his granddaughter Anne, when announcing the box from his "old friend" Thouin, "that they

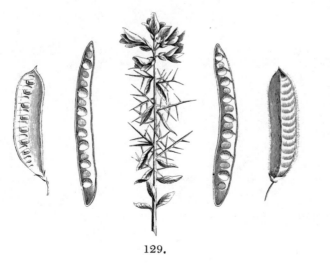

129.

PLAN DE PARIS ET DE SES ENVIRONS,
d'apres la GRANDE CARTE de l'Abbe de la GRIVE. *Par JEAN ROCQUE Topographe de Sa Majeste.*

A LONDRES
chez Robert Sayer Nº 53 Fleet Stree

PARTIE du Grand PARC

A Scale of one Great French League &c

130.

Chapter 8

Environs of Paris: The Road to Versailles
Passy, Auteuil, Sèvres, Chaville, Versailles

THE highway from Paris to Versailles became a much-traveled and familiar road to Jefferson during his five years in France. Leading out of the city from the Place Louis XV, the route followed the right bank of the Seine along the Cours la Reine to the foot of the Colline de Chaillot, where one of Ledoux's new tollhouses at the Barrière de Passy, or Barrière des Bonshommes, marked the city limits. (See Fig. 171.) Then, skirting the heights of Passy on the right, the road passed through the village of Auteuil to the Pont de Sèvres, the first bridge downstream from the Pont Royal. Between these two bridges cross-river traffic was by ferry or small boats. From Sèvres the road led through Chaville to Versailles, the seat of royal power and administrative capital of the kingdom. (Figs. 130, 131.)

A month or more after his arrival in Paris, Jefferson drove out to Versailles to present his credentials. On 15 September 1784, Franklin, Adams, and Jefferson (accompanied by David Humphreys, secretary of the commission) "exhibited officially to the Count de Vergennes Minister and Secretary of State . . . the Commission of the United States in Congress assembled authorizing them to negotiate and conclude a supplementary Treaty between the United States and His Most Christian Majesty."[1] Meanwhile, shortly after his arrival, Jefferson had gone out to call on Dr. Franklin at Passy—the first of many visits there. An entry in his Account Book recording payment of 1 ƒ 4 for "ferriage to & from Passy" on 10 August 1784 indicates that upon that particular occasion he reached the Doctor's residence via the Left Bank.

Franklin had been living since 1777 in one or another of the wings or pavilions of the Hôtel de Valentinois, a spacious estate then owned by Le Ray de Chaumont. Like the neighboring villas, the *hôtel* stood on the crest of the bluff with terraces and gardens leading down to the river (Fig. 132). "You have sat on the terrace," taunts the Gout in the "Dialogue" Franklin printed at Passy for his neighbor Madame Brillon, "you have praised the fine view, and looked at the beauties of the garden below, but you have never stirred a step to descend and walk about in them."[2] The Hôtel de Valentinois has long since disappeared, with only a memorial tablet at the corner of Rue Singer and Rue Raynouard (the old Rue Basse de Passy) to recall the site. Threading his way down to the Seine via the Rue Berton, the modern pilgrim finds only vestiges of the terraces and gardens that once covered these slopes. The towering mass of Le Front de Seine closes the trans-riverine horizon.

The American Commissioners had their first formal meeting at Passy on 30 August 1784 and, out of deference to the Gout (and the Stones), continued to transact their business there until the following spring. Here at Passy Jefferson resumed acquaintance with Franklin, his co-worker at the Continental Congress in 1775–1776, and came to know the other members of Franklin's household, including the Doctor's grandsons, William Temple Franklin, then twenty-two, and Benjamin Franklin Bache, a lad of fifteen. Benny, under his grandpapa's watchful eye, was learning the printer's trade with François Didot, the eminent Parisian printer. In the course of his frequent visits to the Hôtel de Valentinois Jefferson witnessed the ex-

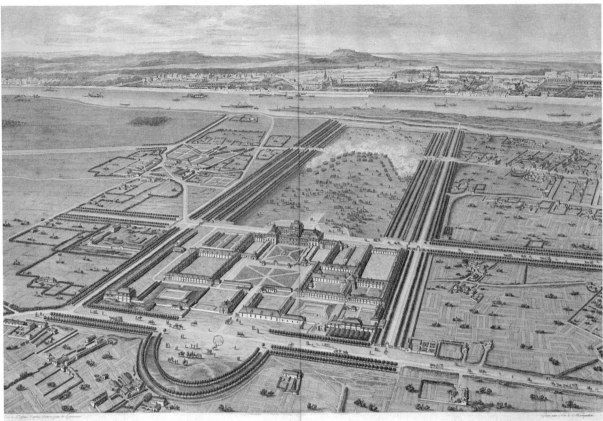

PLAN PERSPECTIF DE L'ECOLE ROYALE MILITAIRE .

131. Beyond the river, right to left: Chaillot, Passy, Auteuil

traordinary respect and veneration enjoyed by Franklin in France. When Franklin left Passy for America on 11 July 1785, in a mule-supported litter thoughtfully provided by the Queen, "it seemed," Jefferson said, "as if the village had lost its patriarch."[3]

With the Patriarch gone, Jefferson's business took him less frequently to Passy. Nevertheless, throughout his stay in Paris, he continued to enjoy "manifold civilities and kindnesses" from acquaintances first made through Franklin. Among them was Louis-Guillaume Le Veillard, resident director of the Eaux de Passy, to whom Franklin had given a manuscript of the autobiography written in part at Passy with Le Veillard's encouragement.[4] The grounds of the "Waters," long known for their medicinal and therapeutic qualities, stretched down to the Seine a bit to the west of the present Pont de Bir Hakeim (formerly Pont de Passy), with the "Rue des Eaux" as a reminder of their heyday.[5]

The house of the Abbés Chalut and Arnoux also boasted an unobstructed view over the river and the city beyond, as John Trumbull's drawings testify (Fig. 133). Trumbull no doubt had his sketchbook with him on 13 August 1786, the day he "dined, in company with Mr. Jefferson, at the Abbés Chalut and Arnoux in Passy." It was, he noted in his diary, "a *jour maigre*, or fast day, but the luxury of the table in soups, fish and fruits, truly characteristic of the opulent clergy of the times."[6] Jefferson enjoyed the table talk as well as the table of these abbés, whom he classed among the "literati" and who were well known to both Franklin and the Adams family. Chalut was a brother of the Farmer General, Chalut de Vérin (see Chapter 2). Arnoux, of Provençal origin, provided Jefferson with fruitful letters of introduction when he made his journey to Southern France in 1787. Among them, one to Madame de Laye, who received Jefferson at the Château de Laye-Epinay

[92]

132. Hôtel de Valentinois, front facing the Seine

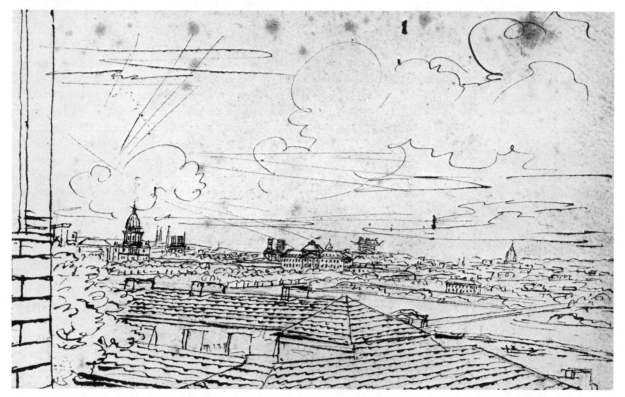

133. View from Franklin's house at Passy, by John Trumbull. Center distance: Ecole Militaire: Church of Ste.-Geneviève, with scaffolding, on horizon

in Beaujolais, where he saw that "delicious morsel of sculpture," Michel-Ange Slodtz's Diana and Endymion.[7]

Still another Passy household known to Jefferson, and to Franklin and Adams before him was the small country seat of the Swiss-born banker Ferdinand Grand (see Chapter 2). "Himself, his Lady, Niece and Sons," John Adams noted in terms that Jefferson could subscribe to, "composed as decent, modest and regular a Family as I ever knew in France."[8]

* * * * * * * * * * * *

The village of Auteuil, a short distance beyond Passy, also became a familiar resort to Jefferson during his first months in Paris. John Adams, the third of the American Commissioners, lived there from August 1784 to May 1785 with his wife Abigail and two children, Miss Abigail and John Quincy, already a much-traveled young man of seventeen. The reunited Adams family, who reached Paris shortly after Jefferson's own arrival, stayed for a few days at the Hôtel d'York in the Rue Jacob (close by Jefferson's lodgings in the Hôtel d'Orléans, Rue des Petits Augustins) before moving into a house at Auteuil rented from the Comte de Rouhault—"distant from the putrid streets of Paris," as Adams put it.[9] He already knew the house well, for he had been Thomas Barclay's guest there in the autumn of 1783 when recuperating from an illness.[10] After enduring for a

134. Hôtel Rouhault (Verrières), garden side. Residence of the Adams family in Auteuil, 1784-1785

year the constant roar of carriages—"like incessant rolls of thunder"—in his lodgings at the Grand Hôtel du Roi, Place du Carrousel, Adams found the "silence of Auteuil" and the "pure air of a country garden" most effective restoratives. He had walked and ridden over the Bois de Boulogne and soon "made myself Master of this curious forest." He had inspected under a caretaker's guidance the "Seat of the famous Boileau" in the Rue des Garennes, then being advertised for sale by Madame Binet, its owner. Had she not declined letting it, Adams noted in his diary, "I should have hired it."

Auteuil proved to be as agreeable to his family as it had when Adams alone was the Barclays' guest there. Thanks to the diary-keeping and letter-writing habits of the Adamses, an extensive record of their residence in Auteuil has survived.[11] "Mr. Jefferson's" name occurs frequently, as a dinner guest or companion on various excursions. "One of the choice ones of the earth," Mrs. Adams said of him, while her daughter termed him "a man of great sensibility and parental affection." The Adams's house in Auteuil, which had earlier been the *folie* of the actresses Les Demoiselles Marie and Claude-Geneviève de Verrières, is still recognizable at 43–47 Rue d'Auteuil in the Sixteenth Arrondissement (Fig. 134). The "delightful and blooming garden" that Abigail Adams exchanged for the "noise and bustle" of London and which once filled the area bounded by present Rues Boileau, Michel-Ange, and Molitor, has gradually been eaten away and now blooms with high-rise apartment houses and office buildings.

As with the "Seat of the famous Boileau," no trace remains of Madame Helvetius's house, situated "but a few doors" from the Adamses on a site corresponding to present No. 59 Rue d'Auteuil. "Notre-Dame d'Auteuil," as Franklin called the widow of the noted *philosophe*, was a well-known figure in the Paris intellectual world, though her informal manners astonished the more straitlaced Adamses. Jefferson met in her salon at Auteuil several of the young literati whose subsequent writings were to interest him deeply: Volney, Destutt de Tracy, and Cabanis, among others.[12] Volney, the author of a *Voyage en Syrie et en Egypte* who later contributed to Jefferson's cabinet the model of an Egyptian

VUE DU CHATEAU DE BELLEVUE,
prise de la Glaciere.
A.P.D.R.

Isle de France

135. Bellevue, Saint-Cloud, with Mont Calvaire (Valérien) on horizon at right. Pont de Sèvres in foreground, and Pont de Saint-Cloud beyond

136. Tipoo Sahib's Ambassadors in the lower park of Saint-Cloud, 1788

pyramid, visited Monticello in 1796 and published in 1803 his *Tableau du Climat et du Sol des Etats-Unis d'Amérique*. Jefferson commenced an English translation of Volney's *Les Ruines, ou Méditation sur les Révolutions des Empires* (1791) but eventually turned the job over to Joel Barlow for completion. He found American publishers and himself revised their translations of Destutt de Tracy's *Commentary and Review of Montesquieu's Spirit of Laws* (Philadelphia, Duane, 1811) and *Treatise on Political Economy* (Georgetown, Milligan, 1817). Jefferson likewise held in esteem the writings of Cabanis, another "investigator of the thinking faculty of man." In 1802, when sending Jefferson a copy of his *Rapports du Physique et du Moral de l'Homme*, Cabanis reminded the President that he had several times had the honor of seeing him at Madame Helvétius's in Auteuil. Madame Helvétius was gone, but he and Abbé de La Roche still lived in the house—"a legacy the more touching because her remains repose in the garden there." In his acknowledgment, written from the White House, Jefferson replied: "It is with great satisfaction . . . I recollect the agreeable hours I have past with yourself and M. de la Roche at the house of our late excellent friend, Made. Helvetius. . . . Auteuil always appeared to me a delicious village, and that the most delicious spot in it."[13]

* * * * * * * * * * * *

From the upper stories of his house at Auteuil, John Adams noted, "you have a View of the Village of Issy, of the Castle Royal of Meudon, of the Palace of Bellevue, of the Castle of the Duke of Orleans at St. Cloud and of Mont Calvaire."[14] After leaving Auteuil and passing over the Pont de Sèvres, the road to Versailles skirted the lower reaches of the Parc de Saint-Cloud, with the Château de Bellevue perched on the heights to the left (Fig. 135). Bellevue (built for Madame de Pompadour by Louis XV) was in Jefferson's time the residence of "Mesdames" Adélaïde and Victoire, aunts of Louis XVI; Saint-Cloud was purchased from the Orleans family in 1785 by Marie-Antoinette. Both these royal residences, with their extensive gardens and terraces, were showplaces for tourists and state visitors. An artist at the Manufacture Royale de Sèvres has

given us a glimpse of one such party of sightseers—the Ambassadors of Tipoo Sahib in the Saint-Cloud gardens (Fig. 136). These envoys from the Sultan of Mysore (who was courting French support in his struggle with the English) inevitably titillated the curiosity of the Parisians and were for a brief moment the talk of the town.[15] Jefferson, who was present at their reception by the King on 10 August 1788, dismissed the "unusual pomp" as a mere "*jeu d'enfants*." His eye nevertheless caught the exotic details of the scene and he regretted that his friend Madame de Bréhan (then absent in America) was not present with her pencil and sketchbook. Madame Vigée-Lebrun, as she relates in her memoirs, seized the opportunity to paint portraits of "Davich Khan" and of "Acbar Ally Khan," the latter with his son. Both portraits were shown at the Salon of 1789, where Houdon's bust of Jefferson was first exhibited.

It was perhaps from Madame de Tessé that Jefferson picked up that phrase "*un jeu d'enfants*." Madame de Tessé was then engaged, at Jefferson's bidding, in the more important business of compiling a list of the American plants she particularly wanted—and "in abundance"—for her garden at Chaville. The Queen, she wrote in a breathless note, had not seen fit to excuse her from the audience of the Indian ambassadors, so that she had been obliged to draw up her want-list in a state of great "consternation."[16] Despite her tiresome duties at Court, she completed the list in time for Jefferson to forward it to John Banister, Jr., of Battersea at Petersburg, Virginia, in hope that the plants could be gathered that autumn and shipped for early spring arrival in France.[17] In this instance the well-laid plans went amiss, for both young Banister and his father died unexpectedly before Jefferson's request reached Virginia. "But," as he had already warned Madame de Tessé, "Botany is the school for patience, and its amateurs learn resignation from daily disappointments."[18]

The Comtesse de Tessé spent a good part of the year at Chaville, where she and the Comte de Tessé had a beautiful estate along the road to Versailles.[19] Like their town house in the Faubourg Saint-Germain (see Chapter 6), the Chaville estate was a Crown property of which the

137. Château de Chaville. Boullée's drawing of front elevation

Comte de Tessé enjoyed the usufruct. Prior to its acquisition by the King in 1695, Chancelier Letellier had built an impressive château here, with grounds and formal gardens in the manner of André Le Nôtre. Soon after the Tessés took possession, the old château, being in poor repair, was demolished. In its place was erected a Neo-classic pavilion designed in 1764 by Etienne-Louis Boullée (Fig. 137). Although the general pattern of the seventeenth-century estate, with its great central axis, was retained, modern gardens in the Anglo-Chinese style were soon laid out adjoining the new château. Winding streams, kiosks, classic columns, a Malbrouck tower, and other *fabriques* adorned these gardens, which earned a place in Lerouge's albums depicting

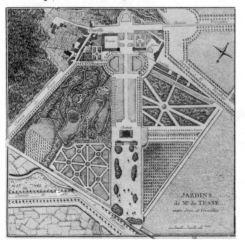

138.

139. "Les Plaisirs de Chaville." Madame de Tessé (reading aloud), Mme de Tott, Comte de Mun, Sénac de Meilhan, Comte de Tessé (asleep), and Baron de Tott (the artist) in background

[97]

"*les nouveaux jardins à la mode*" (Figs. 138, 140). The Comtesse de Tessé's once-fashionable gardens as well as Boullée's pavilion were eventually devoured by suburban developers. Pausing today at the Pointe de Chaville, where the Route des Gardes comes into the road to Versailles (Route Nationale No. 10), one sees only a tangle of drab streets and nondescript villas extending up the slopes toward the Versailles-Montparnasse railway line, which cuts across the Chaville estate that Jefferson knew.

In addition to the gardens, Chaville offered many other pleasures (Fig. 139). There was never a lack of society in the household presided over by Madame de Tessé. Jefferson met there, among others, the Countess's protégée "Madame" de Tott.[20] Like her father Baron de Tott (who had long resided in the Near East) young Sophie-Ernestine had some talent for drawing. Jefferson encouraged her efforts, discussed painting with her, and suggested books to read. During his journey in Southern France he wrote to Madame de Tott and to her "adopted mother" of the treasures he was discovering there. To Madame de Tessé he penned the lines: "Loving,

MONUMENT DANS LES JARDINS DE CHAVILLE. par F. Rotter.
à Mᵈᵉ Tessé, les Colonnes sont de Granit
a la Cᵉᵉ

140.

as you do Madam, the precious remains of antiquity, loving architecture, gardening, a warm sun, and a clear sky, I wonder you have never thought of moving Chaville to Nismes."[21] In her reply Madame de Tessé told Jefferson that she had read his letter aloud to mutual friends—"as, doubtless, they used to read those of the apostles at the gatherings of the early Christians."[22]

As France moved closer to the momentous events of 1789, politics came to be the chief subject of conversation at Madame de Tessé's. Her nephew Lafayette was much in the public eye and her husband was a deputy to the Estates General from the Sénéchaussée du Maine. According to Gouverneur Morris, who dined at her house with Jefferson in March 1789, Madame de Tessé was a "Republican of the first Feather." But her ideas, Morris thought, "were not suited either to the Situation, the Circumstances or the Dispositions of France."[23] As for Jefferson: "He and I differ in our Systems of Politics." When Jefferson left France in September 1789, Madame de Tessé still clung to Jefferson's system, though she was soon to become a convert to Morris's. Meanwhile she surprised Jefferson with a parting gift, which he discovered one evening awaiting him in the hallway of the Hôtel de Langeac."[24] It was an "altar," a garden ornament for the groves of Monticello, consisting of a classic column set on a pedestal inscribed in Latin "to the Supreme Ruler of the Universe, under whose watchful care the liberties of North America were finally achieved, and under whose tutelage the name of Thomas Jefferson will descend forever blessed to posterity." (See Dedication, above.)

One of Jefferson's first errands upon his return to Monticello was to collect and pack with his own hands a shipment of plants for Chaville.[25] By the time they reached France, in the spring of 1790, Madame de Tessé was no longer there to plant them. She had already left for Switzerland, the first stage of an exile that lasted until 1800.[26] Presumably Jefferson never knew that the botanical treasures he had gathered were eventually "nationalized" along with the Chaville gardens and the Tessés' Rue de Varenne mansion. In the autumn of 1792, soon after the proclamation of the French Republic, the *ci-devant* Jardin du Roi in Paris was enriched by trees and shrubs salvaged from émigré estates and former Crown properties.[27] A commission headed by André Thouin, now gardener-in-chief of the Jardin *National*, systematically visited gardens such as Petit Trianon, Bagatelle, Bellevue, and Chaville, in order to select rare exotic species "useful" to the Nation. According to the report on the mission to Chaville (29 October 1792), 188 "individuals" representing 148 species were selected by Thouin in the presence of Madame de Tessé's gardener Cyrus Bowie (who was already seeking means to return to London), and were carted to Paris next day. Among them were a *Magnolia grandiflora*, six varieties of *Quercus caroliniensis*, and two pots of *Laurus sassafras*.

After Madame de Tessé's return from exile, Jefferson again attempted to send her plants and seeds, despite war-troubled seas and the Embargo. She was no longer at Chaville but had started the old life afresh at Aulnay, east of Paris, where she and the Comte de Tessé celebrated their golden wedding at a memorable family gathering in 1805. The Comte de Tessé died in January 1814, the Comtesse a week later. In his last letter to her Jefferson had written from Monticello: "I learn with great pleasure the success of your new gardens at Aulnay. No occupation can be more delightful or useful. They will have the merit of inducing you to forget those of Chaville."[28]

* * * * * * * * * * * *

From Chaville it was only about three miles to the Royal Palace at Versailles. The palace and its dependencies alone constituted a small city (Fig. 141). In addition to the great reception rooms—the *salles d'apparat*—there were apartments for the King, the Queen, and other members of the Royal Family, each with his own military and civil household, as well as quarters for courtiers, ministers, and innumerable retainers. The pomp and circumstance of the Court of Versailles seem to have held little appeal for Jefferson, but as a good diplomat he soon learned the customs and obligatory usages of the palace. His accounts record numerous payments for "chair hire" at Versailles, "for charity" and other incidental expenses. On 1 January 1787, for example, he "gave following *étrennes* at Court": valet

VUE DE LA VILLE ET CHATEAU DE VERSAILLES,
Prise de la hauteur du Bois de Satory au Sud Sud-Est et à coté Thiais du Chateau, dans le haut de l'Étroite qui enfile la tête du Canal et la Porte S.ᵗ Antoine.

141.

de chambre of M. de Vergennes, *96 livres*, to Vergennes' livery servants, 24, and to his Suisse, 24; to M. de Rayneval's Suisse, 24, to his garçon de bureau, 24; to the Coffee men at the Salle des Ambassadeurs, 48, and to the two Suisses there, 24 *livres*. The following day he gave 72 *livres* to the servants of the two "Introductors"—making a grand total of 336 *livres* for New Year's gratuities.

A young traveler whom the American Minister presented at Court has left a more complete account than any written by Jefferson himself. Thomas Lee Shippen of Philadelphia was greatly impressed by his day at Versailles and described it in detail to family and friends back home.[29] "When we were introduced to the King," he noted, "it was after waiting 5 minutes in his antichamber. . . . He was just pulling on his coat, a servant was tying his hair in which there was no powder, while one of his attendants was arranging his sword belt, and when the file of ambassadors Envoys Ministers &c. in full dress . . . were prostrating themselves before him . . . he hitched on his sword and hobbled from one side of the room to the other, spoke 8 words to a few of the ambassadors and 2 to a German Prince who was presented with me, and left the room." Shippen also observed with patriotic pride that "although Mr. Jefferson was the plainest man in the room, and the most destitute of ribbands crosses and other insignia of rank, he was the most courted and most attended to (even by the Courtiers themselves) of the whole Diplomatic corps."

Except for such formal occasions, Jefferson had few direct dealings with the King. Official business was transacted through the King's ministers, Vergennes (who died in 1787), his successor Montmorin, or with permanent career officials such as Hennin or Gérard de Rayneval, who was in charge of North American affairs. The Ministry of Foreign Affairs had its own *hôtel*, which it shared with the Ministry of Marine (then entrusted with consular and colonial affairs), in the Rue de l'Intendance adjoining the Palace.[30] The building, erected in 1759–1760 from designs of Jean-Baptiste Berthier (father of Marshal Berthier), is still standing in present Rue de l'Indépendance Américaine and now houses the Bibliothèque Municipale de Versailles (Fig. 142).

When recalling in his autobiography his mission to the French Court, Jefferson commented that he found the government "entirely disposed to befriend us on all occasions, and to yield us every indulgence, not absolutely injurious to themselves."[31] The Comte de Vergennes, he wrote, "had the reputation with the diplomatic corps of being wary and slippery in his diplomatic intercourse; and so he might be with those whom he knew to be slippery and doublefaced themselves. As he saw that I had no indirect views, practiced no subtleties, meddled in no intrigues, pursued no concealed object, I found him as frank, as honorable, as easy of access to reason as any man with whom I had ever done

business; and I must say the same for his successor Montmorin, one of the most honest and worthy of human beings."

As for Louis XVI, Jefferson wrote, also in his autobiography: "He had not a wish but for the good of the nation, and for that object no personal sacrifice would ever have cost him a moment's regret. But his mind was weakness itself, his constitution timid, his judgment null, and without sufficient firmness even to stand by the faith of his word. His Queen, too, haughty and bearing no contradiction, had an absolute ascendency over him."[32] Balancing this retrospective view, more indulgent comments appear in Jefferson's official dispatches and personal letters of the time.[33] "The King," he told Madison in 1787, "loves business, oeconomy, order and justice. He wishes sincerely the good of his people. He is irascible, rude and very limited in his understanding, religious bordering only on bigotry. He has no mistress, loves his queen and is too much governed by her." Reflecting the relentless antipathy current in the liberal circles he frequented, Jefferson could say little good of Marie-Antoinette. She was not, in his opinion, the angel "gaudily painted in the rhapsodies of the Rhetor Burke." She "led herself to the Guillotine, & drew the king on with her, and plunged the world into crimes and calamities which will forever stain the pages of modern history." "I have ever believed," Jefferson concluded in his autobiography, "that had there been no queen, there would have been no revolution."[34]

Passing from Kings and Queens to "beings of an higher order, the plants of the field," Jefferson could remember, unreservedly, the various gardens created by royalty. One of the early entries in his Paris accounts is "for seeing gardens at Versailles." He could see there, as one still can, the magnificent gardens planned by Le Nôtre as a grandiose setting for Louis XIV's palace (Fig. 143). Beyond them lay the marble palace of Grand Trianon as well as the still later Petit Trianon, the Neo-classic pavilion designed by Gabriel—a forerunner of Boullée's Chaville and Bélanger's Bagatelle.[35] Petit Trianon boasted both a formal French-style garden with clipped hedges and trellised trees and a "natural" English-style garden laid out with the counsel of the Comte de Caraman and the gardener Claude

142. Hôtel de la Marine et des Affaires Etrangères

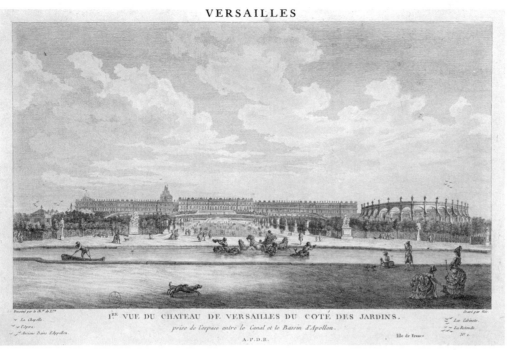

I^{RE} VUE DU CHATEAU DE VERSAILLES DU COTÉ DES JARDINS.
prise de l'espace entre le Canal et le Bassin d'Apollon.
A.P.D.R.

143.

Richard. The grounds of Petit Trianon are an epitome of the taste of the 1780's, with a little theatre designed by Mique, grottos and cascades, a Belvedere, and a Temple de l'Amour (also designed by Mique) set on an islet in a meandering stream (Fig. 144). Bordering a lake is Marie-Antoinette's *hameau*, concerning which Gouverneur Morris remarked: "Royalty has here endeavoured to conceal itself from its own Eye, but the Attempt is vain. A Dairy furnished with the Porcelaine of Sèvres is a Semblance too splendid of rural Life."[36]

I^{ERE} VUE DU CHATEAU DE TRIANON.
prise sur la Rive gauche de la Rivière du Côté du Temple de l'Amour.
A.P.D.R.

144.

VUE DU PAVILLON DE BAGATELLE.
du côté de l'entrée.
Construit en 64 jours sur les desseins d'Alexandre Belanger premier Architecte de M.gr Comte d'Artois.

145.

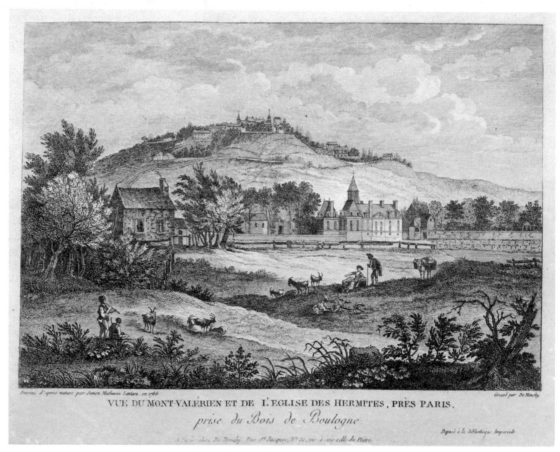

VUE DU MONT-VALÉRIEN ET DE L'EGLISE DES HERMITES, PRÈS PARIS.
prise du Bois de Boulogne.

146. Abbaye de Longchamp: right foreground

Chapter 9

Environs of Paris: Bois de Boulogne, Mont Calvaire, & the Road to Saint-Germain

JEFFERSON's second Paris residence, the Hôtel de Langeac, was situated along one of the main thoroughfares leading out of the city. The Champs-Elysées, or Grand Cours as it was also called (to distinguish it from the Petit Cours or Cours la Reine), led up over the "Etoile" out to the bridge at Neuilly and thence to Saint-Germain-en-Laye and beyond. Before reaching Neuilly the highway skirted the northern edge of the Bois de Boulogne, which extended south to the villages of Boulogne, Passy, and Auteuil. (See Fig. 130.) The Bois covered much the same area as it does today, though its general appearance has undergone a transformation.[1] It was in the mid-nineteenth century that Napoleon III's landscape architects remodeled it and created the "romantic" Bois known to subsequent generations. In Jefferson's day the geometric pattern of roads and lanes was still that of the traditional royal hunting ground (Fig. 147).

Like John Adams, Jefferson soon "made himself master of this curious forest." "The Bois de Boulogne," he wrote Madame de Corny in the summer of 1787, "invites you earnestly to come and survey its beautiful verdure, to retire to its umbrage from the heats of the season. I was through it today, as I am every day."[2] It was this "daily habit of walking in the Bois de Boulogne" that gave him an opportunity to turn over in his mind his "Thoughts on English Prosody," the essay-letter on the measure of English verse intended for the Marquis de Chastellux.[3]

The Bois indeed offered many subjects for meditation and observation. The day Jefferson wrote to Madame de Corny he noticed, when approaching the Bois from the Passy side, that La Muette was for sale and blithely suggested

that she should buy it. The Château de la Muette (originally a hunting lodge as the name implies), rebuilt by Louis XV and much frequented by Louis XVI and Marie-Antoinette soon after their marriage, had by now fallen from royal favor.[4] Its new occupant turned out to be, not Madame de Corny, but Mr. Milne from Lancashire in England, who, under the patronage of the French government, set up a "manufactory of fine cotton thread" there.[5] Milne's son was in the United States investigating cotton production in Georgia and South Carolina and had discussed with Washington at Mount Vernon the improved labor-saving machines his father was introducing in France. During the spring and summer of 1789, Jefferson returned several times to La Muette (once in the company of Gouverneur Morris) to observe Milne's machines in operation. At the request of William Bingham of Philadelphia, who wrote on behalf of the "Society for Encouraging Manufactures," he obtained Milne's price (12,000 *livres tournois*) for a "compleat Sett of Machines for carding and spinning Cotton." To work such a set by hand, Milne explained, "requires five Men, three Women and five Children, but if the Machines are worked by Water there will be no occasion for the Men."

Entering the Bois de Boulogne from Neuilly, Jefferson met a variety of sights. Not far from the bridge was the "Folie Sainte-James," the estate of Monsieur Baudard de Vaudésir, baron de Sainte-Gemmes, *trésorier-général de la Marine*, who had anglicized his name as well as his gardens.[6] The Sainte-James gardens laid out by Bélanger *dans le genre pittoresque*, ran the whole gamut of the fashionable gardener's art,

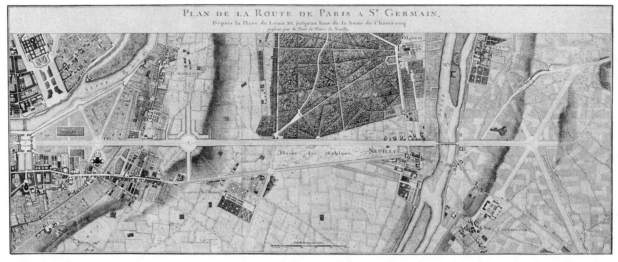

PLAN DE LA ROUTE DE PARIS A St GERMAIN.
Depuis la Place de Louis XV. jusqu'au haut de la butte de Chante-coq
passant par le Pont de Pierre de Neuilly.

147.

including an "Isle des Magnolias" set in an arti-
ficial stream flowing into the Seine. In one of his
rare "town-talk letters" from Paris, Jefferson reported early in 1787 that Monsieur de Sainte-
James's bankruptcy and his taking asylum in the
Bastille was furnishing "matter of astonish-
ment": "His garden at the Pont de Neuilly,
where, on seventeen acres of ground he had laid
out fifty thousand Louis, will probably sell for
somewhat less money."[7]

Farther along, the old Château de Madrid
(dating from the time of King François Premier) was still standing, and beyond that came
Bagatelle, "the prettiest bagatelle in the world,"
as the Prince de Ligne called it[8] (Fig. 145).
This Neo-classic pavilion was built in 1777 for
the Comte d'Artois by his architect François-
Joseph Bélanger, the same who designed the
Folie Sainte-James. Bagatelle, now the property
of the City of Paris, was owned in the course of
the nineteenth century by the fourth Marquess
of Hertford and by Sir Richard Wallace, the
well-known collectors of 18th-century art. Bélanger's pavilion, though coiffed with an inap-
propriate bonnet that distorts the original design,
still stands, but virtually nothing remains of the
original "picturesque" park planted under the
supervision of the Scottish gardener William
Blaikie. It has been eclipsed by latter-day rosa-
ries and other horticultural attractions. Along
this same side of the Bois de Boulogne, where
the racetracks were later built, was a small ham-
let clustered about the mediaeval abbey-church

of Longchamp. Here a ferry crossed the Seine
to the village of Suresnes, behind which rose
Mont Valérien, also known in Jefferson's time
as Mont Calvaire (Fig. 146). Up its slopes pilgrims and penitents followed the Stations of the
Cross to the great Calvary set at the summit.

Every year, on Wednesday, Thursday, and
Friday of Holy Week, Parisians swarmed up the
Champs-Elysées and across the Bois de Boulogne to Longchamp.[9] The excuse for this
springtime rite had originally been to listen to
the fine music at the Tenebrae services in the
abbey there. But, by the 1780's, few of those
who joined the procession ever set foot in the
church despite the dire admonitions of the Archbishop. The Promenade à Longchamp had become, instead, a three-day display, an excuse
to see and be seen (Fig. 148). Fine carriages,
spirited horses, dashing cavaliers and be-jeweled
courtesans vied for attention as they made their
way over the sandy, and sometimes miry roads
of the Bois. Even "the people," workers on foot
and dressed in their Sunday best, joined the
crowd, ogled the pretty women in the liveried
carriages, or made merry in the bursting tav-
erns. "Thus it is," scolded Mercier, "that we
mourn the Passion of Our Lord."

The Hôtel de Langeac provided an exceptionally good vantage point for viewing the annual
Longchamp parade. In 1787, while Jefferson
himself was traveling in southern France, William Short did the honors of the house and unexpectedly found himself enmeshed in delicate

matters of protocol.[10] At Jefferson's suggestion he invited several of their acquaintances to witness the procession. Madame de Tessé—"who had never seen Longchamp, which I hardly supposed any Parisian of her age could say"—accepted with alacrity, but her "daughter" Madame de Tott declined, as she must attend Holy Week services. However, she pointedly added, "Maman has no such scruples and *she* can very well go!" Madame de Tessé, scrupulous where others were concerned if not for herself, strongly advised Short not to invite Madame de Lafayette, whose piety would be shocked at the very thought. Jefferson's landlord, the Comte de Langeac, invited himself and "his sister." Short found him in one of the upstairs rooms, not with his sister, but with three other ladies whom Short "did not know." As Madame de Corny was expected next day, the probable presence of the unknown ladies raised problems of etiquette. To the young host's relief, Madame de Corny did not come until the third evening, when the Comte de Langeac returned, this time with his sister (the Marquise de Chambaraud) and only one of the previous trio (the Comtesse de Neuilly), both of whom were known socially to Madame de Corny. "At length Longchamp is at an end," Short reported to Jefferson. "The company have just left me and I retire from the bustle of the procession to the calmer pleasure of writing to you. My apprehensions as to *convenances* between some of the ladies were without ground."

Again in 1788 Jefferson missed the Longchamp procession (he was touring in Holland and the Rhine Valley) and again his secretary did the honors of the house. Though several of Short's letters for this period are missing, we know that Madame de Corny had asked to take Patsy and Polly "out of the convent sometimes" during their father's absence and particularly wished to bring them to the Hôtel de Langeac "one of the days of Longchamp."[11] Presumably the girls had this pleasure (to the envy of their classmates) and we know for certain that another young American, Thomas Shippen, had the pleasure of riding in the procession in the carriage of "a young Nabob from the East," whose acquaintance he made at Mr. Jefferson's.[12] Young Mr. Ashburnham, who had come from London with letters of introduction from Dr. Richard Price, was the son of the Governor of Bombay.

* * * * * * * * * * * *

Jefferson's own promenades to Longchamp were more like those of Rousseau's *promeneur solitaire*. "The sky is clearing," he announced one October morning in 1787 as he sauntered forth across the Bois de Boulogne, "and I shall away to my hermitage!"[13] His hermitage was across the river from Longchamp on the little mountain of Mont Calvaire, where a community of lay brothers known as the "Hermites"—to distinguish them from the "Prêtres du Calvaire" who served the pilgrimage church—sold wood and honey, *vin de Suresnes* from their vineyards, and fine quality silk stockings from their manufactory[14] (Fig. 149). The Hermits also kept a boardinghouse for paying guests who, as Mercier says, "enjoyed good air, a magnificent view, and found comfort for body as well as for soul." Years later Jefferson's daughter Martha recalled that "whenever he had a press of business," her father "was in the habit of taking his papers and going to the hermitage, where he spent

148. Promenade à Longchamp

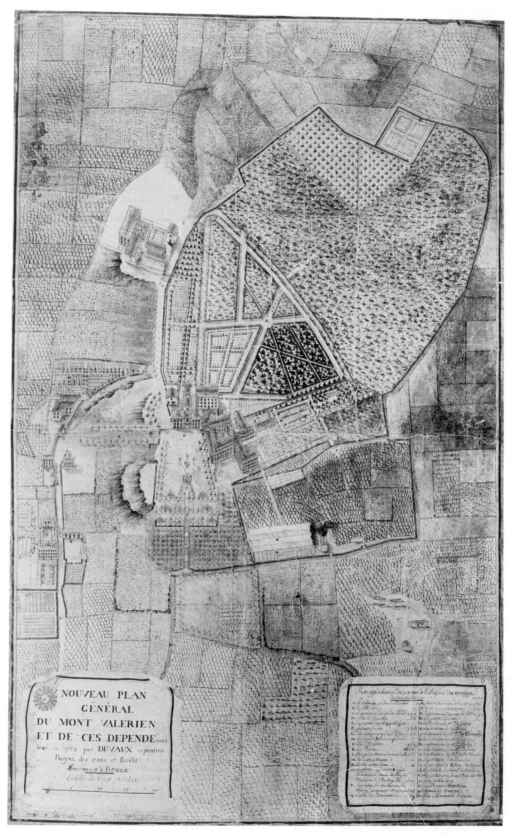

149. According to the key, *3* designates "La Maison des Hermittes," and *4* "leur jardin et leur clos de vignes"

150. Hermits' Account Book, October 1787

151. Jefferson's Account Book, October 1787

The sightly Hermitage was something like a gentlemen's club where the guests found agreeable table companions, exchanged reading matter, and kept abreast of the latest gossip of Court and Town. "If you plan to go to the Hermit brothers tomorrow," one of the habitués (Monsieur Fremyn de Fontenille) wrote Jefferson, "please pay my respects to the gentlemen of our table . . . tell good brother Joseph to tell the cook to have something good for you. If they're not forewarned, the cuisine lacks variety and is very lean."[16]

The Hermits of Mont Calvaire survived the early years of the Revolution thanks to their agricultural labors and stocking manufactory, adjudged "useful to society," but the Priests were dispersed in 1792. After serving for a time as Merlin de Thionville's country estate, the hill resumed its role as a place of pilgrimage during the Empire and Restoration. Since 1840, when fortifications were built there, the summit has been under military jurisdiction. The American Cemetery of Suresnes, where dead of World War I lie buried, is now situated on the lower slopes, covered with vineyards in Jefferson's day. Farther up, a memorial to World War II martyrs of the French Resistance attracts still other pilgrims. Thus, once again, the hill has been reconsecrated, and the old name of Calvary takes on fresh significance.

* * * * * * * * * * * * *

Though Jefferson often took the Longchamp-Suresnes ferry when en route to his Mont Calvaire hermitage, he could also reach Suresnes via the Pont de Neuilly and the village of Puteaux. One Sunday in August 1786, for example, he went with John Trumbull and others to see the crowning of the *Rosière* of Suresnes and returned on foot to Paris over the Pont de Neuilly.[17] The ceremony of crowning with roses "the most amiable, industrious and virtuous maiden of the parish" had been revived at Suresnes and in other villages by Rousseau-minded *âmes sensibles* and had in turn been popularized by fashionable artists of the day (Fig. 152). The Pont de Neuilly—in Trumbull's opinion "a very beautiful stone bridge over the Seine"—was completed in 1774 by a native

sometimes a week or more till he had finished his work. The hermits visited him occasionally in Paris, and the Superior [Paul Ruggieri, alias Brother Placide] made him a present of an ivory broom that was turned by one of the brothers."[15] Jefferson's retreats to the Mont Calvaire hermitage were chiefly in the autumn of 1787 and of 1788, as both his own and the Hermits' accounts attest (Figs. 150, 151).

152. Le Couronnement de la Rosière. Design by J.-B. Huet for a *toile de Jouy*

of Suresnes, Jean-Rodolphe Perronet, *ingénieur des ponts et chaussées*, and at once commanded the admiration of connoisseurs[18] (Fig. 153). Franklin, for example, thought that Thomas Paine (then devising a bridge of his own), should study Perronet's masterpiece. Upon another occasion, when riding in the Bois de Boulogne with Gouverneur Morris, Jefferson took special pains to call his compatriot's attention to the bridge, which, Morris noted, "I had crossed four Times without remarking it and which he says is the handsomest in the World."[19] It was indeed handsome, Morris conceded, "and has, in Appearance at least, Solidity and Lightness as perfectly combined as is possible. For the Rest I am no Judge and therefore refer all final Decision to old Father Time." Perronet's Pont de Neuilly, studied as a model by successive gen-

153.

154.

erations of civil engineers, rebuilt and widened in the twentieth century, is now dwarfed and overshadowed by the skyscrapers of La Défense.

Beyond the Pont de Neuilly, along the road to Saint-Germain, were other sights that caught Jefferson's eye. Near Bougival, for example, he saw the Machine de Marly, the celebrated hydraulic marvel built in the seventeenth century to raise water from the Seine to the aqueduct and reservoirs that fed the cascades and fountains of Versailles and the Château de Marly. He had first paused here to examine its wheels and pumps when on his way from Le Havre to Paris in 1784. The day he went to Saint-Germain with Mrs. Cosway, when "every object was beautiful," it was the "rainbows of the machine of Marly" that caught his fancy. On the heights near the Aqueduct of Marly (Fig. 154) was the village of Lucienne, or Louveciennes, where the charming pavilion designed by Ledoux for Madame Du Barry was situated[20] (Fig. 155), and beyond that, the royal Château de Marly, designed by Mansart for Louis XIV as a "hermitage" or retreat from the greater splendors of Versailles[21] (Fig. 156). Marly, when Jefferson knew it, was enjoying its final years as a royal pleasure ground. Nationalized in 1792, as were other Crown properties, then sold to speculators, the Marly buildings housed for a brief span a cotton manufactory before being demolished by debt-ridden owners for the salvage value of the

156. Château de Marly. Painting by J.-B. Martin, ca. 1710

stone. The great park in which the buildings were set has survived and been carefully reclaimed in recent years. Studying it, as an archaeologist "reads" an ancient site or as Jefferson viewed the "remains of Roman grandeur" in southern France, the old Marly can be reconstructed in the mind's eye. Its general pattern— the central pavilion facing a great rectangular basin flanked on either side by smaller pavilions in descending alignment—bears some resemblance (as the architectural historian Fiske Kimball has suggested) to Jefferson's design for the University of Virginia at Charlottesville.[22]

155.

VUE DU PAVILLON DE LUCIENNE, près de Marli, appartenant à Mᵐᵉ la Comtesse du Bary.

157.

IIᵉ VUE DU CHATEAU DE Sᵗ GERMAIN EN LAYE, prise du Parterre du côté du Nord.

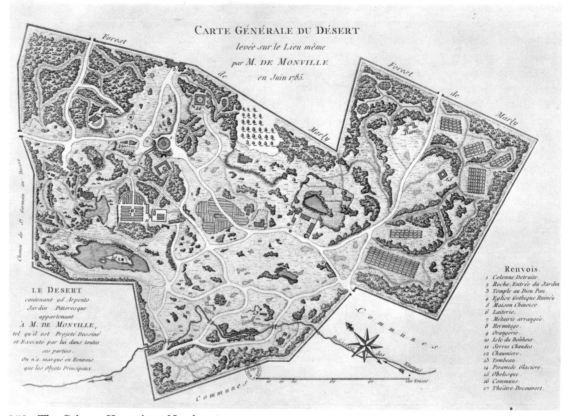

158. The Column House is at Number *1*

159. "How grand the idea excited by the remains of such a column!"

From Marly, the highway led up into the town of Saint-Germain-en-Laye, the site of still another royal château (Fig. 157). Between the château and the forest extends a spacious terrace, set with parterres, and commanding a splendid view that embraces the Aqueduct of Marly on heights at the left and the spires and domes of Paris on the far horizon. Saint-Germain, the birthplace of Louis XIV, was later the seat of the Court of the exiled Stuarts; King James II lies buried in the Church of Saint-Louis not far from the château. The town was considered a healthy country residence for Parisians (one of the *hôtels* of the Noailles family, portions of which still exist, was here) as well as a good place for foreigners to learn French. With a longstanding tradition of English residents and visitors, there were boardinghouses and private homes ready to accommodate them. Several of Jefferson's compatriots resided at Saint-Germain, among them Mrs. Thomas Barclay, whose husband was absent on a mission to the Barbary States.[23] William Short spent a good deal of time there, living with a French family by the name of Royez, "*la plus aimable de la France*," who adopted him as their son.[24] While gaining proficiency in French Short lost his heart, temporarily at least, to the daughter of the house, Hipolite or "Lilite," whom his friends back home in Virginia teasingly referred to as "the fair Pomona of the village" or "the Belle of Saint-Germain."

"Go on then, like a kind comforter," says Jefferson's Heart in the dialogue with his Head, "and paint to me the day we went to St. Germains." "How beautiful was every object! the Pont de Neuilly, the hills along the Seine, the rainbows of the machine of Marly, the terras of St. Germains, the chateaux, the gardens, the statues of Marly, the pavillon of Lucienne. Recollect too Madrid, Bagatelle, the King's garden, the Dessert. How grand the idea excited by the remains of such a column! The spiral staircase too was beautiful. The wheels of time moved on with a rapidity of which those of our carriage gave but a faint idea, and yet in the evening, when one took a retrospect of the day, what a mass of happiness we travelled over!"[25]

The "Dessert" that Jefferson and Mrs. Cosway visited on that memorable summer day in

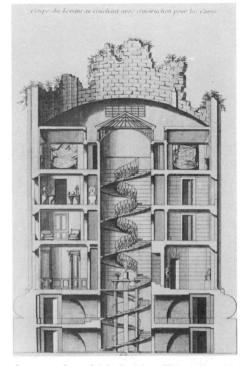

160. Cross-section of M. de Monville's column house

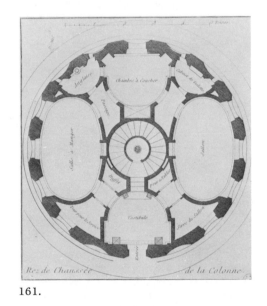

161.

1786 was Le Désert de Retz, the country estate of Racine de Monville, situated some four miles from Saint-Germain, on the edge of the Forest of Marly near the village of Chambourcy[26] (Fig. 158). According to Thiéry's guide for *amateurs* of Jefferson's day, "Everything there seems arranged by the hands of The Graces," or, as a

162. The Chinese House: 5 on the plan (Fig. 158)

Pyramid (serving as an ice-house); a Gothic ruin; and even an "Almost Ruined Little Altar." Monsieur de Monville, himself almost ruined, was forced to sell his property in 1792 to an Englishman with the improbable but somehow appropriate name of Louis Disney Ffytche. By the mid-twentieth century Jefferson's "Dessert" had become a weedy jungle. Due to the cries raised by modern connoisseurs of the Neo-Classic, Pre-Romantic and Surrealistic, and its "classification" as an historic monument, the column house has at last been saved from genuine ruin.

* * * * * * * * * * * *

twentieth-century *amateur* puts it, by some "beckfordizing Walpole." In the heart of M. de Monville's wilderness, designed by him with the assistance of the architect François Barbier, was a huge "ruined" column, inside which living quarters were ingeniously disposed around a central spiral staircase (Figs. 159, 160, 161). Strolling through the grounds, the connoisseur could discover, appropriately placed, a Chinese house, which, said the Prince de Ligne, the Emperor of China himself would not disown (Fig. 162); a Temple to the God Pan; an Obelisk; a

Beyond Saint-Germain, between Mantes and Vernon, a mediaeval donjon perched on the chalk cliffs above the Seine, served as a beacon for travelers along the road to Rouen and Le Havre. The Château de La Roche-Guyon, the country seat of the La Rochefoucauld family (see Chapter 6) nestled at the base of this authentic ruined tower (Fig. 163). On the slopes crowned by the donjon, Jefferson's friend, the Duchesse d'Enville, was laying out modern-style gardens with the assistance of her architect

163. Château de La Roche-Guyon. Drawing by Lespinasse

Montfeu and the counsel of such authorities as J.-M. Morel, author of *La Théorie des Jardins* (1774), and Abbé Delille, whose *Les Jardins, ou l'Art d'embellir les Paysages* (1782), a poem in four cantos, bestowed consecration on the fashionable gardens of the period.[27] Even the doorway of the old donjon was updated with a Neo-classic portico (Fig. 164). The Duchesse d'Enville, like the Comtesse de Tessé and other green thumbs, sought Jefferson's help in obtaining plants and seeds from America. In a gracious note written from La Roche-Guyon on the eve of Jefferson's departure from Paris, she begged him and his daughters to break their journey to Le Havre and use her house as their inn.[28] Jefferson could not accept the Duchesse's hospitality, but a few months later he received via William Short her "Liste Des Grennes que je voudrais avoir De La merique."[29] The desiderata included the *Franklinia alatamaha* as well as such lesser rarities as *Quercus alba* and *Liriodendron tulipifera*, which Jefferson once described as the "Jupiter" and "the Juno of our groves"[30] (Figs. 165, 166, 167). In a subsequent message, the philanthropic Duchesse d'Enville begged Mr. Jefferson "to send her also some Irish potato seed." Jefferson duly executed the commissions, and the seeds eventually reached La Roche-Guyon in time to be planted in the spring of 1792. "They are the more precious to

164. Donjon at La Roche-Guyon with portico added by the Duchesse d'Enville, ca. 1780

us," the Duchesse wrote in acknowledging this *beau présent*, "coming as they do from a man we revere, from a true philosopher in the full meaning of the term." "Those who live to see the trees they produce," she added, "will bless you as long as the mountain of La Rocheguyon stands."[31] Only a few months later tragedy struck the La Rochefoucauld family. Through the troubled years ahead, William Short, who took to heart the trials of the "old lady" and became the intimate friend of the widowed "young duchess," often resided at La Roche-Guyon.[32] For a time it almost seemed that he was its chatelain.

165.   166. "The Jupiter. . . ."   167. "and the Juno of our groves"

L'AN I.er DE LA RÉVOLUTION

À UN PEUPLE LIBRE.

Se vend, à Paris, chez le S.t Vieilh de
Varenne, Auteur de la Collection des Drapeaux,

Rue S.t Antoine, au Magazin des
demolitions de la Bastille.

168.

Chapter 10

Adieu to Jefferson's Paris

"I THINK I have somewhere met with the observation," Abigail Adams told Jefferson when she was leaving the French capital for London, "that nobody ever leaves Paris but with a degree of tristeness."[1] Jefferson was no exception to the rule, though his "tristeness" when he left Paris on 26 September 1789 was mitigated by the conviction that he would be back again the following spring after a few months' leave at Monticello. As things turned out, he never saw Paris again. Instead, he accepted the post of Secretary of State in President Washington's cabinet, assumed his new duties in New York in March 1790, and at the end of that year, when the seat of government was transferred, moved on to Philadelphia. Thus, the Paris Jefferson took leave of—the city that would live on in his memory—was still the Bourbon Paris of the Ancien Régime. Already, however, it was the stage for new actors in a drama entitled in Jefferson's words, "the First Chapter of the History of European Liberty." (Fig. 168.)

The Paris winter of 1788–1789 had been exceptionally cold. The temperature went "as low as 9.° below nought, that is to say 41.° below freezing by Farenheit's thermometer."[2] "We have had such a winter," Jefferson reported to a New York correspondent, "as makes me shiver yet whenever I think of it. All communications were almost cut off. Dinners and suppers were suppressed, and the money laid out in feeding and warming the poor, whose labours were suspended by the rigour of the season. Loaded carriages past the Seine on the ice, and it was covered with thousands of people from morning to night, skaiting and sliding. Such sights were never seen before, and they continued two months."[3] The government kept great fires burning at all the cross-streets, bread was distributed daily, and the parish priests collected subscriptions from the well-to-do. The American Minister, for example, gave the Curé de Chaillot 42 *livres* on two successive weeks in January. "Fur gloves for Patsy" and another pair for himself cost him 6 *livres* each.[4] Being, as he said, "an animal of a warm climate, a mere Oran-ootan," Jefferson found this cold Paris winter a severe personal trial.[5] Furthermore, his daughters were sick and home with him for a time at the Hôtel de Langeac under the care of Dr. Richard Gem, the English-born doctor with whom he discussed declarations of rights and such doctrines as "The Earth belongs in Usufruct to the Living."[6]

"The change in this country, since you left it," Jefferson wrote David Humphreys, "is such as you can form no idea of. The frivolities of conversation have given way entirely to politics —men, women and children talk nothing else: and all, you know, talk a great deal."[7] All the world was electioneering. Paris seemed a desert, for "everybody" (including such friends as the Marquis de Lafayette) had gone to the country to choose or be chosen deputies to the States General. Though Jefferson considered the public mind, as he observed it in Paris, "almost thoroughly ripe for a just decision of the great question of voting by orders or by persons," he foresaw some difficulties in the size of the projected assembly. Twelve hundred persons, of any rank and of any nation, "would with difficulty be prevented from tumult, and confusion," but when they were to compose an assembly for which no rules of debate had been established, "and to consist moreover of Frenchmen among

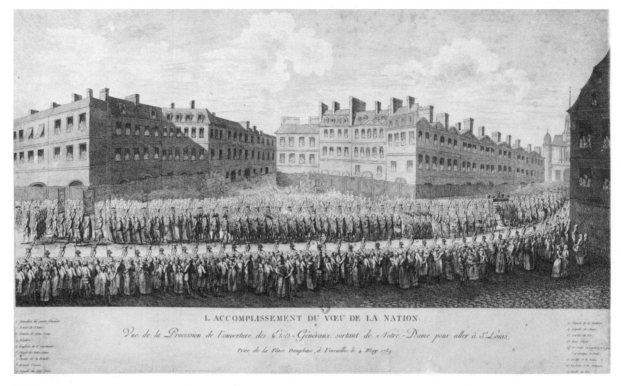

L'ACCOMPLISSEMENT DU VŒU DE LA NATION.

Vue de la Procession de l'ouverture des États-Généraux sortant de Notre-Dame pour aller à St Louis.

Prise de la Place Dauphine à Versailles le 4 May 1789.

169.

whom there are always more speakers than listeners," he confessed he "apprehended some danger."[8]

The deputies elected to represent the three orders—Nobility, Clergy, and Third Estate—assembled in Versailles in the spring of 1789, at the same time that congressmen elected under the new United States Constitution were gathering in New York for the inauguration on 30 April of President Washington. On May 2nd the King received the deputies in the Salon d'Hercule at the royal palace. On the 4th a spectacular procession crossed the town from the Church of Notre-Dame to the Church of Saint-Louis (Fig. 169). On the 5th the assembly of the Estates General was formally opened in the hall built for the occasion on the premises of the Hôtel des Menus Plaisirs, a half-mile or so from the château along the Avenue de Paris. The administrative department known as the "Menus Plaisirs" had offices here as well as warehouses for the storage of scenery and the other paraphernalia of royal ceremonies and pageantry. A temporary hall had been set up for the Assembly of Notables in 1787, but a still larger one was

needed to accommodate the deputies to the Estates and the expected throng of ticket-holding spectators, estimated at 2,000 by Jefferson. The impressive hall, inspired by the basilicas of antiquity, was designed by Pierre-Adrien Pâris, who had often in the course of his duties as architect of the Menus Plaisirs designed stage settings. During March and April workmen and decorators strained valiantly to have all in readiness.[9]

Jefferson was of course present at the May 5th opening (Fig. 170). "Viewing it as an Opera," he said, "it was imposing." "As a scene of business the king's speech was exactly what it should have been and very well delivered. Not a word of the Chancellor's [Barentin, Garde des Sceaux] was heard by anybody, so that I never heard a single guess at what it was about. Mr. Necker's was as good as such a number of details would permit it to be. . . . If the king will do business with the tiers etat which constitutes the nation, it may be well done without priests or nobles."[10]

During the ensuing months Jefferson frequently returned to the Salle des Menus Plaisirs.

The debates were so interesting, he told John Trumbull, "as to carry me almost every day to Versailles."[11] Eagerly following the debates, he watched the business "checked by a disagreement between the orders," then interrupted briefly when the Tiers on 20 June, finding themselves locked out of the customary meeting place, adjourned to the Jeu de Paume and "bound themselves by an oath never to separate of their own accord till they had settled a constitution for the nation on a solid basis." On the 22nd the Commoners, joined by a majority of the Clergy and many Nobles, met in the Church of Saint-Louis. "When Jefferson and I went there to hear the discussions," Filippo Mazzei recalled in his memoirs, "he stopped at the threshold, looked in and said: 'This is the first time that churches have been made some good use of.' "[12]

"At this moment," Jefferson reported on 29 June, "the triumph of the Tiers is considered as complete. Tomorrow they will recommence business, voting by persons on all questions. . . . All danger of civil commotion here is at an end."[13] On July 4th a party of Americans (including Monsieur et Madame Lafayette) gathered at the Hôtel de Langeac to celebrate "the anniversary of our Independence" and offer a congratulatory address (composed by the Connecticut wit, Joel Barlow) to the man "who sustained so conspicuous a part in the immortal transactions of that day."[14]

Despite Jefferson's prediction, "civil commotion"—"fermentation," "turbulence," "great tumults," a "dangerous scene of war," as he at various times phrased it—was soon to disturb the Paris scene. On the 8th he felt obliged to inform Montmorin that his *hôtel* had been robbed three times and requested that police protection be extended to the whole quarter by lodging a corps de garde in the vacant *douane* at the former Grille de Chaillot.[15]

On the 12th (the day the King dismissed M. Necker, the popular finance minister) the unpopular tollhouses—Ledoux's "little palaces"—

170.

171. This tollhouse, known as the Barrière de Passy or Barrière des Bonshommes, was at the base of the Colline de Chaillot opposite the Champ de Mars

were sacked and blackened by incendiaries (Fig. 171). That same day, when passing through the Place Louis XV in his carriage, Jefferson observed a body of the Prince de Lambesc's cavalry drawn up at the entrance to the Tuileries Gardens and a menacing crowd stationed near the piles of stones collected there for the construction of the new Pont Louis XVI. "I passed thro' the lane they had formed, without interruption. But the moment after I had passed, the people attacked the cavalry . . . and the showers of stones obliged the horse to retire"[16] (Fig. 172). "The people now armed themselves with such weapons as they could find in armorers' shops and private houses . . . and were roaming all night, through all parts of the city, without any decided object." To maintain public order and redirect popular feeling a Paris citizens' guard (*milice bourgeoise*) was formed on the 13th with Lafayette—"Restorer of Liberty in America and Defender of her Rights in France" —as its first commander-in-chief (Fig. 173). Milliners' shops were besieged for the cockades "of white, blue and pink-coloured ribbon" that had become the patriots' badge[17].

It was at the De Cornys' house in the Chaussée d'Antin—"where all is beautiful"—that Jefferson heard news of the storming of the Bastille on July 14th. He had a narrative of the transactions from Monsieur Ethis de Corny himself, one of the deputies sent by the city committee to ask arms for the National Guard from M. de Launay, Governor of the Bastille[18] (Fig. 174).

Following an inconclusive parley, "the people rushed forward, and almost in an instant were in possession of a fortification . . . of infinite strength. . . . They took all the arms, discharged the prisoners and such of the garrison as were not killed in the first moment of fury; carried the Governor and Lieutenant Governor to the Place de Grève (the place of public execution), cut off their heads, and sent them through the city, in triumph, to the Palais Royal." In the course of the next few days, Jefferson's Account Book tells us, he paid 6# for "seeing Bastille"—already being demolished—and soon thereafter contributed 60# "for widows of those who were killed in taking the Bastille."

Throughout the Paris tumults of that summer, "Mr. Short and myself," Jefferson reported to Jay, "have been every day among them in order to be sure of what was passing . . . for nothing can be believed but what one sees, or has from an eye witness."[19] Years later he reminded the Scottish philosopher Dugald Stewart that the two of them had together seen (on 17 July) "Louis XVI led in triumph by his people through the streets of his capital."[20] "The king's carriage was in the center, on each side of it the assembly, in two ranks afoot, at their head the Marquis de la Fayette as Commander-in-chief, on horseback, and Bourgeois guards before and behind. About 60,000 citizens of all forms and conditions, armed with the muskets of the Bastille and Invalides, as far as they would go, the rest with pistols, swords, pikes, pruning hooks, scythes &c. lined all the streets thro' which the procession passed, and with the crowds of people in the streets, doors and windows, saluted them everywhere with cries of 'vive la nation.' "[21] At the Hôtel de Ville Monsieur Bailly presented and put into the King's hat the popular cockade; on the return the cries were "vive le roy et la nation!" (Figs. 175, 176). The band of the Gardes Françaises, with a sense of the appropriate, played the refrain from Grétry's *Lucile*: "Où peut-on être mieux qu'au sein de sa famille?" The King was conducted back to his palace at Versailles, and thus concluded, in Jefferson's words, "such an Amende honorable as no Sovereign ever made, and no people ever received."

"The tumults of the city had pretty well subsided," Jefferson wrote to James Madison on 22

12 Juillet à 7 Heures du Soir

Le Prince de Lambesc, à la tête de Royal Almand,
parait au Pont-Tournant des Thuilleries, et massacre
un malheureux Vieillard qui cherchait à se retirer
avec un ami

172. Place Louis XV, 12 July 1789

Formation de la Garde Nationale

Le 13 Juillet a cinq heures du soir, toutes les Classes de Citoyens
se rendirent armées a la Place de Greve. Une troupe, portant les
Armes du Garde Meuble, s'yporta en Triomphe, un homme du
peuple, tenant l'epée d'Henri IV, ne voulut point la troquer contre
une épée a poignée fine que lui offroit un particulier : Non Non
dis ait il, celle ci est plus fine; elle vient du bon Roi Henri

173. Arms from the Garde-Meuble collection. The cockaded clown, lower right,
holds a sword *"qui vient du bon Roi Henri"*

Prise du gouverneur de la Bastille;
le 14 Juillet 1789.

174. 14 July 1789

Le Roi sortant de l'Hôtel de Ville
Montre au Peuple la Cocarde Nationale.

175. 17 July 1789

July, "but to-day they have been revived by a new incident. Foulon, one of the fugitive ministers was taken in the country . . . and brought to Paris. . . . He was forced from the hands of the gardes Bourgeoises by the mob, was hung, and after severing his head, the body was dragged by the enraged populace thro' the principal streets of Paris"[22] (Fig. 177). By the end of July, following such "paroxysms" and the King's recall of M. Necker, tranquillity seemed "pretty well established in the capital" and the National Assembly—still meeting in the Salle des Menus Plaisirs at Versailles—set seriously about the work of drafting a constitution. The "Declaration of the Rights of Man and of the Citizen," intended as a preamble to the Constitution proper was already "on the carpet" and was adopted on 20–28 August. Meanwhile, as a corollary action, the Assembly on the night of 4 August had (on the motion of Lafayette's brother-in-law the Vicomte de Noailles) "mowed down a whole legion of abuses"—"abolished all titles of rank, all the abusive privileges of feudalism, the tithes and casuals of the Clergy, all Provincial privileges, and, in fine, the Feudal regimen generally."[23] "It is impossible," Jefferson told Madison, "to desire better dispositions towards us, than prevail in this assembly. Our proceedings have been viewed as a model for them on every occasion; and tho' in the heat of debate men are generally disposed to contradict every authority urged by their opponents, ours has been treated like that of the bible, open to explanation but not to question."[24]

177. Heads of Foulon and Bertier de Sauvigny (his son-in-law) paraded around the Halle aux Bleds, 22 July 1789

Although Jefferson attempted to preserve "the character of a neutral and passive spectator" appropriate to his diplomatic status, he nevertheless found himself a consultant, if not an actual participant in the Assembly's debates. As an artisan of the American Revolution and author of the Declaration of Independence, he was a living authority whose counsel was eagerly sought. On one occasion he did, to be sure, decline an invitation from Champion de Cicé, Archbishop of Bordeaux, to meet with the committee charged with drafting the Constitution, pleading his foreign diplomat's status in reply to the Archbishop's argument that "there are no foreigners when the happiness of mankind is at stake."[25] But he could not evade Lafayette's urgent appeal: "I beg for liberty's sake you will break every engagement to give us a dinner to-morrow Wenesday. We shall be some members of the National Assembly—eight of us whom I want to coalize as being the only means to prevent a total dissolution and civil war. The diffi-

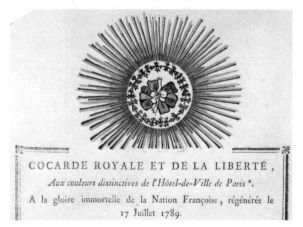

COCARDE ROYALE ET DE LA LIBERTÉ,
Aux couleurs distinctives de l'Hôtel-de-Ville de Paris.
A la gloire immortelle de la Nation Françoise, régénérée le 17 Juillet 1789.

176.

culty between them is the King's veto. . . . These gentlemen wish to consult you and me, they will dine tomorrow at your house as mine is always full. I depend on you to receive us."[26]

The eight duly arrived at the Hôtel de Langeac on 26 August: Lafayette, Duport, Barnave, Lameth, Blacons, Mounier, LaTour Maubourg, and d'Agoult. Describing the scene in his memoirs, Jefferson wrote: "The cloth being removed and wine set on the table, after the American manner, the Marquis introduced the objects of the conference. . . . The discussions began at the hour of four, and were continued till ten o'clock in the evening; during which time I was a silent witness to a coolness and candor of argument unusual in the conflicts of political opinion; to a logical reasoning, and chaste eloquence, disfigured by no gaudy tinsel of rhetoric or declamation, and truly worthy of being placed in parallel with the finest dialogues of antiquity, as handed to us by Xenophon, by Plato, and Cicero. The result was an agreement that the king should have a suspensive veto on the laws, that the legislature should be composed of a single body only, and that to be chosen by the people. This Concordate decided the fate of the constitution."[27]

Next morning Jefferson called on the Comte de Montmorin and explained "with truth and candor, how it had happened that my house had been made the scene of conferences of such a character." The Minister told him that he already knew everything which had passed and "that so far from taking umbrage at the use made of my house . . . he earnestly wished I would habitually assist at such conferences, being sure I should be useful in moderating the warmer spirits, and promoting a wholesome and practical reformation only."

The "spirit of revolution" was the leit-motif of the many letters Jefferson wrote from Paris in the summer of 1789. His own mood may have varied from day to day, or according to his correspondents—guarded and factual in the official dispatches to Jay, reassuring to those he knew to be skeptical or faint-hearted, enthusiastic with the true believers in the cause—but there is no mistaking his essentially optimistic frame of mind. "I have so much confidence in the good sense of man, and his qualifications for self-government," he wrote in one of his less-guarded moments, "that I am never afraid of the issue where reason is left free to exert her force; and I will agree to be stoned as a false prophet if all does not end well in this country. Here is but the first chapter of the history of European liberty."[28]

When the October Days came round Jefferson was already homeward bound and so did not witness the procession (Lafayette again at its head) that brought the King and Royal Family back to Paris for good. The role of Versailles was at an end. The National Assembly soon followed the King and resumed its debates in the Salle du Manège in the gardens adjoining the Tuileries Palace, once again a royal residence. The last of the Concerts Spirituels to be held there in the Salle des Machines took place in November 1789. Later on, in 1793, the concert hall that Jefferson had known was transformed (still in the Neo-classic manner) into a meeting place for the Convention charged with framing a Constitution for the First French Republic.[29]

* * * * * * * * * * * *

John Jay's letter of 19 June 1789 informing Jefferson that the President had granted his request for leave and that the Senate had confirmed William Short's appointment as chargé d'affaires finally reached Paris late in August.[30] Following an illness that confined him to his house for a week in early September, the American Minister made his round of farewell visits, official and personal, and set off for Le Havre on the 26th. (Figs. 178, 179.) A considerable shipment of baggage, sent down the Seine by diligence d'eau, had preceded him: hampers of wine, trunks and numbered boxes containing books, pictures, Houdon busts of John Paul Jones, plants (pear, peach, and almond among them), Martha's harpsichord, "the pedestal for Fayette's bust," as well as a phaeton and a "chariot."[31]

The next year, when Jefferson knew he would not be returning, an even weightier cargo of souvenirs de Paris followed. During the summer of 1790 William Short, with the assistance of the maître d'hôtel, Adrien Petit, supervised the packing done by Grevin, maître-layetier. By

178. Passport for the American Minister, "his family, servants, baggage and carriages," signed by Louis XVI, countersigned by Montmorin

179. Laissez-passer for "M. Jefferson, his daughters, and their servants" issued by the Commune de Paris, endorsed by Lafayette as commander of the National Guard

July 4th Short could report that "Petit and the packers are going on with the greatest expedition possible. I foresee no delay unless the fever of going to work at the Champ de Mars [where preparations for the Fête de la Fédération on the 14th were under way] should take possession of the packers. . . . Petit still continues his determination not to go to America, unless he should hear farther from you."[32] On 4 August Short wrote: "Your furniture is at length all packed up, and the last articles are this moment gone to Neuilly to meet the vessel which is to take them in there. They are all plumbed so as not to be opened any where. They will be received at Havre by M. de la Motte, who promises to take charge of them."[33]

The shipment comprised 86 crates, all meticulously listed in Grevin's invoice, containing more wine, books, pictures, busts, scientific instruments, as well as the household furnishings from the Hôtel de Langeac and additional purchases made by Short at Jefferson's direction.[34] There were dishes, silver, kitchenware, a blue silk ottoman, mirrors, armchairs crimson and blue, damask curtains, toiles de Jouy, wallpaper from Arthur's on the Boulevards and, to crown it all, Madame de Tessé's gift, the altar for the groves of Monticello. (See Dedication, above.)

It also devolved upon Short to terminate the lease of the Hôtel de Langeac (whose owner, like others of his class, was by now in Switzerland), discharge the servants, sell the horses, and dispose of the remaining effects. Petit, the maître d'hôtel, went home to his family's farm in the province of Champagne, but after receiving an eloquent plea expressed in Jefferson's best French, eventually decided to join *"le Roy des maîtres"* (as he described Jefferson) and *"rester toujours"* in his service.[35] He reached Philadelphia in July 1791 and presided over Jefferson's

ADIEU TO JEFFERSON'S PARIS

household there until January 1794, when the Secretary of State relinquished his duties and retired—temporarily—to Monticello.[36]

When Petit arrived in Philadelphia, he brought with him still further reminders of Jefferson's Paris, including a sealed package containing the protocolic *présent du Roi* to departing diplomats.[37] The official register of such presents describes Jefferson's only as a *boîte à portrait* valued at 15 *livres*, 174 (a bit less than the one presented in 1785 to Franklin, the work of Solle and Sicardi, set with 421 brilliants and valued at 16 *livres*, 103). Acceptance of the gift had cost Jefferson considerable anguish, for he was acutely aware of both the European diplomatic custom and the proviso in the new U.S. Constitution (Art. I, Sec. 9) enjoining American officials from accepting presents from "any King, Prince, or foreign state" without the consent of Congress. Not wishing to have the matter "laid on the gridiron of debate in Congress," the Secretary of State resolved his dilemma by accepting the gift but having the brilliants removed from the box and the proceeds from their sale applied to the reciprocal presents customarily expected from departing diplomats at the Court of Versailles by the Introducteur des Ambassadeurs (Tolozan) and his Secretary (Sequeville). Jefferson did not begrudge them their present, for, as he told William Short, such gifts were their livelihood. The whole transaction was accomplished under Short's discreet supervision, with a banking partner of Ferdinand Grand, J.-A. Gautier, extracting the stones from the box with his own hands. Nothing of all this transpired at the time. Nor is it known what subsequently happened to the King's mutilated *présent de congé* delivered in Philadelphia by Petit. That same summer, the new French Minister to the United States, Ternant, brought with him for presentation purposes twenty copies of the King's portrait engraved by Bervic after Callet's painting.[38] Jefferson was presumably one of the favored (as was Washington) for he was later to list as No. 42 in his "Catalogue of Paintings etc. at Monticello," hanging in the parlour, middle tier (between "Susanna and the elders" copied from Coypel and a print of Bonaparte): "Louis XVI. a print. a present from the king to Th:J." The print is not now at Monticello, but

it must have been similar to the Bervic-Callet portrait reproduced here (Fig. 180).

"The principal small news" brought by Petit from Paris, Jefferson wrote his daughter Martha (by now the mistress of her own household and mother of her first child, Anne Cary Randolph), "is that Panthemont is one of the convents kept up for education, that the old Abbess is living, but Madame de Tonbenheim dead, that some of the nuns have chosen to rejoin the world, others to stay, that there are no English pensioners there now, Botidoux remains there, &c. &c. &c. Mr. Short lives in the Hotel d'Orleans Rue des Petits Augustins where I lived when you first went to Panthemont."[39] Martha herself had earlier received a lengthy journal-letter from her classmate Botidoux relaying convent gossip during the autumn and winter following the Jeffersons' departure.[40] Mademoiselle "Botte," who evidently enjoyed playing the radical amidst the conservative *dames pensionnaires*, recounted with relish the escapade of one of the nuns who had rejoined the world under somewhat unusual circumstances: poor Sister Catherine broke out through the Panthemont kitchen door, ran into the Rue du Bac, apron and all, and then to the Faubourg Saint-Antoine, where she took refuge with an *aubergiste* friend. On the way she stopped at Monsieur Marat's, who published the rather muddled story of her tribulations in his paper *L'Ami du Peuple*! All of which, according to Botidoux, "*a fait un bruit terrible dans La Maison*," &c. &c. &c.

* * * * * * * * * * * *

William Short's letters—both the official dispatches reporting political developments and his private communications giving small news of mutual friends—long continued to be one of Jefferson's links with Paris. Short's disillusionment with the course the Revolution was taking soon became evident, but Jefferson himself only gradually and reluctantly abandoned the optimistic beliefs he held at the time he left the Paris scene. Years later, in 1815, when reviewing with Lafayette "the crimes and cruelties" through which France had passed, he was able

LOUIS SEIZE.
ROI DES FRANÇAIS, RESTAURATEUR DE LA LIBERTÉ.
PRESENTÉ AU ROI et à L'ASSEMBLÉE NATIONALE. Par l'Auteur.

180. A print similar to this (engraved by Bervic after Callet), recorded by Jefferson as "a present from the King to Th:J.", once hung in the parlor at Monticello

[124]

to rationalize his false prophecies by re-affirming his faith in democratic government while admitting that the French, at least in 1789, were unprepared for it.[41] During the intervening years, he had corresponded at rare intervals with friends in France. News also came to him through French visitors to America, from *émigrés* in the legal sense of the word, or travelers who found it expedient to be removed from the uncertainties of life at home. Jefferson was thus aware of the tragedies that befell many of his Paris acquaintances. "My own affections have been deeply wounded by some of the martyrs to the cause," he told Short when attempting to bolster the younger man's faltering faith. But, he added in words that seem callous even when read in the context of an intimate and confidential correspondence, "I deplore them as I should have done had they fallen in battle."[42]

The Dialogue of the Head and the Heart continued. Jefferson's Head directed his official dealings with France, as Secretary of State and later as Vice-President and President, never losing sight of what he believed the true interests of the United States. Nevertheless, he was ever ready to "turn for a moment from the barren field of politics to the rich map of nature"[43] and discuss scientific and literary subjects with French correspondents. Nor was he averse (as in the negotiations for Louisiana) to make "private friendships instrumental to the public good by inspiring a confidence which is denied the public, and official communications."[44] After his release from the burdens of public office—especially after 1815, when books, seeds, and wine from France could reach him without interference from the "pirates of the seas"—his Heart could have free rein. "Now that Bonaparte is put down," he told Short when the latter was contemplating taking up permanent residence abroad, "France, freed from that monster, must again become the most agreeable country on earth."[45] He could indulge, too, in "idle reveries . . . of seeing all my friends of Paris once more, for a month or two; a thing impossible, which, however, I never permitted myself to despair of."[46]

In such a mood Jefferson penned his classic tribute to France, including the lines: "A more benevolent people, I have never known, nor greater warmth and devotedness in their select friendships. Their kindness and accommodation to strangers is unparalleled, and the hospitality of Paris is beyond anything I had conceived to be practicable in a large city. Their eminence, too, in science, the communicative dispositions of their scientific men, the politeness of the general manners, the ease and vivacity of their conversation, give a charm to their society to be found nowhere else."[47]

The length of Jefferson's tether might be reduced, as he once said, but he still had with him at Monticello the "treasure of art, science and sentiment" amassed during his years in Paris.[48] When Daniel Webster visited Monticello in December 1824, he noted that "dinner is served in half Virginian, half French style, in good taste and abundance. No wine is put on the table till the cloth is removed." Jefferson was easy and natural in conversation, the New England visitor found. The leading topics to which his mind habitually turned were: "early anecdotes of revolutionary times; French society, politics, and literature such as they were when he was in France, and general literature; and the Virginia university. On these three general topics he has much to say, and he says it all well."[49] The historian Henry Adams, when attempting to fathom the puzzling intricacies he found in Jefferson's personality, concluded that "with all his extraordinary versatility of character and opinions, he seemed during his entire life to breathe with perfect satisfaction nowhere except in the liberal, literary, and scientific air of Paris in 1789."[50]

Abbreviations

Works frequently cited in the notes are abbreviated as follows:

Papers
Julian P. Boyd et al., eds., *The Papers of Thomas Jefferson*, 19 vols. as of 1975 (Princeton, N.J., Princeton University Press, 1950——). *Index* covering Vols. 1-18 (1760 through January 1791), 3 vols., compiled by Elizabeth J. Sherwood, Ida T. Hopper, Delight Ansley.

TJ, *Autobiography*
References are to Volume ı of P. L. Ford, ed., *The Writings of Thomas Jefferson* (New York, 1892-1899), where the uncompleted autobiography (written in 1821) is at pp. 1-153

Gallet (72)
Michel Gallet, *Stately Mansions: Eighteenth Century Paris Architecture* (New York, Praeger, 1972; London ed. titled: *Paris Domestic Architecture of the Eighteenth Century*), which is a revised and enlarged edition of Gallet's *Demeures parisiennes: L'Epoque de Louis XVI* (Paris, 1964)

Mercier
Sébastien Mercier, *Tableau de Paris*, 12 tomes (Amsterdam, 1782-1788)

Morris, *Diary*
Beatrix Cary Davenport, ed., *A Diary of the French Revolution by Gouverneur Morris*, 2 vols. (Boston, Houghton Mifflin, 1939)

Neo-Classicism
Council of Europe exhibition catalogue: *The Age of Neo-Classicism* (Arts Council of Great Britain, 1972)

Sowerby
E. Millicent Sowerby, comp., *Catalogue of the Library of Thomas Jefferson*, 5 vols. (Washington, D.C., Library of Congress, 1952-1959)

Thiéry
Luc-Vincent Thiéry, *Guide des Amateurs et des Etrangers voyageurs à Paris*, 2 vols. (Paris, Hardouin & Gattey, 1787)

Trumbull, *Autobiography*
Theodore Sizer, ed., *The Autobiography of Colonel John Trumbull* (New Haven, Conn., Yale University Press, 1953)

Notes

CHAPTER 1: *Summary View*

1. Ledoux, *De l'architecture considérée sous le rapport de l'art, des moeurs et de la législation* (Paris, 1804). Marcel Raval and J.-Ch. Moreux, *Claude-Nicolas Ledoux, 1756-1806* (Paris, 1945), Part IV, "Les Propylées de Paris," pp. 65-67, Pl. 258-329. Other modern studies of Ledoux by Geneviève Levallet-Haug, Emil Kaufmann, Yvan Christ, et al.

2. TJ to David Humphreys, 14 Aug. 1787, *Papers* 12: 32-33.

3. *Ibid.*

4. Mercier, t. XI, 1-2, unnumbered chapter, "Il fait bon crier un peu."

5. Janinet, *Vues pittoresques des principaux édifices de Paris* (Paris, 1792), published shortly before the fall of the monarchy.

6. Mercier, t. I, Chap. 88, "On bâtit de tous côtés." The best study of building activity during this period is Gallet (72); this well-illustrated work includes an invaluable "Register of Architects." See also Michel Gallet, "Palladio et l'architecture française dans la seconde moitié du XVIII siècle," *Les Monuments Historiques de la France*, 1975, No. 2 (special Palladio number), pp. 43-55.

7. TJ to James Madison, 2 August 1787, *Papers* 11: 662-668. Account Book, 5 Jan. 1787: "pd. Goldsmith for Tableau de Paris 10 *f*." Sowerby, No. 3890.

8. TJ to Buchanan and Hay, 13 Aug. 1785, *Papers* 8: at p. 367.

9. Sébastien Mercier, *Paris pendant la Révolution (1789-1798), ou Le Nouveau Paris*, nouvelle édition, 2 vols. (Paris, Poulet-Massis, 1862), II, Chap. CXX, "La Ville de Paris en relief."

CHAPTER 2: *Center of Paris*

1. Jefferson's so-called account books for 1783–1790 —more properly described as his Memorandum Books or Journal of Expenditures—are in Massachusetts Historical Society, Boston. An annotated edition by James A. Bear, Jr., is in preparation. Units of French money under the Ancien Régime were the *livre tournois* (or *franc*), the *sol* (or *sou*), and the *denier*. 12 *deniers* equaled 1 *sol*; 20 *sous* equaled 1 *livre*. Arithmetical operations were thus similar to those used with English money prior to the recent adoption of the decimal unit.

The coin called a *franc* was no longer current under Louis XVI, but the word was still common as a synonym for *livre*. Jefferson writes, for example, "18 *f* 10", which may be read as 18 *livres*, 10 *sous*. The decimal system was adopted during the French Revolution by a decree of 1795.

2. Watin's directory, *Etat actuel de Paris* (1788), places the Hôtel d'Orléans at No. 23 Rue de Richelieu, which corresponds to present No. 30, eastern side of street, opposite the Fontaine Molière and Rue Thérèse (Rue du Hazard on our map, Fig. 15). Auguste Vitu, "La Rue Richelieu depuis sa création" (appendix to his *La Maison mortuaire de Molière*, Paris, 1883), pp. 104, 168. Jefferson's hotel is not to be confused with the Left Bank hotel of the same name (Rue des Petits Augustins, present Rue Bonaparte) to which he subsequently moved, or with still another Hôtel d'Orléans located within the Palais Royal enclosure, arcade No. 116 (Watin; Thiéry, I, 286).

3. Mercier, t. X, Chaps. 819-821.

4. In addition to Mercier, Thiéry, Restif de la Bretonne, there are many other contemporary descriptions, such as Mayer de Saint-Paul's *Tableau du Nouveau Palais-Royal* (1788), from which our Fig. 17 is taken. Charles Marionneau, *Victor Louis* (Bordeaux, 1881). Victor Champier and G. Roger Sandoz, *Le Palais-Royal*, 2 vols. (Paris, 1900). E. Dupezard, *Le Palais-Royal de Paris: Architecture et décoration de Louis XV à nos jours* (Paris, 1911). Pierre D'Espezel, *Le Palais-Royal* (Paris, 1936).

5. TJ to David Humphreys, 14 Aug. 1787, *Papers* 12: 32-33.

6. TJ to James Currie, 14 Jan., 5 Feb. 1785, *Papers* 7: 604-606, 635.

7. Mercier, t. X, Chap. 819.

8. Thiéry, I, 273-274. The original numbering of the Palais-Royal arcades is still in use. Beginning at southwestern corner of the rectangle: Nos. 1–78, western (Rue de Montpensier) side; Nos. 79–102, northern (Rue de Beaujolais) side; Nos. 103–180, eastern (Rue de Valois) side.

9. *Tableau du Nouveau Palais-Royal*, I, 55-61.

10. Thiéry, I, 271-272. Max Aghion, *Le Théâtre à Paris au XVIII* *siècle* (Paris, n.d.), pp. 279-282, 288-302. The Variétés was at this location only from January 1785 to spring of 1789. Present Théâtre des Variétés, Boulevard Montmartre, dates only from 1807.

NOTES

11. Mme de Marmontel to TJ, 13 Oct. 1786, *Papers* 10: 459.

12. Dates from TJ's Account Book. Programs in *Journal de Paris*.

13. Thiéry, I, 279-280. Sowerby, No. 1174. According to TJ's Account Book, 1 April 1786, he bought in London a set of chessmen for 18 shillings.

14. Thiéry, I, 239-262, lists the paintings in the Palais-Royal collection. Chastellux to TJ, 3 Sept. 1785, *Papers* 8: 471-472.

15. René Hennequin, *Edme Quenedey . . . portraitiste au physionotrace* (Troyes, 1926-27); *Les Portraits au physionotrace . . . catalogue nominatif, biographique et critique . . . Estampes de Chrétien et de Quenedey* (Troyes, 1932). Successive locations of Quenedey's studio in vicinity of Palais-Royal are discussed in Hennequin's *Quenedey*, pp. 24-26, and shown on map, Pl. II. Announcement cited here is in *Les Portraits*, pp. 5-6. When TJ visited it, the studio was in the Hôtel de Lussan (no longer standing) on the site of present No. 42, Rue Croix des Petits Champs, near corner of Rue Coquillière.

16. H. C. Rice, Jr., "A 'New' Likeness of Thomas Jefferson," *William & Mary Quarterly*, 3rd series, VI (Jan. 1949), 84-89. *Papers* 14: xlii-xliv. Alfred L. Bush, *The Life Portraits of TJ* (Charlottesville, 1962), pp. 20-22.

17. TJ to Anne Willing Bingham, 7 Feb. 1787, *Papers* 11: 122-124.

18. Mercier, t. x, Chap. 820.

19. Arthur Young, *Travels in France and Italy during the Years 1787, 1788 and 1789* (London, 1792, and later editions), under date 14 Oct. 1787. Henri Sée's translation, *Voyages . . .*, 3 vols. (Paris, 1931) has excellent introduction and notes.

20. Thiéry, I, 413-419, Pl. 6. Gabriel Vauthier, "La Halle au Blé 1758-1811," *Bulletin Soc. Hist. de Paris*, LV (1926), 62-68. Bib. Nat., Cab. Est., Va. 230.d.

21. Fiske Kimball, "Jefferson and the Public Buildings of Virginia," *Huntington Library Quarterly*, XII (Feb., May 1949), 115-120, 303-310. H. C. Rice, Jr., "A French Source of Jefferson's Plan for the Prison at Richmond," *Journal Soc. Architectural Historians*, XII, No. 4 (Dec. 1953), 28-30.

22. Trumbull, *Autobiography*, p. 120.

23. Helen D. Bullock, *My Head and My Heart: A Little History of Thomas Jefferson and Maria Cosway* (New York, 1945). Lyman H. Butterfield and Howard C. Rice, Jr., "Jefferson's Earliest Note to Maria Cosway with Some Facts and Conjectures on His Broken Wrist," *William & Mary Quarterly*, 3rd series, V (Jan. 1948), 26-33. Since the appearance of this article, date and place of the accident (Cours la Reine) have been confirmed by Le Veillard's letter to Wm. Temple Franklin, Paris, 20 Sept. 1786 (MS, Am. Phil. Soc.).

24. TJ to Maria Cosway, 12 Oct. 1786, *Papers* 10: 443-455.

25. Paul F. Norton, "Jefferson's Plans for Mothballing the Frigates," *U.S. Naval Inst. Proceedings*, 82, No. 7 (July 1956), 736-741. Jefferson recalled his scheme in letter to Lewis M. Wiss, 27 Nov. 1825 (MS, LC).

26. Sowerby, No. 4183.

27. Paul F. Norton, "Latrobe's Ceiling for the Hall of Representatives," *Journal Soc. Architectural Historians*, X, No. 2 (1951), 5-10.

28. Sigfried Giedion, *Space, Time and Architecture* (Cambridge, Mass., 1947), p. 110, Fig. 52.

29. Robert Hénard, *La Rue Saint-Honoré, des origines à la Révolution* (Paris, 1908).

30. Mercier, t. I, Chap. 39.

31. Thiéry, I, 224-227. Hippolyte Gautier, *L'An 1789* (Paris, n.d.), p. 375, ill.

32. Account Book: 16 June 1787, 30 April 1789, 27 May 1789. Programs in *Journal de Paris*.

33. Watin, *Etat actuel de Paris* (1788) and *Almanach de Paris* (1789) list the Houdetot residence at what was then No. 331.

34. Thiéry, I, 120-121. Gallet (72), pp. 68, 139 *s.v.* Antoine.

35. Thiéry, I, 126. J. Vacquier, et al., *Les Vieux Hôtels de Paris* (Paris, 1914 . . .), IX, "Place Vendôme."

36. Abbés Arnoux and Chalut to TJ, 13 Nov. 1785, *Papers* 9: 28-29.

37. Watin, *Etat* (1788) places the "bureau de M. Grand, banquier" at No. 21, Rue Neuve des Capucines. This would have been just around the corner from the Place Vendôme in present Rue des Capucines, approximately No. 5.

38. Purchases from Noseda, Account Book: 9 Sept., 16 Oct. 1785, 11 July, 30 Aug. 1787, 7 Feb., 15 May 1788, 30 April 1789. From Daguerre: 22 Oct. 1784. From Dupuis: 21 April 1785. Dupuis's receipted bill (purchases made by Short for TJ), 21 June 1790, is reproduced in Marie Kimball, *The Furnishings of Monticello* (1940), p. 4.

39. *Papers* 15, xxvii-xxix, xxxiv, ill. Julian P. Boyd, "Thomas Jefferson and the Roman Askos of Nîmes," *Antiques*, 104, No. 1 (July 1973), 116-124, ill. Monelle Hayot, "J. B. C. Odiot le prince des orfèvres," *L'Estampille*, No. 59 (Nov. 1974), pp. 7-16. Pierre Kjellberg, "Pour devenir compétent en orfèvrerie de l'Empire," *Connaissance des Arts*, No. 155 (Jan. 1965), pp. 30-38. The firm of Odiot is still in existence (7 Place de la Madeleine).

40. Mercier, t. ii, Chap. 173. TJ to Anne Willing Bingham, 7 Feb. 1787, *Papers* 11: 122-124. *Papers* 8: 66n-67n, citing description of Mlle Bertin's establishment in Miss Abigail Adams's journal (9 March 1785).

41. TJ to Caspar Wistar, Jr., 21 June 1807, L.C.

CHAPTER 3: *Center of Paris*

1. Young, *Travels*, 14 Oct. 1787.

2. Thiéry, i, 96-104. Comte de Fels, *Ange-Jacques Gabriel, Premier Architecte du Roi* (Paris, 1924, 2nd ed.). Gallet (72), pp. 161-162 *s.v.* Gabriel. *Louis XV* (exhibition cat., Hôtel de la Monnaie, Paris, 1974), Nos. 16-17.

3. Sowerby, No. 4211. *Neo-Classicism*, No. 1252.

4. TJ to Virginia Delegates in Congress, 12 July 1785, *Papers* 8: 289-290.

5. TJ memorandum on his rate of walking, *Papers* 11: 484n, repr. in Edward Dumbauld, *Thomas Jefferson, American Tourist* (Norman, Oklahoma, 1946), facing p. 17. Pedometer described in TJ to James Madison, 3 May 1788, *Papers* 13: 129-133. Account Book: 7 Feb. 1788, purchase of pedometer from Noseda.

6. Thiéry, i, 98n-100n. J.-R. Perronet, *Description des projets et de la construction des Ponts de Neuilly, de Mantes, d'Orléans & autres*, 3 vols. (Paris, Imprimerie Royale, 1782-1789), Pont Louis XVI in Vols. ii and iii. Dartein, "Le Pont de la Concorde sur la Seine, à Paris (1786-1791)," *Annales des Ponts et Chaussées, Mémoires et Documents*, 8th series, xxiv (1906), 88-148. M.-L. Levent, "La Construction du Pont Louis XVI," *Bulletin Musée Carnavalet*, 7, No. 1 (June 1954), pp. 9-15.

7. Martial de Pradel de Lamase, *L'Hôtel de la Marine, le monument et l'histoire* (Paris, 1924).

8. TJ to L'Enfant, 10 April 1791, Saul K. Padover, ed., *Thomas Jefferson and the National Capital* (Washington, 1946), pp. 58-59.

9. Thiéry, i, 93-94. Léon Gruel, *La Madeleine* (Paris, 1910). Gallet (72), pp. 151, 153, *s.v.* Contant, Couture. Pérouse de Montclos, *Boullée* (Paris, 1969), p. 155, Figs. 56-61. *Neo-Classicism*, No. 1059.

10. Account Book: 18 March 1785. Thiéry, i, 94n. M. Gallet, "Un Modèle pour la Madeleine," *Bulletin Musée Carnavalet*, 18e Année, No. 1 (June 1965), pp. 14-19.

11. TJ to J. Buchanan and W. Hay, 13 Aug. 1785, *Papers* 8: 366-368. TJ, *Autobiography*, pp. 63-64.

12. Clérisseau to TJ, 4 Dec. 1787, *Papers* 12: 393.

13. TJ to Clérisseau, 2 June 1786, Clérisseau to TJ, same date, *Papers* 9: 602-603. *Ibid.*, 637-638 (Instruc-

tions for unpacking model, by Bloquet, a *stuccateur*, probably an assistant to Fouquet, the model-maker); xxvii (note on model, repr. facing p. 226). Account Book: 22 May 1786, "pd Fouquet for the state of Virginia for model of the capitol in plaister 372 f." A plaster model of the Pont Louis XVI, now in the Musée Carnavalet, is signed: "Ce modelle a été/ exécuté par Fouquet,/ rue pagevin N.° 16/ en 1788." Cf. *Bulletin Musée Carnavalet* (June 1954), repr. p. 11 and p. 15, n. 7. Watin's *Etat* (1787), i, 85, lists the "Bureau du voyage pittoresque de la Grèce" at No. 16 Rue Pagevin (a street then in vicinity of the Place des Victoires). The *Voyage* is the great illustrated work compiled by Choiseul-Gouffier. In his *Autobiography* (p. 64) Jefferson states that the model for the Richmond capitol "was executed by the artist whom Choiseul-Gouffier had carried with him to Constantinople, and employed, while Ambassador there, in making those beautiful models of the remains of Grecian architecture which are to be seen at Paris."

14. Marcel Poëte, *Au Jardin des Tuileries* (Paris, 1924). Yvan Christ, *Le Louvre et les Tuileries* (Paris, Editions TEL, 1949).

15. Thiéry, i, 303n, 398-399. *Journal de Paris*, 16 Sept. 1784ff. Jefferson subscribed to this paper throughout his stay in Paris (annual subscription, 30 *f*).

16. TJ to Francis Hopkinson, Annapolis, 18 Feb. 1784, *Papers* 6: 541-543. TJ to Philip Turpin, Annapolis, 28 April 1784 (with sketches copied from Faujas de Saint-Fond, *Description des expériences de la machine aérostatique de MM. Mongolfier*); TJ to James Monroe, Philadelphia, 21 May 1784; *Papers* 7: 134-137, 279-281.

17. Hester Lynch Piozzi, *Observations and Reflections made in the course of a Journey through France, Italy and Germany* (London, 1789), i, 22-24. M. Tyson and H. Guppy, eds., *The French Journals of Mrs. Thrale and Doctor Johnson* (Manchester, 1932), pp. 203-204.

18. TJ to Francis Hopkinson, 13 Jan. 1785, to James Monroe, 14 Jan., *Papers* 7: 602-603, 607-608; to Charles Thomson, 21 June 1785, *Papers* 8: 245-246.

19. Account Book: 18 June 1786. *Journal de Paris*, 13 June 1786ff. *Journal Polytype: Partie des Arts Utiles*, i, No. 18 (27 June 1786), facing p. 302, plate showing Tétu's "aerostat."

20. Thiéry, i, 397.

21. Account Book: 13 June 1785.

22. TJ to Madame de Tessé, Nîmes, 20 March 1787, *Papers* 11: 226-228.

23. Georges Lenôtre, *Les Tuileries: Fastes et maléfices d'un palais disparu* (Paris, 1933). Yvan Christ, *Le Louvre et les Tuileries* (Paris, 1949).

24. Trumbull, *Autobiography*, p. 96.

25. Michel Brenet (pseud. Marie Bobillier), *Les*

Concerts en France sous l'Ancien Régime (Paris, 1900).

26. Mercier, t. VII, Chap. 556.

27. Thiéry, I, 391-394. Albert Babeau, "Le Théâtre des Tuileries sous Louis XIV, Louis XV et Louis XVI," *Bulletin Soc. Hist. de Paris*, XXII (1895), 130-188.

28. Account Book: 8 Sept., 20 Oct. 1784; 3 April, 5 May, 15 Aug., 25 Dec. 1785; 2 Feb., 15 June, 8 Sept., 1 Nov. 1786; 2 Feb. 1788; 12 April 1789. Entries for 10 May 1786, 12 April 1789 mention concert tickets without specifying the Concerts spirituels. Programs in *Journal de Paris*.

29. A. B. Shepperson, "A Harpsichord for Monticello," in *John Paradise and Lucy Ludwell* (Richmond, 1942), Chap. 11.

30. Helen Cripe, *Thomas Jefferson and Music* (Charlottesville, 1974). Appendix II, pp. 105ff., is an inventory of "Collections of Jefferson Family Music" now at Monticello or University of Virginia.

31. Thiéry, I, 327-380. Louis Hautecoeur, *Histoire du Louvre* (Paris, 1927). Yvan Christ, *Le Louvre*.

32. Communication from Archivist, Institut de France, to H. C. Rice, 27 Nov. 1946.

33. Sophie von La Roche, *Journal einer Reise durch Frankreich* (Altenburg, 1787), pp. 169-170.

34. Christiane Aulanier, *Histoire du Palais et du Musée du Louvre: (2) Le Salon Carré* (Paris, 1950); summary in *Musées de France*, 1949, special number, "Le Salon Carré et son histoire."

35. TJ to John Trumbull, 30 Aug. 1787, *Papers* 12: 69.

36. Salon catalogues, reprinted in *Collection des Livrets des anciennes expositions depuis 1673 jusqu'en 1800* (Paris, Liepmannssohn, 1870).

37. TJ to William Short, 6 April 1790, *Papers* 16: 318-324. Short commissioned Joseph Boze to paint Lafayette's portrait, completed in December 1790. *Papers* 16: 318; *Papers* 18: 32, 356, 450. Repr., *Papers* 5: 185. The portrait is now in the Mass. Historical Society.

38. TJ to Mme de Bréhan, 14 March 1789, *Papers* 14: 655-656.

39. Gerda Kircher, "Chardins Doppelgänger," *Der Cicerone* (Leipzig), XX (1928), 95-101. Present whereabouts of Roland de la Porte's "Crucifix," if it has survived, has not been determined. It probably resembled the Crucifix by Boilly reproduced in exhibition catalogue, *French Painting 1774-1830* (Grand Palais, Detroit, Met. Museum, 1974-75), No. 9.

40. TJ to Mme de Tott, 28 Feb. 1787; Mme de Tott to TJ, 4 March; TJ to Mme de Tott, 5 April; *Papers* 11: xxxi (ill. following p. 414), 187-188, 198-199, 270-273. Cf. *French Painting 1774-1830*, No. 52, repr. color and black and white.

41. TJ to L'Enfant, 10 April 1790, above, n. 8. Jefferson had in his library Claude Perrault's treatise on the five orders of columns (Sowerby, No. 4182) as well as Perrault's edition of Vitruvius (Sowerby, No. 4173).

CHAPTER 4: *New Quarters*

1. Jacques Silvestre de Sacy, *Alexandre-Théodore Brongniart* (Paris, 1940), pp. 16-20, 34-48, Pl. V-XI, XVI-XIX. M. Raval and J.-Ch. Moreux, *Claude-Nicolas Ledoux* (Paris, 1945), "Plan de Paris," facing p. 9, Pl. 22-45.

2. *Papers* 7: 442-443. Original in Archives Nationales, Minutier Central des Notaires de la Seine, fonds LXXIX, liasse 255. Cf. H. C. Rice, Jr., "The Paris Depository for Notarial Archives," *American Archivist*, XIV, No. 2 (April 1951), 99-104.

3. Thus in Account Book and elsewhere. Letters from Henry Martin, 7 Dec. 1784, 4 Feb. 1785, forwarded to Jefferson from his former transient lodgings, are re-addressed to "Cul de sac thetbou hautel landron," *Papers* 7: 557, 635. Jefferson himself never used this designation and no other authority for it has been found.

4. TJ to John Jay, 15 May 1788, *Papers* 13: 161-164.

5. Account Book for this period.

6. Account Book: 21 Oct. 1784. TJ to Buchanan and Hay, 13 Aug. 1785, *Papers* 8: 366-368.

7. Catalogues of the sales are listed in F. Lugt, *Répertoire des catalogues des ventes publiques* (The Hague, 1938-1964), I, Nos. 3791, 3832. Jefferson's "Catalogue of Paintings etc. at Monticello" (MS, *ca.* 1809, ViU) mentions five items (TJ Nos. 4, 22, 23, 34, 35) purchased from St. Séverin collection and gives references to the sale catalogue (Nos. 36, 248, 215, 306, 59). Another such list (this one unnumbered), printed in Marie Kimball, *Jefferson: The Scene of Europe* (New York, 1950), mentions the five St. Séverin paintings, and also a single De Billy item with reference to the sale catalogue (No. 21). A marked copy of the De Billy catalogue (Bib. de Versailles) records purchaser of item 21 as "Saubert," which suggests that Jefferson acquired it through an agent or intermediary. A marked copy of the Dupille de Saint-Séverin catalogue (Heim collection, Paris) mentions "L'Envoié d'Amérique" as purchaser of items 36, 59, but his name is not noted for Nos. 215, 248, 306. Jefferson's Account Book, Feb. 1785, records substantial payments "for pictures," without specifying the sale or the subjects.

8. Information about servants is derived from Account Book. Re James Hemings: "pd. the Traiteur 150 f being the half of what I am to pay him for

teaching James, the other half to be paid when he is taken away" (16 Dec. 1784); "pd. Combeaux balance of James's apprenticeship 150" (2 Feb. 1786).

9. John Adams to TJ, Quincy, 22 Jan. 1825, Lester J. Cappon, ed., *The Adams-Jefferson Letters* (Chapel Hill, 1959), II, 606-607.

10. TJ to James Monroe, 18 March 1785, *Papers* 8: 42-45.

11. Account Book.

12. TJ to William Short, Monticello, 30 Sept. 1790, *Papers* 17: 543-546.

13. Silvestre de Sacy, *Brongniart* (Paris, 1940), pp. 17-20, Pl. VI.

14. Gilbert Chinard, *Trois Amitiés françaises de Jefferson* (Paris, 1927), pp. 145-238.

15. TJ to Mme de Corny, 26 Oct. 1788, *Papers* 14: 37-38.

16. Mme de Corny to TJ, 17 May 1801, Chinard, *Trois Amitiés*, pp. 202-204.

17. Thiéry, I, 140-141. Mercier, t. II, Chap. 193. Prince de Ligne, *Coup d'oeil sur Beloeil et sur une grande partie des Jardins de l'Europe* (ed. Ganay, 1922), p. 176. Abbé J. Delille, *Les Jardins, ou l'art d'embellir les paysages* (Reims, 1785, 6th ed.), Chant I, pp. 14, 103. *Re* gardens in general: Ernest de Ganay, *Les Jardins de France et leur décor* (Paris, 1949).

18. Plans for development of grounds at Monticello, Account Book 1771, in E. M. Betts, ed., *Jefferson's Garden Book* (Philadelphia, 1944), pp. 25-27.

19. Boutin [Simon-Charles Boutin (1720-1794)] to TJ, 14 Sept. 1787, *Papers* 12: 120.

20. Mercier, *Nouveau Paris*, Chap. 167 (1862 ed.), II, 152-156).

21. *Journal de Madame Cradock: Voyage en France, 1783-1786*, trans. Balleyguier (Paris, 1896), pp. 35-36. Claude Ruggieri, *Précis historique sur les Fêtes et Spectacles et les Réjouissance publiques* (Paris, 1830). Programs for spectacles in *Journal de Paris*. The firm of Ruggieri is still in existence.

22. Watin, *Etat* (1787) places Malesherbes's "cabinet d'histoire naturelle" at No. 17 Rue des Martyrs. Watin (1788) lists Malesherbes at No. 10 Rue des Martyrs. *Almanach Royal* (1789): "Rue des Martyrs, Barrière Montmartre." Cité Malesherbes, off present No. 59 Rue des Martyrs, is presumably on site of former Malesherbes estate.

23. TJ to James Madison, 20 June 1787; TJ to John Jay, 21 June 1787; *Papers* 11: 482, 490. Malesherbes to TJ, 6 May 1786, *Papers* 9: 452-453, and Index, *s.v.* Malesherbes, for other evidence of the cordial relationship.

24. Boissy d'Anglas to TJ, 2 April 1820, MS draft, Andre deCoppet Collection, Princeton Univ. Library.

25. Chinard, *Trois Amitiés*, pp. 14-61. Watin, *Etat* (1788), under No. 38 Rue Rochechouart, lists "M. le marquis de Brehan, & Dlle . . . , son épouse; M. le comte Louis de Brehan; M. le comte de Moustier, ministre plénipotentiaire près les Etats Unis d'Amérique." Same edition of Watin also lists "M. le comte de Brehan" at No. 16 Rue Cadet and "M. le comte de Moustier" at No. 27 Rue Cadet. The Rue Rochechouart was, as now, a prolongation of Rue Cadet.

26. Thiéry, I, 534-540.

27. Account Book: 26 April, 9 Oct. 1785, 20 Jan. 1786. Programs in *Journal de Paris*.

28. TJ to Mrs. Adams, 27 Dec. 1785, *Papers* 9: 126.

29. TJ to Mrs. Cosway, 13 Oct. 1786, *Papers* 10: 458-459.

30. Thiéry, I, 182-185, Pl. 4.

31. Max Aghion, *Le Théâtre à Paris au XVIIIe siècle*, pp. 161-187.

32. TJ to William Short, Aix, 29 March 1787, *Papers* 11: 253-255. H. & A. Le Roux, *La Dugazon* (Paris, 1926). *Songs and Duets by Mrs. Cosway* (*ca.* 1786), a copy of which she sent to Jefferson, contains an Italian paraphrase of Mme Dugazon's famous song: "Mais je regarde . . . hélas! . . . hélas! / Le bien-aimé ne revient pas!" Bullock, *Little History*, p. 51.

33. TJ to Mrs. Cosway, 12 Oct. 1786, *Papers* 10: at p. 452.

34. J. Q. Adams, *Memoirs*, ed. Charles Francis Adams (Philadelphia, 1874-1877), VIII, 246-247.

35. Henry Adams to Elizabeth Cameron, Paris, 29 Dec. 1891, *Letters of Henry Adams, 1858-1891*, ed. W. C. Ford (Boston, 1930), pp. 533-534.

36. Thiéry, I, 148. *Journal de Madame Cradock*, pp. 72-73, entry for 10 Aug. 1784. Henri Clouzot, *Le Papier peint en France du XVIIe au XIXe siècle* (Paris, 1931), pp. 16-17, Pl. XVI.

37. Account Book: 2 Feb., 1 July 1786, 17 Feb. 1787. TJ to Short, with instructions for procuring household goods, *Papers* 16: 318ff. Jefferson's desiderata in wall paper are described in detail at p. 322. Short's reply, *ibid.*, 501. Arthur & Robert's receipted invoice, 29 July 1790, *Papers* 18: 34n. Marie Kimball, *The Furnishings of Monticello*, p. 21.

CHAPTER 5: *New Quarters: Faubourg du Roule*

1. TJ to the Rev. William Smith, 19 Feb. 1791, *Papers* 19: 112-114.

2. TJ to Abigail Adams, 4 Sept. 1785, *Papers* 8: 472-473.

3. Thiéry, I, 42. Following Jansen's death the estate passed to the Comtesse de Marbeuf. H. Bonnardot, *Monographie du 8ᵉ arrondissement* (Paris, 1880), pp. 127-128 *s.v.* Rue Lincoln. *Papers* 10: 332n. Plan in Lerouge, *Jardins Anglo-Chinois*, Cahier 6, Pl. 24.

4. Text of lease is in *Papers* 8: 485-492, with private agreement of same date and modifications of both documents dated 30 March 1789. The latter reduced the annual rent to 3,000 *livres* (real rent, 6,000 *livres*). Termination of the lease is discussed in Short to TJ, Paris, 29 June 1790, *Papers* 16: 582-585, and TJ to Short, Monticello, 30 Sept. 1790, *Papers* 17: 543-546.

5. René Dupuis, "Le Pavillon de Langeac à la Grille de Chaillot," *Bulletin Soc. historique et archéologique des VIIIᵉ et XVIIᵉ arrondissements de Paris*, new series, No. 10 (1933), 159-170. H. C. Rice, Jr., *L'Hôtel de Langeac: Jefferson's Paris Residence, 1785-1789* (Paris and Monticello, 1947), which reproduces additional drawings not included in the present work.

6. TJ to Langeac, 12 Oct. 1786, *Papers* 10: 455-456; TJ to Coulon, 30 Aug. 1788, *Papers* 13: 548-549; TJ to Langeac, 15 Feb. 1789, *Papers* 14: 556-557.

7. Thiéry, I, 54. *Neo-Classicism*, No. 487, *s.v.* Berthélemy. *French Painting 1774-1830*, No. 2, *s.v.* Berthélemy. Another ceiling painted by Berthélemy for a Chalgrin-designed building can be seen above the main stairway in the Hôtel de La Vrillière at 2, Rue Saint-Florentin (branch offices of the United States Embassy).

8. TJ to Madison, 25 May 1788, *Papers* 13: 201-203.

9. Thiéry, I, 44-45, 47-51. TJ to the Rev. James Madison, 2 Oct. 1785, *Papers* 8: 574-575 and note. Beaumarchais wrote the prospectus for this enterprise and was later involved in a controversy with Mirabeau concerning its financial management.

10. TJ to Short, 21 May 1787, *Papers* 11: at p. 373; TJ to Col. Nicholas Lewis, 17 Sept. 1787, *Papers* 12: 134-136; TJ to Lewis, 11 July 1788, *Papers* 13: at p. 343.

11. TJ to Baron Geismar, 13 July 1788, *Papers* 13: 356-357.

12. Gaston Galtier, *La Viticulture . . . d'après les Notes de Voyage de Thomas Jefferson* (Montpellier, Editions "La Journée Vinicole," 1953). Account Book. *Papers*: Index, *s.v.* Bondfield, Lambert, Lur-Saluce, Parent, Rochegude, vineyards, wine.

13 TJ, *Autobiography*, p. 90.

14. *Papers* 10: at p. 453. Sowerby, No. 219, citing Fulwar Skipwith to TJ, 15 Jan. 1805, *re* "poor old Latude."

15. Maria Cosway to TJ, ca. 1 Dec. 1787, *Papers* 12: 387.

16. Account Book: 9 June 1786.

17. Thiéry, I, 54-55. Edward Carrington to TJ, 14 May, 17 May 1788; TJ to Crèvecoeur, 9 Aug. 1788; *Papers* 13: 156-157n, 172, 485-487.

18. Trumbull, *Autobiography*, pp. 92-93, 146-147, 152 and n. 290, citing Trumbull to his brother Jonathan, Paris, 6 Feb. 1788. TJ to Trumbull, 13 Nov. 1787; Trumbull to TJ, 7 Dec. 1787; Trumbull to TJ, 22 Feb. 1788; *Papers* 12: 358, 405-406, 622. Trumbull's "first idea" for his "Declaration" with TJ's floor plan of Independence Hall on same sheet, dated by Trumbull Sept. 1786, repr. *Papers* 10: xxvii-xxviii. Trumbull's sketch and notes on French officers' uniforms, repr. *Papers* 12: xxxv.

19. Bush, *Life Portraits*, pp. 17-19. Theodore Sizer, *Works of Col. John Trumbull* (New Haven, 1967, rev. ed.), pp. 45-46, Figs. 119, 157, 160, 161. The three miniatures are described and reproduced in *Papers* 10: xxix-xxx; *Papers* 14: xxxv-xxxviii. E. P. Richardson, "A Life Drawing of Jefferson by John Trumbull," *American Art Journal*, Nov. 1975, pp. 4-9, attributes to Trumbull the pencil portrait that came to the Maryland Historical Society with papers of Benjamin H. Latrobe (cf. Bush, No. 11) and believes that it was drawn in Paris.

20. Thiéry, I, 73-74. Gallet (72), p. 142, *s.v.* Bélanger.

21. Thiéry, I, 75-77, Pl. 1. Gallet (72), p. 149, *s.v.* Chalgrin.

22. Fiske Kimball, "A Church Designed by Jefferson," *Architectural Record*, 53 (Feb. 1923), pp. 184-186. F. D. Nichols, *TJ's Architectural Drawings* (Boston and Charlottesville, 1961, rev. 3rd ed.), p. 9.

23. Thiéry, I, 58-60.

24. *Ibid.*, 62-64. Gallet (72), p. 163, *s.v.* Girardin. A. Masson, *Un Mécène bordelais: Nicolas Beaujon* (Bordeaux, 1937).

25. TJ to Démeunier, 29 April 1795, *Selected Writings of TJ*, A. Koch and W. Peden, eds. (New York, Modern Library, 1944), pp. 533-534.

26. Mariette, *Description des travaux qui ont précédé, accompagné et suivi la fonte en bronze . . . de la statue equestre de Louis XV* (Paris, 1768) includes plates showing grounds and buildings of the City Foundry. Maurice Dumolin, "La Maladerie et le Fief du Roule," *Bulletin Soc. Hist. de Paris*, 57 (1930), pp. 74-76.

27. Houdon to Bachelier, 11 Oct. 1794, in Giacometti, *Houdon* (1919), I, 160-164.

28. *Journal de Paris*, 24 Sept. 1788. Paul Vitry, "Notes sur les différents logements et ateliers occupés par J.-A. Houdon," *Archives de l'Art français*, I (1907), 217-220.

29. The fullest record of TJ's relations with Houdon is in *Papers* (cf. Index). Gilbert Chinard, *Houdon in America* (Baltimore, 1930). On Houdon in general: works by Charles H. Hart and E. Biddle, Georges Gia-

cometti, Louis Réau; H. H. Arnason's *Sculpture by Houdon* (Worcester, Mass., Art Museum exhibition catalogue, 1964) and his *The Sculptures of Houdon* (New York, 1975).

30. TJ to William Temple Franklin, 7 May 1786, *Papers* 9: 466-467.

31. Account Book: 6 May 1785, 14 July 1785, 22 Dec. 1787. Undated memorandum (LC) in Chinard, *Houdon*, p. 37.

32. Trumbull, *Autobiography*, p. 99, 6 Aug. 1786.

33. TJ to Joseph Hopkinson, 23 June 1792; Hopkinson to TJ, 29 June 1792; TJ to Hopkinson, 11 July 1792; Mass. Hist. Soc. The present whereabouts of this small plaster Diana, if it has survived, is not known to the author. The Diana is not specifically mentioned in Grevin's 1790 packing list, but a reference to a plaster vestal virgin (Crate 42) suggests that TJ may also have acquired a small version of Houdon's Vestal. *Papers* 18: 36n. Arnason (1975), pp. 11-13.

34. *Procès-Verbaux des 15 & 28 Septembre 1786, relatifs à la reception du buste de M. le marquis de La Fayette, à l'Hôtel-de-Ville de Paris* (Philadelphia [Paris], M. Carey, 1786), reprinted with appendix and notes by Gilbert Chinard (Institut Français de Washington, 1955). *Papers* 10: 407-410, 414-416.

35. William Short to William Nelson, 25 Oct. 1786, cited in *Papers* 10: 416n.

36. M. Tourneux, ed., *Procès-Verbaux de la Commune de Paris, 10 août 1792–1er juin 1793* (Paris, 1894), p. 6.

37. *Papers* 15: xxxvi-xxxvii. Bush, *Life Portraits*, pp. 23-26. Max Terrier, "Le Buste de Thomas Jefferson par Houdon," in *Jefferson* (brochure, Amis du Musée de Blérancourt, 1965), pp. 6-8. Extant examples of the Jefferson bust (excluding modern casts) include one in marble (Boston Museum of Fine Arts) and four in plaster (American Philosophical Society, New-York Historical Society, Musée de Blérancourt [our Fig. 84], private collection).

38. A variant version of the Boilly painting reproduced here as our Fig. 85 (Musée de Cherbourg), showing Houdon modeling the head of Laplace, is in the Musée des Arts Décoratifs, Paris. *Neo-Classicism*, Nos. 35, 36. Arnason (1975), Figs. 205, 206.

CHAPTER 6: *Left Bank*

1. Account Book: 10 Aug., 17 Oct. 1784 (payment to "Mad^me Mayan"). Watin (1788) places the Hôtel d'Orléans, "garni," at what was then No. 34 Rue des Petits Augustins. This would have been on eastern side of present Rue Bonaparte between corner of present Rue Jacob (formerly Rue du Colombier) and Rue Visconti (formerly Rue des Marais). The latter street bounded the grounds of the Hôtel de La Rochefoucauld. The Hôtel d'Orléans was much frequented by English and Americans. John Jay was living there in

the autumn of 1782 (cf. John Adams, *Diary* 3: 37-38, 53, 79). George Craufurd, the English envoy, resided there in 1784 (cf. *Papers* 8: 363n.).

2. Chastellux, *Travels in North America*, ed. H. C. Rice, Jr. (Chapel Hill, 1963), I, 17, n. 67. The site is between Rue du Bac and Gare d'Orsay, now occupied by Caisse d'Amortissement et des Dépôts et Consignations.

3. Chastellux to TJ, 24 Aug. 1784, *Papers* 7: 410-411.

4. TJ to Chastellux, 2 Sept. 1785, *Papers* 8: 467-470. Chastellux's description of Jefferson at Monticello is in *Travels*, II, 389-396.

5. TJ to Mme Chastellux, 10 July 1796, cited in Chastellux, *Travels*, II, 577-578, n. 17.

6. Thiéry, II, 590-591. H. Thirion, *Le Palais de la Légion d'Honneur, ancien Hôtel de Salm* (Versailles, 1883). Gallet (72), p. 75, Pl. 153-157. *Neo-Classicism*, No. 1303. Claude Ducourtial-Rey, *La Légion d'Honneur: Palais et Musée* (Paris, museum brochure, ca. 1970).

7. TJ to L'Enfant, 10 April 1791, above, Chap. 3, n. 8.

8. *La Fayette* (exhibition catalogue, Archives Nationales, 1957), Nos. 548-552. Photo. of the still extant adjoining house, known as l'Hôtel Turgot, is in René Huyghe, *Hommage à Frits Lugt* (Paris, Institut Néerlandais, 1971). Yvon Bizardel, "French Estates, American Landlords," *Apollo*, CI, No. 156 (Feb. 1975), 113.

9. Lafayette to TJ, Hartford, Conn., 11 Oct. 1784, *Papers* 7: 438-439. *Re* Lafayette's Indians: L. Gottschalk, *Lafayette between the American and the French Revolution (1783-1789)* (Chicago, 1950), pp. 433-434; *Papers* 9: 262n.

10. Lafayette to his wife, 1784, cited in André Maurois, *Adrienne, ou la Vie de Mme de La Fayette* (Paris, 1960), p. 154.

11. G. Mareschal de Bièvre, *L'Hôtel de Villeroy et le Ministère de l'Agriculture* (Paris, ca. 1924). Gallet (72), p. 154 *s.v.* Debias-Aubry, p. 173 *s.v.* Le Roux. This Rue de Varenne *hôtel* is not to be confused with the Hôtel de Tessé, No. 1 Quai Voltaire, built for the mother-in-law of TJ's Comtesse de Tessé and from which paneling is now installed in the Metropolitan Museum of Art.

12. Chinard, *Trois Amitiés*, pp. 66-143.

13. Martha Jefferson to Eliza House Trist [after 24 Aug. 1785], *Papers* 8: 436-439.

14. Thiéry, II, 568-569. François Rousseau, "Histoire de l'Abbaye de Pentemont," *Mémoires Soc. Hist. de Paris*, 45 (1918), pp. 171-227. Marcel Fosseyeux, "Une Abbesse de Panthemont au XVIIIe siècle: Madame de Béthisy-Mézières," *Revue du Dix-huitième siècle*, v (1918), 1-16.

15. Martha Jefferson to TJ, 25 March 1787, *Papers* 11: 238-239. Letters of Jefferson to and from his daughters are grouped in E. M. Betts and James A. Bear, Jr., eds., *The Family Letters of Thomas Jefferson* (Columbia, Missouri, 1966).

16. Martha J. to TJ, 3 May 1787, *Papers* 11: 333-334.

17. Maurice Dumolin, "Notes topographiques sur le Couvent de Pentemont," *Bulletin Soc. d'Hist. et d'Archéologie des VIIᵉ et XVᵉ arrondissements de Paris*, No. 29 (Aug. 1926), pp. 72-95. R.-A. Weigert, "Un Centenaire: le Temple de Pentemont, 1846-1946," *Bulletin Soc. d'Hist. du Protestantisme français*, Jan.-March 1947, pp. 13-32.

18. Martha J. to Mrs. Trist, *Papers* 8: 436-439.

19. Martha J. to TJ, 27 May 1787, *Papers* 11: 380-381.

20. TJ to Martha J., 28 June 1787, *Papers* 11: 503.

21. Martha J. to TJ, 9 April 1787, *Papers* 11: 281-282.

22. TJ to Mary Jefferson Bolling, 23 July 1787, *Papers* 11: 612-613.

23. J.-A. Tronchin, dispatch of 10 March 1788, Archives de l'Etat de Genève; *Papers* 14: xli.

24. *Journal and Correspondence of Miss Adams*, ed. De Windt (New York and London, 1841-1842), I, 23-27, entry for 14 Oct. 1784: "Mr. Jefferson sent us cards yesterday to admit us to see the ceremony of taking the veil in the convent where his daughter is to receive her education."

25. Sowerby, No. 1540.

26. *Papers* 14: 356n-357n.

27. Thiéry, II, 376-391, 692, Pl. 4. Gallet (72), p. 157 *s.v.* De Wailly, p. 181 *s.v.* Peyre the Elder. Gallet, "Un Projet de Charles de Wailly pour la Comédie Française," *Bull. Musée Carnavalet*, 18, No. 1 (June 1965), 3-13. *Louis XV* (exh. cat., 1974), No. 26.

28. Account Book. *Journal de Paris*.

29. TJ to Jay, 6 Aug. 1787, *Papers* 11: 698-699, and Index for other references to Beaumarchais.

30. Sowerby, Nos. 4592, 4594, 4923.

31. Thiéry, II, 473-482. Mercier, t. IX, Chap. 735. *Almanach des Monnoies* (Paris, 1784ff). Fernand Mazerolles, *L'Hôtel des Monnaies* (Paris, 1907). Gallet (72), p. 139 *s.v.* Antoine. Pérouse de Montclos, *Boullée* (1969), pp. 58-60, Pl. 16-22. *Louis XV* (exh. cat., Hôtel de la Monnaie, 1974), Nos. 30-43.

32. *Papers* 7: 150ff, at p. 186 (4).

33. *Papers* 16: 602ff.

34. TJ to Jay, 9 Jan. 1787, 1 Feb. 1787 (with enclosure, Droz to Grand, 16 Jan. 1787), *Papers* 11: 29-33, 99-103.

35. TJ to Ferdinand Grand, 23 April 1790, *Papers* 16: 368-369, and Index, *s.v.* Droz, for subsequent correspondence. Don Taxay, *The U.S. Mint and Coinage* (New York, 1966).

36. "Notes on American Medals Struck in France," *Papers* 16: xxxv-xli, 53-59.

37. TJ to William Short, 30 April 1790, *Papers* 16: 395-396. TJ to Moustier, 2 March 1791; TJ to Short, 8 March 1791; *Papers* 19: 357, 424-426. Only two copies in gold and eight in copper were struck from original die; cf. note to our Fig. 106, p. 145.

38. Thiéry, I, 378-379. Account Book: 8 March 1785, "Pd at Cabinet of Medals, 6 f." Mazerolles, *L'Hôtel des Monnaies*, pp. 35-45.

39. Antoine Guillois, *La Marquise de Condorcet: Sa famille, son salon, ses amis, 1764-1822* (Paris, 1897).

40. *Papers* 10: 452 (in Head and Heart Dialogue).

41. Sowerby, Nos. 2467, 2468, and Index, *s.v.* Condorcet.

42. "Jefferson's Notes from Condorcet on Slavery," *Papers* 14: 494-498. *Papers* 15: Editorial Note, 386-387.

43. Condorcet to TJ, 12 Sept. 1789, *Papers* 15: 419.

44. Philip Mazzei's Memoranda Regarding Persons and Affairs in Paris, ca. July 1784, *Papers* 7: 386-391.

45. Emile Rousse, *La Roche-Guyon: Châtelains, Château et Bourg* (Paris, 1892), pp. 294ff and genealogical chart, p. 490.

46. Abigail Adams to E. Cranch, 10 May 1785, *Letters of Mrs. Adams*, ed. Charles Francis Adams (Boston, 1848, 4th ed.), pp. 249-251. John Adams, *Diary* 4: 66-67.

47. TJ to Duchesse d'Enville, 2 April 1790, *Papers* 16: 290-291. When forwarding her reply to TJ (27 July 1790, *Papers* 17: 286-287) William Short noted that it was sealed only with a wafer "because she complies with the decree in not making use of her arms."

48. Morris, *Diary*, I, 220-221. L. Gottschalk and M. Maddox, *Lafayette in the French Revolution: Through the October Days* (Chicago, 1969), pp. 291-292.

49. TJ to Duc de La Rochefoucauld, 3 April 1790, *Papers* 16: 296-297.

50. "Testament . . . Mars 1794, écrit sur la feuille de garde de l'histoire d'Espagne," *Oeuvres de Condorcet*, ed. A. Condorcet O'Connor and M. F. Arago (Paris, 1847-1849), I, 624-625.

51. Lafayette to TJ, 14 Aug. 1814, in Chinard, ed.,

Letters of Lafayette and Jefferson (Baltimore, 1929), pp. 340-347.

52. Yvon Bizardel and H. C. Rice, Jr., " 'Poor in Love Mr. Short,' " *William & Mary Quarterly*, 3rd series, XXI, No. 4 (Oct. 1964), 516-533.

53. Short to TJ, 21 Oct. 1819, *The Jefferson Papers*, Mass. Hist. Soc. Collections, 7th series, I (Boston, 1900), 288-289.

54. TJ to Short, 31 Oct. 1819, *Selected Writings of TJ*, A. Koch and W. Peden, eds. (New York, Modern Library, 1944), at p. 696.

CHAPTER 7: *Quartier Latin and Jardin du Roi*

1. TJ to Samuel H. Smith, 21 Sept. 1814, cited in *Papers* 18: 35n; MS in L.C.

2. TJ to James Madison, 25 May 1784, *Papers* 7: at p. 288.

3. Account Book. Sowerby, No. 4889. George B. Watts, "Thomas Jefferson, the 'Encyclopédie' and the 'Encyclopédie méthodique,' " *French Review*, XXXVIII, No. 3 (Jan. 1965), 318-325. Royez to TJ, 25 Aug. 1789, *Papers* 15: 356. TJ to Short, 24 Jan. 1791, *Papers* 18: 600-603.

4. H. C. Rice, Jr., "Thomas Jefferson à Strasbourg (1788)," *Cahiers alsaciens d'archéologie, d'art, et d'histoire* (1958), 137-144, Fig. 5 (Koenig's bookshop).

5. TJ to George Ticknor, 19 March 1815, cited in *Papers* 13: 204n.

6. TJ to Francis Hopkinson, 6 July 1788, *Papers* 13: 309. Hopkinson to TJ, 23 Oct. 1788; Franklin to TJ, 24 Oct. 1788; *Papers* 14: 32-33, 36.

7. TJ to C. W. F. Dumas, 9 June 1788, *Papers* 13: 246-247. A 4-page Prospectus (in French) and incomplete file (Nos. 7-16, Feb.-April 1788), "published by Pissot Bookseller, Quai des Augustins N⁰ 21" and "printed for Pissot, by Clousier, Printer to His Majesty, rue de Sorbonne," are in the Bib. Nat., 4⁰ Nd. 54. Complete title: *The General Advertiser, for Great Britain, Ireland and the United States of America*. Not to be confused with a London periodical of similar title or with B. F. Bache's *General Advertiser*, which began publication in Philadelphia in Oct. 1790. TJ Account Book: 1 Jan. 1789, "pd. subscription to Pissot's paper for coming year 48#." Not in Sowerby.

8. TJ to Francis Hopkinson, 1 Aug. 1787, *Papers* 11: at p. 657.

9. TJ to James Monroe, 26 May 1795, cited in Sowerby, V, p. 189; MS in Monroe Papers, L.C.

10. TJ to Thomas Payne (London bookseller), 2 Oct. 1788, *Papers* 13: 650-652.

11. TJ to Lucy Ludwell Paradise, 1 June 1789, *Papers* 15: 162-163.

12. Correspondence *re* Ramsay's history is brought together in Sowerby, Nos. 488-489.

13. Account Book: 20 Sept. 1788. TJ to La Vingtrie, 12 Feb. 1788, *Papers* 12: 586-587n. TJ to Gallimard, 29 July 1788, *Papers* 13: 430-431n. Sowerby, No. 2567.

14. Froullé to TJ, 17 Feb. 1787; TJ to John Adams, 23 Feb., 23 July, 1787; *Papers* 11: 163, 177, 610-611. John Adams to TJ, 25 Aug. 1787, *Papers* 12: 56.

15. Coolie Verner, "Mr. Jefferson Makes a Map," *Imago Mundi*, XIV (1959), 96-108.

16. TJ to Barrois, 22 June 1787; TJ to Morellet, 2 July 1787; *Papers* 11: 500, 529-531. J. M. Carrière, "The Manuscript of Jefferson's Unpublished Errata List for Abbé Morellet's Translation of the *Notes on Virginia*," in *Papers Bibliographical Soc. Univ. Virginia*, I (1948-1949), 3-24.

17. Maille's printed price-list, repr. *Papers* 14: xxxv.

18. Sowerby, No. 4167. Coolie Verner, "Mr. Jefferson Distributes His Notes," New York Public Library *Bulletin*, April 1952.

19. The three separate items were: (1) *Draught of a Fundamental Constitution for the Commonwealth of Virginia*, 14 pp., 1785 (*Papers* 6: 305n-306n); (2) *Notes on the Establishment of a Money Unit, and of Coinage for the United States*, 14 pp., 1785 (*Papers* 7: 186n, TJ to Charles Thomson, 14 July 1785, *Papers* 8: 295); (3) *An Act for Establishing Religious Freedom, passed in the Assembly of Virginia in the beginning of the year 1786*, 4 pp., 1786. For other printings of the *Act*, see *Papers* 2: 550n-552n. "The Virginia act for religious freedom has been received with infinite approbation in Europe and propagated with enthusiasm. I do not mean by the governments, but by the individuals which compose them"; TJ to Madison, 16 Dec. 1786, *Papers* 10: 603-604.

20. Account Book: 1 Aug. 1785. Passports issued by TJ, 1785-1789, *Papers* 15: 483-487. Example of passport (issued to John Lamb, 5 Nov. 1785), *Papers* 8: xxix; another example (William Langborn, 15 June 1786), Princeton Univ. Library, Rush Papers. TJ to Pierres, 12 Jan. 1787; Pierres to TJ, 15 Jan. 1787; *Papers* 11: 38-39, 45. P.-D. Pierres, *Description d'une nouvelle presse d'imprimerie* (Paris: Imprimé chez l'Auteur, par sa nouvelle presse, 1786).

21. "The Consular Convention of 1788," *Papers* 14: 66ff, with repr. of the first page of Clousier's printing, facing p. 72.

22. "Documents Concerning the Whale Fishery," *Papers* 14: 217ff.

23. Account Book: 9 Nov. 1788 (Corneillon), 17 Oct. 1788 (Crepy). Blank specimens of Crepy's ruled paper are preserved at Monticello; Bear, *Curator's Report 1962*, p. 17.

24. Thiéry, I, 719-723. A. G. Camus, *Histoire et procédés du polytypage et de la stéréotypie* (Paris,

Baudoin, An X-1801), pp. 43-45. "Polytype and Other Methods of Printing," *Papers* 10: 318ff.

25. TJ to James Madison, 8 Feb. 1786, *Papers* 9: at p. 267.

26. Hoffman's estimate, *Papers* 10: 325.

27. Entry in Hoffman's record book communicated to author by André Jammes in 1958. Hoffman's journal-books for 1785-1786 have subsequently been acquired by the Newberry Library, Chicago; cf. exhibition catalogue, *The Scholar Printers* (1964), p. 55, No. 60.

28. Ed. note, Calonne to TJ, Fontainebleau, 22 Oct. 1786, *Papers* 10: 474-478.

29. TJ to Pierre Samuel Dupont, ca. 5 Nov. 1787; Dupont to TJ, 5 Nov. 1787; *Papers* 12: 325-327. "De Nemours" was later added to the name to distinguish it from another Dupont, also a member of the National Assembly.

30. TJ to Ezra Stiles, 1 Sept. 1786, *Papers* 10: 316-318.

31. *Papers* 10: 325. Another specimen of a manuscript duplicated by Hoffman—Lafayette's "Résumé de mon avis au Comité du Commerce"—is reproduced, *Papers* 9: facing p. 386, and discussed, 344n-345n.

32. Thiéry, II, 172-184. Muséum National d'Histoire Naturelle, *Exposition du Troisième Centenaire*, catalogue ed. Léon Bultingaire (Paris, 1935). Yves François, "Buffon au Jardin du Roi (1739-1788)," in *Buffon* (Muséum, series "Les Grands Naturalistes Français," 1952), pp. 105-124.

33. Jefferson, *Notes on the State of Virginia*, introduction and notes by William Peden (Chapel Hill, 1955).

34. TJ to Chastellux, 7 June 1785, *Papers* 8: 184-186.

35. Buffon to TJ, 31 Dec. 1785, *Papers*, 9: 130-131.

36. Buffon to TJ, 27 March 1787, *Papers* 15: 635.

37. Notes of Mr. Jefferson's Conversation at Monticello, 1824, Charles M. Wiltse and Harold D. Moser, eds., *Papers of Daniel Webster* (Hanover., N.H., University Press of New England for Dartmouth College, 1974——), Correspondence I, 370-378.

38. TJ to Francis Hopkinson, 3 Jan. 1786, *Papers* 9: 148-149.

39. TJ to Rev. James Madison, 19 July 1788, *Papers* 13: 379-383.

40. Anna Clark Jones, "Antlers for Jefferson," *New England Quarterly*, XII, No. 2 (June 1939), 333-348. *Papers*, vols. 7-13: see Index, *s.v.* moose.

41. Daubenton to TJ, 2 Oct. 1787; Lacépède to TJ, 25 Oct. 1787; *Papers* 12: 197, 287-288.

42. Sowerby, No. 640, with correspondence of Faujas de Saint-Fond and TJ.

43. Sowerby, No. 1050, with correspondence of Lacépède and TJ.

44. H. C. Rice, Jr., "Jefferson's Gift of Fossils to the Museum of Natural History in Paris," American Philosophical Society, *Proceedings*, 95, No. 6 (Dec. 1951), 597-627.

45. TJ to Ezra Stiles, 10 June 1784, *Papers* 7: 304-305. *Notes on Virginia*, ed. Peden, p. 45.

46. "Memorandum on a Tour from Paris to Amsterdam, Strasbourg and back to Paris," entry for 19 April 1788, *Papers* 13: 27. Preliminary sketch of moldboard, *Papers* 13: xxv-xxvi, repro. facing p. 16. Thomas Mann Randolph, Jr., to TJ, 23 April 1790, *Papers* 16: 370-371n. *Thomas Jefferson's Farm Book*, ed. E. M. Betts, (Princeton, 1953), pp. 47-64.

47. Société Centrale d'Agriculture du Dépt. de la Seine, *Mémoires d'Agriculture, d'Economie rurale et domestique*, VII (An XIII-1805), Séance, 8 Floréal (28 April 1805).

48. A. Guillaumin and V. Chaudun, "La Collection de modèles réduits d'instruments agricoles et horticoles du Muséum," Muséum National d'Histoire Naturelle, *Bulletin*, 2nd series, XVI, No. 2 (March-April 1944), 137-141. Block at right in our Fig. 126 has inscription in Thouin's handwriting: "Bloc de bois propre à fournir une oreille de charrue taillée d'après les principes de M. Thomas Jefferson, président des Etats unis d'Amérique. Envoyé par l'auteur en 1801, au Prof. Thouin." Other models and drawings of the Jefferson moldboard are preserved in the Conservatoire National des Arts et Métiers.

49. André Thouin, *Cours de culture et de naturalisation des végétaux*, publié par Oscar Leclerc, son neveu et son aide au Jardin du Roi, 3 vols. and 1 vol. of plates (Paris, 1827), I, 457-458, and Pl. 23, Fig. 9.

50. TJ to Bernard McMahon, 28 Dec. 1808, *Jefferson's Garden Book*, ed. Betts, pp. 383-384.

51. TJ to Martha Jefferson Randolph, 18 Oct. 1808, *Family Letters*, pp. 351-352.

52. Anne Randolph Bankhead to TJ, 26 Nov. 1808, *Family Letters*, pp. 365-366.

53. *Garden Book*, pp. 446, 480.

54. TJ to Dr. John P. Emmet, 27 April, 12 May 1826, *Garden Book*, pp. 619-620.

CHAPTER 8: *Road to Versailles*

1. Minutes of the Commissioners, cited in *Papers* 7: 420n.

2. "Dialogue between Franklin and the Gout," *Writings*, ed. Smythe, VIII, 154ff.

3. TJ to Rev. William Smith, 19 Feb. 1791, *Papers* 19: 112-114.

4. TJ to Le Veillard, 9 May 1786, *Papers* 9: 483-498. TJ to Le Veillard, 5 April 1790, *Papers* 16: 306.

5. Louis Batave, "Les Eaux de Passy au 18ᵉ siècle," *Revue du Dix-huitième siècle*, II (1914), 113-127. Commission municipale du Vieux Paris, *Procès-Verbaux*, Année 1920, pp. 183ff.

6. Trumbull, *Autobiography*, p. 116, diary entry for 13 Aug. 1786. *Papers* 8: 92n.

7. François Souchal, *Les Slodtz: sculpteurs et décorateurs du Roi (1685-1764)* (Paris, 1967), Chap. 2, "Diane et Endymion," pp. 189-194, 659-660 (No. 148), Pl. 14a-15a. Souchal, "Hommage aux Slodtz," *Connaissance des Arts*, No. 199 (Sept. 1968), pp. 64-69, with color repr. of "Diane et Endymion" at p. 69.

8. John Adams, *Diary* 2: 303; 4: 64.

9. *Ibid.*, 3: 171.

10. *Ibid.*, 3: 143-146.

11. H. C. Rice, Jr., *The Adams Family in Auteuil, as Told in the Letters of Abigail Adams, 1784-1785* (Boston, Mass. Hist. Soc., 1956).

12. Gilbert Chinard, *Volney et l'Amérique, d'après . . . sa correspondance avec Jefferson* (Baltimore and Paris, 1923); *Jefferson et les Idéologues* (Baltimore and Paris, 1925). Sowerby, *s.v.* Cabanis, Destutt de Tracy, Volney. Jean Gaulmier, *Volney: Un Grand témoin de la Révolution et de l'Empire* (Paris, 1959), includes extracts from Volney's journal of his visit to Monticello in June 1796.

13. TJ to Cabanis, 13 July 1803, Chinard, *Idéologues*, pp. 25-26. Sowerby, No. 1246. MS in L.C.

14. Adams, *Diary* 3: 145.

15. *Papers* 13: xxx-xxxi and ill. facing p. 481. TJ to Moustier, 9 Aug. 1788; TJ to Jay, 10 Aug. 1788; *Papers* 13: 491-492, 496-497. A. M. de La Vaissière and B. de Montgolfier, "Une Tasse de Sèvres commémorant l'Ambassade de Tipoo-Saïb," *Bulletin Musée Carnavalet*, 14ᵉ Année, No. 1 (June 1961), pp. 9-11. Marcelle Brunet, "Incidences de l'Ambassade de Tipoo-Saib (1788) sur la Porcelaine de Sèvres," *Cahiers de la Céramique*, No. 24 (1961), pp. 275-284.

16. Mme de Tessé to TJ, Chaville, 7 Aug. 1788, *Papers* 13: 476-477.

17. TJ to John Banister, Jr., 9 Aug. 1788, *Papers* 13: 483-485. Duncan Rose to TJ, Battersea near Petersburg, 26 Feb. 1789, *Papers* 14: 592-593.

18. TJ to Mme de Tessé, 25 April 1788, *Papers* 13: 108-109.

19. Vte de Grouchy, "Meudon, Bellevue et Chaville," Soc. de l'hist. de Paris et de l'Ile-de-France, *Mémoires*, XX (1893), 51-206. Abbé Dassé, *Chaville historique* (Chaville and Paris, 1897). Pérouse de Montclos, *Boullée* (Paris, 1969), pp. 82-86, Figs. 32-36.

20. *Papers* 10: 157n-160n.

21. TJ to Mme de Tessé, Nîmes, 20 March 1787, *Papers* 11: 226-228.

22. Mme de Tessé to TJ, 30 March 1787, *Papers* 11: 257-260.

23. Morris, *Diary*, I, 6, 113.

24. TJ to Mme de Tessé, 27 Aug. 1789; Mme de Tessé to TJ, 29 Aug. 1789; *Papers* 15: 363-364, 371. Bush, *Life Portraits*, pp. 27-29, Fig. 5. "The Comtesse de Tessé's parting gift to Jefferson in 1789," *Papers* 18: xxxiii-xxxiv.

25. TJ to Mme de Tessé, Alexandria, Va., 11 March 1790, *Papers* 16: 226-228.

26. Mme de Tessé to TJ, Reuchenette près Bienne, Switzerland, 6 July 1790, *Papers* 17: 8-9. Morris, *Diary*, II, 140, entry for 6 March 1791, noting message from Mme de Tessé via d'Agout.

27. Bib. Centr. du Muséum National d'Histoire Naturelle, MS 306: a dossier *re* the "Commission de la recherche des plantes dans les jardins de la liste civile et dans ceux des émigrés (1792-1793)," from papers of André Thouin.

28. TJ to Mme de Tessé, 8 Dec. 1813, Chinard, *Trois Amitiés*, pp. 136-143, where Aulnay (Seine-St.-Denis) is mis-transcribed "Avenay."

29. Thomas Lee Shippen to Dr. William Shippen, Jr., 14 Feb.–26 March 1788, excerpts in *Papers* 12: 502n-504n.

30. Charles Hirschauer, "Jean-Baptiste Berthier et la décoration de l'Hôtel de la Guerre et des Affaires Etrangères," *Revue de l'Histoire de Versailles et de Seine-et-Oise*, XXXII, No. 2 (April-June 1930), 137-157. René Pichard du Page, *La Bibliothèque de Versailles et le Musée Lambinet* (Paris, 1935).

31. TJ, *Autobiography*, pp. 90-91.

32. *Ibid.*, pp. 121-122.

33. TJ to J. Madison, 20 June 1787, *Papers* 11: 480-484. TJ to John Browne Cutting, 24 July, 23 Aug. 1788, *Papers* 13: 403-407, 538-539. TJ to John Jay, 9 May, 17 June 1789, *Papers* 15: 110-113, 187-193,

34. TJ, *Autobiography*, p. 140.

35. Gallet (72), p. 161 *s.v.* Gabriel, p. 176 *s.v.* Mique. *Neo-Classicism*, Nos. 1106-1107.

36. Morris, *Diary*, I, 78.

CHAPTER 9: *Road to Saint-Germain*

1. Thiéry, I, 13n. Gallet (72), pp. 102-103. David H. Pinkney, *Napoleon III and the Rebuilding of Paris* (Princeton, 1958), pp. 95-100.

2. TJ to Mme de Corny, 30 June 1787, *Papers* 11: 509-510.

3. TJ to Chastellux, [Oct. 1786], *Papers* 10: 498-499n.

4. Thiéry, I, 13-15. Cte. de Franqueville, *Le Château de la Muette* (Paris, 1917). *Louis XV* (exh. cat., 1974), Nos. 14-15.

5. Washington to TJ, 13 Feb. 1789, *Papers* 14: 546-549. TJ to William Bingham, 25 Sept. 1789, with Milne's memorandum enclosed, *Papers* 15: 476-477n. Morris, *Diary*, I, 9-10 (11 March 1789), 51 (24 April 1789). Ch. Ballot, *L'Introduction du machinisme dans l'industrie française* (Paris, 1923).

6. Thiéry, I, 33-39. E. de Ganay, *Les Jardins de France* (Paris, 1949), pp. 235-237. Gallet (72), p. 142 *s.v.* Bélanger, Figs. 172-173. Georges Pillement, *Les Hôtels d'Auteuil au Palais-Royal* (Paris, 1952), pp. 20-21, Pl. XII.

7. TJ to Anne Willing Bingham, 7 Feb. 1787, *Papers* 11: 122-124.

8. Account Book: 24 Aug. 1788. Thiéry, I, 25-30. E. de Ganay, *Châteaux et Manoirs de France: Ile-de-France*, V (Paris, 1939), pp. 5-9, Pl. 1-5. Gallet (72), p. 142 *s.v.* Bélanger, Figs. 174-175. *Neo-Classicism*, No. 999.

9. Thiéry, I, 25. Mercier, t. II, Chap. 122. J. Q. Adams, *Memoirs*, ed. C. F. Adams (Philadelphia, 1874-1877), I, 13 (diary for 25 March 1785 describing procession to Longchamp).

10. William Short to TJ, 26 March, 4 April, 6 April, 1787, *Papers* 11: 239-241, 267-270, 274-277.

11. Short to TJ, 14 March 1788, *Papers* 12: 667-668.

12. Thomas Lee Shippen to Dr. William Shippen, Jr., *Papers* 12: 504n. Richard Price to TJ, introducing Mr. Ashburnham, ca. March 1788, not April as in *Papers* 13: 119-120.

13. TJ to Mme de Corny, 18 Oct. 1787, *Papers* 12: 246-247.

14. Pontbriand, *Pèlerinage du Calvaire sur le Mont Valérien . . . avec des figures* (Paris, Babuty, 1779), TJ's copy, Sowerby, No. 1541. Mercier, t. VII, Chap. 561. Jacques Hérissay, *Le Mont-Valérien* (Paris, 1934). H. C. Rice, Jr., "Les Visites de Jefferson au Mont-Valérien," Soc. Hist. de Suresnes, *Bulletin*, III, No. 13 (1953-1954), 46-49. *Papers* 12: 199n.

15. Sarah N. Randolph, *The Domestic Life of TJ* (Charlottesville, Va., 1947, 3rd ed.), p. 48.

16. Fremyn de Fontenille to TJ, 23 Oct. 1787; TJ (in French) to Fremyn de Fontenille, 24 Oct. 1787; *Papers* 12: 258-259, 265.

17. Trumbull, *Autobiography*, pp. 98-99, diary entry for Sunday, 5 Aug. 1786. *Papers* 10: 251n-252n.

18. Jean-Rodolphe Perronet, *Description des projets et de la construction des Ponts de Neuilly, de Mantes, d'Orléans et autres* (Paris, Imprimerie Royale, 2 vols. and supplement, 1782-1789). Thiéry, I, 39. Dartein, "La Vie et les Travaux de Jean-Rodolphe Perronet, *Annales des Ponts et Chaussées, Mémoires et Documents*, 8th series, XXIV (1906), 5-87. *Neo-Classicism* pp. 989-990. TJ to Franklin, 23 Dec. 1786, erroneously reporting death of Perronet, who died only in 1794, *Papers* 10: 624. Franklin to TJ, 19 April 1787, *Papers* 11: 301-302. Models of the bridge (now on display in the Musée Carnavalet) could be seen at the Ecole des Ponts et Chaussées, then located in the Hôtel Bruant, Perronet's residence, Rue de la Perle, in the Marais. Thiéry, I, 586-589.

19. Morris, *Diary*, I, 83, entry for 19 May 1789.

20. Raval and Moreux, *Ledoux*, p. 52, Figs. 64-69. *Neo-Classicism*, Nos. 1203-1205.

21. J. and A. Marie, *Marly* (Paris, Editions TEL, 1947).

22. Conversation with Fiske Kimball at Marly, June 1947. Marie Kimball, *Jefferson: The Scene of Europe* (New York, 1950), pp. 165-166. F. D. Nichols, Introduction to 1968 reprint of Kimball's *TJ Architect*, p. ix.

23. TJ correspondence with Mary Barclay, e.g., Mrs. Barclay to TJ, 11 Nov. 1787, *Papers* 12: 343.

24. Yvon Bizardel and H. C. Rice, Jr., "'Poor in Love Mr. Short,'" *Wm. & Mary Quarterly*, 3rd series, XXI, No. 4 (Oct. 1964), 516-533.

25. TJ to Maria Cosway, 12 Oct. 1786, *Papers* 10: at pp. 445-446.

26. Thiéry, *Guide . . . aux Environs de Paris* (1788), t. II, 348. Mercier, t. X, Chap. 795. Prince de Ligne, *Coup d'oeil sur Beloeil* (ed. Ganay), pp. 222-223. L. H. Butterfield and H. C. Rice, Jr., "Jefferson's Earliest Note to Maria Cosway," 26-33. Osvald Sirén, *China and the Gardens of Europe of the Eighteenth Century* (New York, 1950). Colette, "Le Désert de Retz," *Paradis terrestre* (photos by Izis-Bidermanas, Lausanne, Guilde du Livre, 1953), pp. 59-81. Cyril Connolly and Jerome Zerbe, *Les Pavillons: French Pavilions of the Eighteenth Century* (New York, 1962), pp. 150-151. Gallet (72), pp. 35, 141 *s.v.* Barbier. Pérouse de Montclos, *Boullée*, pp. 73-77. *Neo-Classicism*, Nos. 996-997.

27. Emile Rousse, *La Roche-Guyon* (Paris, 1892), pp. 302-304. Ganay, *Les Jardins de France* (Paris, 1949), p. 153.

28. Mme La Rochefoucauld d'Enville to TJ, 19 Sept. 1789, *Papers* 15: 454.

29. Mme d'Enville's List of seeds, enclosed in Short to TJ, 14 June 1790, *Papers* 16: 503-504. Short to TJ, 3 Oct. 1790, *Papers* 17: 558-560.

30. So described in TJ to Mme de Tessé, 26 Oct. 1805, *Trois Amitiés*, pp. 129-132.

31. Mme d'Enville to TJ, 13 Feb. 1792, MS, L.C.

32. George Green Shackelford, "William Short: Diplomat in Revolutionary France, 1785-1793," Am. Phil. Soc., *Proceedings*, 102, No. 6 (Dec. 1958), 596-612. Yvon Bizardel, "Un Américain [William Short] à la découverte de l'Auvergne en 1801," *Revue de la Haute-Auvergne*, XXXVIII (Oct.-Dec. 1963), 425-437.

CHAPTER 10: *Adieu to Jefferson's Paris*

1. A. Adams to TJ, 6 June 1785, *Papers* 8: 178-181.

2. TJ to Jay, 11 Jan. 1789, *Papers* 14: at p. 429.

3. TJ to Mme de Bréhan, 14 March 1789, *Papers* 14: 655-656.

4. Account Book: 1, 6, 8, 13, Jan. 1789.

5. TJ to Maria Cosway, 14 Jan. 1789, *Papers* 14: 445-446.

6. Notes on Dr. Gem, *Papers* 15: 384n-387n.

7. TJ to Humphreys, 18 March 1789, *Papers* 14: at p. 676.

8. TJ to Thomas Lee Shippen, 11 March 1789, *Papers* 14: 638-640.

9. Gallet (72), p. 179 *s.v.* Pâris. *Neo-Classicism*, No. 1251. A.-Ch. Gruber, *Les Grandes Fêtes et leurs décors à l'époque de Louis XVI* (Geneva, 1972), pp. 144-148, Figs. 101-105.

10. TJ to William Carmichael, 8 May 1789, *Papers* 15: 103-105.

11. TJ to Trumbull, 18 June 1789, *Papers* 15: 199-200.

12. Filippo Mazzei, *Memoirs*, trans. H. R. Marraro (New York, 1942), p. 316. Mazzei's *Memorie* were first published in Italian at Lugano, 1845-1846.

13. TJ to Jay, 29 June 1789; to Trumbull, 29 June; *Papers* 15: at pp. 222, 224.

14. A Fourth of July Tribute to Jefferson, *Papers* 15: 239-241.

15. TJ to Montmorin, 8 July 1789, *Papers* 15: 260-261.

16. TJ, *Autobiography*, pp. 134-135.

17. *Re* cockades: John Browne Cutting to TJ, Bordeaux, 21 July 1789, *Papers* 15: at p. 293.

18. TJ, *Autobiography*, pp. 136-137.

19. TJ to Jay, 19 July 1789, *Papers* 15: at p. 290.

20. TJ to Dugald Stewart, 26 April 1824, cited in *Papers* 15: xxxiii-xxxiv.

21. TJ to Jay, 19 July 1789, *Papers* 15: at p. 289. TJ, *Autobiography*, p. 139.

22. TJ to Madison, 22 July 1789, *Papers* 15: 299-301.

23. TJ to Jay, 5 Aug. 1789, *Papers* 15: 333-334. TJ, *Autobiography*, p. 149.

24. TJ to Madison, 28 Aug. 1789, *Papers* 15: at p. 366.

25. Archbishop of Bordeaux to TJ, Versailles, 20 July 1789; TJ (in French) to Archbishop of Bordeaux, 22 July 1789; *Papers* 15: 291, 298.

26. Lafayette to TJ, 25 Aug. 1789, *Papers* 15: 354-355. Louis Gottschalk and Margaret Maddox, *Lafayette in the French Revolution: Through the October Days* (Chicago, 1969), pp. 227-229.

27. TJ, *Autobiography*, pp. 145-146.

28. TJ to Diodati, 3 Aug. 1789, *Papers* 15: 325-327. Count Diodati was minister plenipotentiary of the Duke of Mecklenburg-Schwerin at the Court of Versailles. At the time TJ's letter was written he was absent from Paris and residing temporarily in Geneva.

29. Yvan Christ, *Le Louvre et les Tuileries* (Paris, 1949). Fig. 114. *Neo-Classicism*, pp. 544-545, 976 *s.v.* J.-P. Gisors.

30. Jay to TJ, 19 June 1789, *Papers* 15: 202-203.

31. List of Baggage Shipped by Jefferson from France, ca. 1 Sept. 1789, *Papers* 15: 375-377.

32. Short to TJ, 7 July 1790, *Papers* 17: 10-14.

33. Short to TJ, 4 Aug. 1790, *Papers* 17: 315-318.

34. Short to TJ, 7 Nov. 1790 and ed. note summarizing Grevin's invoice, *Papers* 18: 30-39. Julian P. Boyd, "Jefferson's French Baggage, Crated and Uncrated," Mass. Hist. Soc., *Proceedings* (1971), Vol. 83, pp. 16-27. Grevin's address (cf. last page of his packing list) was Rue du Coq-St. Honoré (present Rue de Marengo) in a building owned by the Oratorian Fathers.

35. Petit to TJ, 3 Aug. 1790, *Papers* 17: 297-298. TJ to Petit, 25 Jan. 1791, *Papers* 19: 76-77. TJ to Martha Jefferson Randolph, *Family Letters*, p. 88.

36. Dumas Malone, *Jefferson and His Time*, II, 391-392; III, 167.

37. Jefferson's Policy concerning Presents to Foreign Diplomats, *Papers* 16: 356-368, at p. 366. TJ to Short, 24 Jan. 1791, *Papers* 18: 600-603. "Registre journal des présens faits au nom du Roi dans le département des Affaires étrangères depuis 1753 à 1791," Archives Min. Affaires Etrangères, Mémoires et Documents: France, Vol. 2095, at fol. 40. A. Maze-Sencier, *Le Livre des collectionneurs* (Paris, 1885), *re* Présents du Roi, boîtes à portrait, tabatières diplomatiques, etc.

38. Dossier *re* "gravure du Roi par Bervic, 1783–1791," Arch. Aff. Etr. *Re* Charles-Clément Bervic (1756–1822): Bib. Nat. Cab. Est., *Inventaire du Fonds français: Graveurs du 18ᵉ siècle*, A. Roux ed., ɪɪ, 466ff. Antoine-François Callet (1741–1823): *French Painting 1774–1830* (1974), No. 17.

39. TJ to Martha J. Randolph, 24 July 1791, *Family Letters*, p. 88.

40. Botidoux's journal-letter to Martha, Nov. 1789-May 1790, ᴍs, ViU. Bear, *Curator's Report, 1969*, pp. 14-15. *Papers* 16: at pp. 130, 135n, 273, 386, 388.

41. TJ to Lafayette, 14 Feb. 1815, G. Chinard, ed., *Letters of Lafayette and Jefferson*, pp. 367-373.

42. TJ to Short, 3 Jan. 1793, P. L. Ford, ed., *Writings of TJ*, vɪ, 153-157.

43. TJ to Lacépède, 24 Feb. 1803, cited in Sowerby, No. 1044.

44. TJ to James Monroe, 8 Jan. 1804, P. L. Ford, ed., *Writings of TJ*, x, 60-61.

45. TJ to Short, 28 Nov. 1814, ᴍs, L.C.

46. TJ to Lafayette, 14 Feb. 1815, above, n. 41.

47. TJ, *Autobiography*, pp. 148-149.

48. TJ to Maria Cosway, 21 May 1789, *Papers* 15: at p. 143.

49. C. M. Wiltse and H. D. Moser, eds., *Papers of Daniel Webster*, Correspondence ɪ, 370-380: Notes of Mr. Jefferson's Conversation at Monticello, 1824; Webster to Jeremiah Mason, 29 Dec. 1824.

50. Henry Adams, *History of the United States of America during the first Administration of Thomas Jefferson* (New York, 1889), ɪ, 143-146, in Chap. 5, "Intellect of the Southern States."

List of Illustrations

Frontispiece. Vue de la Cour du Louvre prise sous le Vestibule de la Colonnade. Engr. Née after Meunier. *Voyage pittoresque de la France*: Dépt. de Paris, No. 83. Boston Athenaeum.

Page v. Mme de Tessé's parting gift to Jefferson, 1789. Drawing, perhaps by Cornelia Jefferson Randolph, showing the "altar" which once stood in the entrance hall of Monticello, where, with inscription turned to the wall, it served as the base for Ceracchi's bust (1791) of Jefferson. Pedestal and bust were lost in Library of Congress fire, 1851. University of Virginia Library, Manuscripts Dept. Photo. Univ. Va. Graphic Communications Service.

1. *Plan de la Ville de Paris et de ses anciennes clôtures comparées avec celle faite sous le règne de Louis XVI, 1787.* Engr. P. F. Tardieu. Bib. Nat. Cartes, Ge.C.3694. Photo. B.N.

2. Barrière (Pavillon) de Saint-Denis. Pen and wash drawing by Misbach. Musée Carnavalet. I.E.D. 5166. Photo. Bulloz.

3. Barrière d'Enfer. Engr. Le Campion after Sergent. *Vues pittoresques des principaux édifices de Paris*, No. 65. Bib. Nat. Est., Ve.348. Photo. B.N.

4. Barrière du Trône. Engr. Le Campion after Sergent. *Vues pittoresques*, No. 99. Bib. Nat. Est., Ve.348. Photo. B.N.

5. Rotonde de la Villette. Photo. H. C. Rice, 30 April 1950.

6. Rotonde de Monceau. Pen and wash drawing by J.-B. Maréchal, 1787. Musée Carnavalet, D.6175. Photo. Bulloz.

7. Rotonde de Monceau. Photo. Ed. G.A.L.F., ca. 1948.

8. Demolition of houses on Pont au Change. Oil ptg. by Hubert Robert, 1788. Musée Carnavalet, P.172. Photo. Bulloz.

9. Demolition of houses on Pont Notre-Dame. Oil ptg. by Hubert Robert, 1786. Musée Carnavalet, P.173. Photo. Bulloz.

10. *Vues pittoresques*, title-page. Bib. Nat. Est., Ve.348. Photo. B.N.

11. Pont de Louis XVI. Medal by Benjamin Duvivier, 1788. Musée Carnavalet, N.54. Photo. Bulloz.

12. New Church of Ste.-Geneviève as originally designed by J. G. Soufflot. Engr. Charpentier, 1757. Example of print owned by Jefferson. T.J. Memorial Foundation. Photo. E. Roseberry.

13. Construction of Hôtel de Salm. Oil ptg. by unidentified artist, ca. 1786. Musée Carnavalet, P.692. Photo. Giraudon.

14. Festival of Pales, 1784. Terra cotta model by Jean-Guillaume Moitte for bas-relief on exterior wall of Hôtel de Salm, above entrance door, behind portico, courtyard side. Philadelphia Museum of Art, Gift of Orville H. Bullitt, 1929. Photo. Phila. M. A.

15. Detail from: *Nouveau Plan Routier de la Ville et Faubourgs de Paris. Avec ses Principaux Edifices.* Par M. Pichon, Ingénieur Géographe. Chez Esnauts et Rapilly, rue St. Jacques à la Ville de Coutances. Année 1787. Gravé par Glot. E. Voysard sc. Bib. Hist. Ville de Paris, A.300. Photo. A. Méheux.

16. Jefferson's Account Book, July-August 1784. Mass. Hist. Soc., Boston.

17. Mayer de Saint-Paul, *Tableau du Nouveau Palais-Royal* (Paris, 1788), t. II, Pl. facing p. 1. Author's Collection.

18. Interior View of Circus, Palais-Royal. Engr. Née after Meunier. *Voyage pittoresque de la France*: Dépt. de la Seine, No. 96. Boston Athenaeum.

19. Variétés Amusantes. Engr. J. Dambrun. *Les Délices du Palais-Royal* (Paris, 1786), Pl. 7. Bib. Nat. Est., Ef.71.fol. Photo. B.N.

73. Hôtel de Langeac, plan of garden drawn by Jefferson. Huntington Library, San Marino, Cal. Photo. H.L. Cf. Nichols, *T.J.'s Arch. Drawings*, Check List No. 246.

74. Pompe à feu de Chaillot, river side. Anon. engraving. Bib. Nat. Est., Va.316. Photo. B.N.

75. Portrait of Jefferson. Miniature in oils by John Trumbull, formerly owned by Mrs. Angelica Schuyler Church. Metropolitan Museum of Art, New York. Photo. Met. Mus.

76. Jefferson's calling card, engraved and printed in Paris. Cf. TJ Account Book: 22 March 1785, 11 Feb. 1786. T.J. Memorial Foundation. Photo. Ed. Roseberry.

77. Stables of the Comte d'Artois. Drawing by [Bélanger?]. Bib. Nat. Est., Va.280. Photo. B.N.

78. Church of Saint-Philippe du Roule. Engr. Née after Lallemand. *Voyage pittoresque*: Isle de France, Monumens de Paris, No. 60. Bib. Nat. Est. Photo B.N.

79. Hospice Beaujon, designed by Girardin, 1784-1785. Present No. 206 Rue du Faubourg Saint-Honoré. Photo. Chauvin, July 1948. Author's Collection.

80. Diana by J.-A. Houdon. Bronze. Musée du Louvre.

81. Houdon's Washington, full-length in marble, commissioned by State of Virginia. Capitol, Richmond, Virginia. Photo. Va. State Library.

82. Lafayette's face, plaster by Houdon, 1785. Formerly Fabius Collection, from Château de Chavaniac. Cornell University, Ithaca, N.Y. (acquired 1964). Photo. Giraudon.

83. Houdon's bust of Lafayette in marble, commissioned by State of Virginia. Capitol, Richmond, Virginia. Photo. Va. State Library.

84. Houdon's bust of Jefferson, in plaster painted terra-cotta color. Musée de Blérancourt (acquired 1963). Photo. Musées Nationaux.

85. Houdon in His Studio. Oil ptg. by Louis-Léopold Boilly, 1804. Musée de Cherbourg. Photo. Archives Photographiques.

86. Detail, *Nouveau Plan Routier*, above, Fig. 15.

87. Marquis de Chastellux. Miniature by unidenti-fied artist. Courtesy of the late Duc de Duras. Photo. Michel Chalufour. Author's Collection.

88. Marquise de Chastellux, née Marie-Brigitte Plunkett. Photograph of a miniature, now lost. Courtesy of Comte Louis de Chastellux.

89. Hôtel de Salm, Rue de Bourbon [Lille] side. Engr. Née after Meunier. *Voyage pittoresque*: Dépt. de la Seine, No. 89. Boston Athenaeum.

90. Anastasie, George-Washington, and Virginie de Lafayette with bust of their father. Miniature on ivory by unidentified artist, ca. 1786. Private collection. Photo. Giraudon.

91. Former Hôtel de Tessé (Villeroy), now Ministry of Agriculture, 78 Rue de Varenne. Photo. Chauvin, May 1948. Author's Collection.

92. Mme de Tott painting portrait of Mme de Tessé. Miniature on ivory, probably by Baron de Tott, the young lady's father. Courtesy of Comte de Pusy Lafayette. Photo. Hervochon.

93. Architect's plan for Panthemont church, cross section and profile. Engr. Le Canu [after François Franque]. *Encyclopédie*, Planches I (1762): Architecture, Pl. 21. Princeton Univ. Library.

94. Temple de Pentemont, 106 Rue de Grenelle. Photo. Chauvin, May 1948. Author's Collection.

95. Journal of Receipts, Abbaye Royale de Panthemont, 1785. Archives Nationales, H^5 4036. Photo. Soc. Fr. du Microfilm.

96. Martha Jefferson. Miniature by Joseph Boze, 1789. Hugh Campbell Wallace Collection, U.S. Embassy, Paris. Photo. U.S.I.S., Gabriel Grosseure.

97. Gold ring decorated with blue enamel. Engraved inside: "Martha Jefferson 1788." T.J. Memorial Foundation (cf. Curator's Report for 1962). Photo. R. Thompson.

98. Miniature, oil on paper, of Martha Jefferson's Panthemont schoolmate, Marie-Jacinthe de Botidoux. T.J. Memorial Foundation (cf. Curator's Report for 1963). Photo. R. Thompson.

99. La Forest, *Méthodes d'instruction . . .* (1784), Sowerby No. 1540. Library of Congress. Photo. L.C.

Index

INDEX

Dugazon, Mme Louise, actress, 33,
47-48, Fig. 64
Dugnani, papal nuncio in Paris, 68
Dumaniant (Antoine-Jean Bourlin),
actor and dramatist, 16
dumb-waiter, 15
Dupille de Saint-Séverin, art sale,
40, Fig. 55
Dupont (de Nemours), Pierre-Samu-
el, 31, 83
Duport, Adrien, member Constituent
Assembly, 121
Dupré, Augustin, medalist, 71-72,
Figs. 105, 106
Dupuis, household furnishings, 23
Dutertre, artist, Figs. 64, 101
Duvaux, surveyor, Fig. 149
Duvivier, Benjamin, medalist, 5, 71,
Figs. 11, 105

Eaux de Passy, 92
Ecole Royale des Mines, 72
Ecole Royale Militaire, 25, Figs.
131, 133
Ecuries du Comte d'Artois, 55, Fig.
77
Eglises (churches): Capuchin Noviciate, 6, 37, Fig. 49; Madeleine,
6, 26; Notre-Dame (Versailles),
116, Fig. 169; Notre-Dame de Lorette, 43; Saint-Eustache, 18, 37;
Saint-Germain l'Auxerrois, 35;
Saint-Louis (St.-Germain-en-Laye),
111; Saint-Louis (Versailles),
116, 117; Saint-Louis d'Antin, 6,
37; Saint-Philippe du Roule, 6,
55, 57, Fig. 78; Saint-Roch, 21,
23; Saint-Sulpice, 6; Sainte-Geneviève (Panthéon), 6, Figs. 12, 133
Elbée, sister d', 66
Emmet, Dr. John P., 89
Encyclopédie, 17, 22, Fig. 93
Encyclopédie méthodique, 77, Fig.
129
engravers (all references here are to
Figure numbers): Alix, P. M., 60;
Bartolozzi, F., 28; Bellet, 155;
Benard, 129; Berthault, 171; Ber-
thet, 31, 37, 111, 172; Bervic,
C.-C., 180; Bettini, F., 140; Bornet,
C., 66; Charpentier, J; Chrétien,
G.-L., 23; Dambrun, J., 19, 148,
168; Eustache de St. Fare, J.-F.,
147, 153; Fiesinger, G., 108; Gabriel, 165, 167; Glot, 15; Guyard,
J.-B., 65; Helman, 170; Ingouf,
142; Janninet, 64, 101; Jourdan,
F., 27, 49; Le Campion, 3, 4; Le
Canu, 93; Le Mire, 34; Maleuvre,
125; Martinet, F.-N., 68; Martini,
P.-A., 42; Masquelier, 38, 131,
135; De Monchy, 146; Née, Fran-
çois-Denis, frontispiece, 18, 32,
47, 61, 63, 78, 89, 100, 121, 131,
141, 143, 144, 145, 157; Plée,
166; Perrier, 33; Prieur, 57; Roma-

net, A., 24; Sellier, 114; Tardieu,
P.-F., 1, 147; Voysard, E., 15
Enville, duchesse d' (Louise-Elisa-
beth de la Rochefoucauld), 20, 73-
74, 75, 112-113
Eppes, Francis and Elizabeth, 42
Estates-General (1789), 115-116,
Figs. 169, 170
Etoile, 51, 103

Fantocinni (marionettes), 16
Farmers-General, city wall, 3-4, 8,
37; tobacco monopoly, 53
Faubourg: du Roule, 6, 8, 9, 11, 50-
59; Saint-Antoine, 11, 49, 123;
Saint-Germain, 5, 9, 11, 26, 61-
68; Saint-Honoré, 5, 9; Saint-Mar-
cel, 11; Saint-Victor, 83
Faujas de Saint-Fond, Barthélemy,
geologist, 86, 129 n16
Favart, Charles-Simon, dramatist, 47
Ferat, P. S., Fig. 176
Fête de la Fédération (1790), 122
Février, restaurant, 15
Ffytche, Louis Disney, 112
fireworks, 44
Florian, Jean-Pierre, Claris de, dram-
atist, 48, Fig. 65
Flouest, J., artist, Fig. 65
Foacier, Maître, notary, 37
Fondation Salomon Rothschild, 55
Fontainebleau, 33, 44
Fossier, artist, Fig. 114
fossils, Jefferson's gift to Muséum,
86-87, Fig. 124
Foulis, printer of Glasgow, 81
Foulon, Joseph-François, 120, Fig.
177
Foundry of City of Paris, 55
Fouquet, model-maker, 27
Fourcroy, Antoine-François de,
chemist, 86
Franklin, Benjamin, 19, 22, 51, 52,
56, 73, 79, 80, 81, 86, 94, 108,
123; Avis à ceux qui voudraient
émigrer en Amérique, 78; bust by
Houdon, 56, 59, 75; residence in
Passy, 91-92, Figs. 132, 133
Franklin, William Temple, 91
Franque, François, architect, Fig.
93
Fremyn de Fontenille, 107
Freudenberg, artist, Fig. 24
Front de Seine (Le), 91
Froullé, J.-F., bookseller, 77, 78-79

Gabriel, Jacques-Ange, architect, 6,
25, 26, 100
Garamond, Claude, typefounder,
31, 81
Garde-Meuble, Hôtel du, 26, Figs.
32, 35, 173
gardens, English style, 43; Bagatelle, 104; Beaujon, 55; Boutin
(Tivoli), 43; Chaville (Tessé),
97-98; Désert de Retz, 111-112;

Jansen, 51; La Roche-Guyon,
112-113; Petit Trianon, 100-101;
Sainte-James, 103-104
Gates, Horatio, Saratoga medal by
Gatteaux, 71, Fig. 105
Gatteaux, Nicolas-Marie, medalist,
71, Fig. 105
Gautier, J.-A., banker, 123
Geismar, baron, 52
Gem, Dr. Richard, 115
The General Advertiser, English-
language newspaper published in
Paris, 78
Gérard de Rayneval, Joseph-Mathi-
as, 99, 100
Giornowich, composer, 21
Girardin, Nicolas-Claude, architect,
55
Gluck, Christoph Willibald, com-
poser, 45
Gossec, François-Joseph, composer,
30
Grand, Ferdinand, banker, 23, 71,
123; house in Passy, 94
Grand Trianon, 100
Grande Galerie du Louvre, 31
Grasse, François-Joseph-Paul, comte
de, portrait painted by Trumbull,
54
Greene, George Washington, 53
Greene, Nathanael, 53; Eutaw
Springs medal by Dupré, 71, Fig.
105
Grétry, André, composer, 22, 45,
47, 48, 118
Grevin, packer, 121-122
Grille de Chaillot, 11, 26, 51, 54,
117, Fig. 68
Grive, abbé de la, cartographer, Fig.
130
Grosse, composer, 21
Grotte Flamande, restaurant, 15
Guérin, J., artist, Fig. 108
Guerre ouverte, ou Ruse contre Ruse
(Dumaniant), 16
Guimard, Mlle, house, 42, Fig. 57
Guireaud de Talairac, François, Jef-
ferson's landlord, 37-38, 42

Halle aux Bleds (grain market), 6,
18-21, Figs. 26, 27, 177
Hamerville, Jacques-Guillaume,
bookbinder, 81
Händel, Georg Friedrich, composer,
30
Haussman, baron Georges, 10
Haydn, Franz Joseph, composer,
21, 30
Helvétius, Mme, house in Auteuil,
94-96
Hemings, James, servant, 13, 40
Hennin, government official, 100
Hermits of Mont-Calvaire, 105-107,
Figs. 146, 149, 150
Herodiade, painting by Vouet ac-
quired by Jefferson, 40, Fig. 56